Elaine C. Smith is one of Scotland's best-loved entertainers, an actress, comedienne, writer and columnist. Her numerous television performances include roles in *Naked Video*, *City Lights* and *Two Thousand Acres of Sky*. She is perhaps best known for her acclaimed portrayal of Mary Doll in the award-winning BBC comedy *Rab C. Nesbitt*. Since 2008, Elaine has been touring with the original production of the hit play *Calendar Girls*, which had a hugely successful run in London's West End. She is to take over the lead role in the current tour in autumn 2010.

Elaine was appointed to the Scottish Broadcasting Commission in 2007 and is chair of the Scottish Independence Convention. Elaine is also a patron of many charities in Scotland, from the Children's Parliament and Scottish Youth Theatre to Relationships Scotland and Zero Tolerance. She holds honorary doctorates from Dundee and Glasgow universities. Elaine has recently been given a Women of Influence award for her charity and campaigning work and her achievements as an actor and entertainer. She lives in the East End of Glasgow with her husband and two daughters.

Nothing Like a
DAME
My Autobiography

ELAINE C. SMITH

MAINSTREAM
PUBLISHING

EDINBURGH AND LONDON

This edition, 2010

First published in Great Britain in 2009 by
MAINSTREAM PUBLISHING COMPANY
(EDINBURGH) LTD
7 Albany Street
Edinburgh EH1 3UG

ISBN 9781845965914

Rab C. Nesbitt © Ian Pattison 1990
'The Four Marys' was first published in 1802 in
Sir Walter Scott's *Minstrelsy of the Scottish Border*
'Mother Glasgow': words and music by Michael Marra
'Wan Singer, Wan Song': words and music by Dave Anderson

A catalogue record for this book is available
from the British Library

Typeset in Caslon and Gill Sans

Printed in Great Britain by
CPI Cox and Wyman, Reading, RG1 8EX

1 3 5 7 9 10 8 6 4 2

CONTENTS

For Bob, Katie and Hannah, the loves of my life

For Louise and Diane, for just being my sisters,
and for making my life richer, more joyous and easier on this
planet (and for the hairdos which are just as important)

For Jimmy, Brian, Jack, Harry and Tess
for making our family complete

And for Dad for his knowledge of the Spitfire, the Mosquito,
the Hurricane, the construction of the Forth Road Bridge,
just what the ball-bearing has done for civilisation and
for his ability to fix just about everything

And, of course, for Stella

FOREWORD

Elaine C. Smith is an extraordinary woman. Her life has not turned out as it was supposed to, as this memoir testifies. Yet her journey was never going to be ordinary because of the special combination of qualities she embodies. Her huge talent as an actress, entertainer and comedienne – onstage and television – has brought her considerable public acclaim in Scotland and her recent triumph in the London's West End, starring in *Calendar Girls*, has introduced her to a wider, adoring audience. It is no more than she deserves.

For me, Elaine represents so much that is precious about Scotland – the earthiness and wit, the warmth and compassion, the social conscience and passion for justice. One of the reasons she has come to be so loved by the general public is because, despite her success and celebrity, she has always remained natural and unaffected, with her feet firmly planted on the ground. She is everyone's sister, with traces of all our mothers. She has the ability to tell it like it is, without cruelty but with astute humour and wicked observation. For women, she is a beacon. For men, she is at once delicious and terrifying.

I have spent some of the most hilarious evenings in her company but I have also had the good fortune to know that her rich seams of comedy come from the wisdom of experience. Her own life has not been without pain and loss but she has drawn on it for lessons about life, and her willingness to share those truths has made her iconic.

The west of Scotland is a rare place and Elaine's own family history weaves together many strands that are familiar to those who hail from this part of the world. It is a place in which religion and politics are bread and butter, a place of long memories and short fuses, of bitter wrangles and quick tongues, but it is also a place of touching generosity and fierce loyalties. The ties of family bind tightly. Elaine has always felt that in order to tell her own story she had to tell the story of her mother, Stella, whose marriage outside of her faith took her on a trajectory that undoubtedly affected the choices Elaine herself eventually made in her own life.

Stella's death had an enormous effect on Elaine. For so much of her life, Elaine had carried Stella's secrets and ambitions, with a frequent reversal of the mother/daughter roles, but Stella's courageous struggle with cancer restored an equilibrium. Stella showed herself resourceful and inspirational as her life ebbed away and it left Elaine stranded in a new place, seeing her mother with a different focus and understanding better why they were both the women they were.

Elaine C. Smith's autobiography is authentic, honest and inspirational. It just leaves you thinking: What a dame!

Baroness Helena Kennedy

INTRODUCTION

I'm in my kitchen, in Glasgow, emptying the dishwasher and suddenly I burst into tears. Bob, my husband, turns in shock and asks, 'What is it?' I keep sobbing until I catch my breath and summon the strength to splutter, 'I don't want to go!'

Until that point, I hadn't known my true feelings. I was simply enjoying having an entire three days back in my home (after a gruelling twenty-week tour), to do the mundane things such as emptying the dishwasher. The sobs seemed to get worse after I finally let those words out. I didn't know why I felt the way I did but somewhere in my subconscious it just welled up and I felt terrified. I wanted to stay where I was.

Bob put his arms around me, rubbed my back and said, 'Come on, it'll be fine. It's all right, it'll be fine. Once you're there you'll have a great time. This is exactly the right thing for you to do and it's right that you do it now.'

Bob has this wonderful knack of immediately having empathy for the way a person is feeling; he doesn't sit in judgement or get angry at stupidity. If the kids drop or break things he doesn't shout and accuse, he simply says 'It's an accident – nobody meant it.' I am the one that rants about how stupid and idiotic they've been and that they should pay more attention. When the going gets tough, Bob has a strength and ability to be positive, which is strange for a man who is generally a 'glass half empty' kind of guy. But in times of crisis, there is no one better – calm, understanding and showing neither anger nor blame.

He knew how scared I was and how confused I felt about the life I was leading. I hadn't slept in my own bed for more than three nights in months, I kept questioning the stupidity of going off and doing a show that took me away from what I loved most in the world – my girls, Bob, the home and life we'd built around us.

Now please, don't get me wrong – compared to what some people have to endure on this planet what I was going through was nothing. So, no, I wasn't being carted off to prison or to a war zone. My kids weren't being taken into care by social services and I wasn't about to endure any of the horrors that people go through every day of their lives. I am aware that I am one of the lucky ones, though not without my share of grief or torment. But it's all relative, innit? And, yes, I know that there are actors up and down the land who would have swapped places with me in a second to have a shot at going into the West End of London for a run in the hit show *Calendar Girls* – it's the stuff of dreams for any actor. All the while, this commentary was running through my head as I was standing there, in tears, in my kitchen.

But the truth was I just didn't want to leave.

In my wee world, I was knackered! A twenty-week theatre tour of the United Kingdom; performing eight shows a week; travelling on Sundays – either to the next gig or for a twenty-hour visit home; writing a weekly column as well as writing and performing a two-week run of my stand-up show in Glasgow. And all of this was following on from an arduous, but rewarding, tour throughout Scotland of *The Rise and Fall of Little Voice*, which I starred in and also helped produce. I had only managed to steal a one-week break in the summer, so the thought of four solid months in London, away from everyone and everything I love, just felt like a step too far. It had been 20 years since I had even contemplated working away from Scotland because, in general, my life was good – a great husband, kids, family, friends and career. So why move?

Yet, as a young 19-year-old drama student, I had that same head full of broken bottles and dreams of London and the glittering West End that every other young hopeful before me has ever had. I dreamed of being in those shows like the ones I'd seen in movies and on TV. I wanted to be in musical theatre more than anything in the world.

I even headed off on my own in the summer of 1978 to stay with my then 80-year-old Uncle Jimmy in Hounslow (which was as near to London as I could get at the time). He was my grandmother's brother, and though brought up in Lanarkshire, he'd left after his return from the navy after the First World War when he had discovered that the 'Land Fit for Heroes' had no jobs for those seeking to apply for positions. He walked from Motherwell to Clydebank (a good 25 miles) to try and get a job in the shipyards – but found nothing. So he jumped a train and headed south, never to return, as over time he made a very successful life in London.

So when I said I wanted to go to London, and on my own, my mum relented as long as I was staying with someone from our family. I wrote to Uncle Jimmy and he invited me to stay – it would be my first real adventure. He was a widower by this time, and lived alone, so I think he was glad of the company. He came all the way up to meet me at Euston Station and then we got the London Underground to where he lived. Early in the morning, for the next few days, I travelled up to the famous sights of Piccadilly and Shaftesbury Avenue so that I could drink it all in.

That first morning was wonderful. Getting off the tube in Piccadilly and emerging to the neon signs, the iconic Eros statue, and the sheer buzz and life of the capital city was just amazing. I walked for miles and miles and couldn't believe that I was actually there in Regent Street or at Marble Arch – at once so strange and yet familiar to me.

I queued to see shows like *Evita* with Elaine Paige and David Essex, and *A Chorus Line*. I loved every minute of it and dared to dream that maybe one day I would be in a musical myself. I didn't want to be Elaine Paige, I wanted to be Barbara Dickson of course. I had first seen her on TV when she was appearing on stage in Willy Russell's *John, Paul, George, Ringo and Bert*, and she'd recently had a big hit with 'Another Suitcase in Another Hall' from *Evita*. She was a fellow Scot, and I had never seen another Scotswoman do anything like that, so it was inspiring for me. Broadway was, naturally, where I really wanted to be because I preferred American shows, but then who didn't? However, the sad reality was that I hadn't a clue where to start or how to get an audition.

After my trip, I headed back to Edinburgh to do a postgraduate teacher-training year at Moray House College, with the aim of pursuing a career in education – which I have to say I loved and was really happy to do. The dream of a career in the West End was put well and truly on the back burner.

So here I was, at the ripe old age of 50, about to realise a dream I'd long ago discarded, and I simply felt terrified. I wasn't frightened of the work or my ability to do it, but I think I was scared of the change that it would bring to my life. I suppose we all fear change at some subliminal level. As the saying goes, 'people prefer death to change'. Maybe I was afraid that I would like it too much and not want to come home, as so many of my fellow thespians have done over the years.

Anyway, in true 'Smith' style, I wiped the tears away, packed my suitcase and got on with it. Yes, I know it was a small drama in the great scheme of things – and I hope you'll allow these few paragraphs of self-indulgence, but that's all I will allow, because that Scottish puritanical voice in my head kicks in with, 'Oh, for God's sake, give yourself a shake, lady, you're not going off to the trenches!' So I felt the fear and did it anyway, when what I really wanted to do was feel the fear and go back to my bed. I packed (again) and headed to the airport (again).

I wasn't feeling that brilliant as I got off the train at Paddington Station in London. and asked a cab to take me to the Noël Coward Theatre in St Martin's Lane. Somewhere in my head I was still in Glasgow and not quite ready for the sheer onslaught of London's energy. I was totally preoccupied and unprepared for what was about to happen.

As the cab approached the theatre, we stopped in the busy traffic at the lights at the bottom of Monmouth Street and I looked up and saw a huge yellow sunflower surrounded by flashing lights. As we got nearer, I realised that underneath it said *Calendar Girls*. My heart flipped. Oh shit! This was actually for real. I got out of the cab and started to laugh out loud as I looked up at a huge photo of myself announcing 'ELAINE C. SMITH as Miss JULY'. In that moment, I was 19 again.

I slunk past with my head down along the lane, a bit embarrassed at the photo, and past my favourite restaurant in London – J. Sheekey's

– and into the stage door of the theatre. My dressing room was lovely, with fresh flowers, brand-new white fluffy towels and a box of Molton Brown goodies from our producers and Cameron Mackintosh. A far cry from the community centre toilets I've had to change in at various times in my career.

Well, hen, you're in the West End now. There, on the wall, was a framed poster of Dave Allen, who had appeared at this theatre (when it was previously named The Albery) and that made me smile, as he was my mother's favourite comic of all time. I took off my coat and a white feather floated to the ground. Yes, my mother was with me too – well, I suppose there was no way I was getting to the West End without her.

On our noticeboard, we had a fantastic photo of all the actresses in *Madame de Sade*, which was playing at the Wyndham's Theatre next door – and not just any actresses. The cast was headed by the one and only Dame Judi Dench and the photograph was signed by all nine actresses as they welcomed our own cast of nine to what they had nicknamed 'Vagina Alley'. All these talented women in two shows – sharing the 'Alley', pardon my French! All the while I was thinking: 'This wasn't supposed to happen. I'm a lassie from a wee bloody mining village in Lanarkshire, in Scotland, and here I am – in a dressing room, in a beautiful theatre, in a hit show, in London's glittering West End.' I'd taken the job as a bit of an adventure, a celebration of turning 50 and at the same time to take a risk, and move out of my comfort zone. But truthfully, I had always felt deep down that I had been so fortunate in life, both professionally and personally, and if that was it, then I was very happy. But this was all way more than I had ever expected. I sat down and asked the question 'How the hell did I end up here?'

CHAPTER I

BEGINNINGS

You see, I was supposed to be a good girl. I was supposed to behave, to speak when spoken to, to know my place, to conform, to believe in God, to eat little amounts of food (and never get fat), to do well at school (but not too well because then you're a 'brainbox' and too smart for your own good), to get a good job, to become a teacher if I could, then get married and have kids. Overall, to live happily ever after, that was the life I was supposed to occupy; and I have to admit that I wanted that life too. I wanted to fit in with the world I had been born into.

But hard as I tried (and I bloody tried, but it just didn't work out that way), I guess I was just destined for other things. Well, if you believe in all that. I realise now of course that had it all worked out the way it was supposed to, and if I had been able to live the life of the 'good girl' I wouldn't have had this mostly wonderful life I have thus far enjoyed, and for that I am very grateful. But it didn't stop my trying to get it right. And before you start thinking that me not being a good girl is going to lead to a steamy showbiz tale of sex, booze and debauchery, I have to say that I am sorry to disappoint . . . that isn't my story.

The thing is, although I wasn't good in the sense of conforming like a wee girl from Lanarkshire was supposed to do, I was never actually really, really bad. As far as debauchery goes, I suppose at worst it was a puff of a joint and a bottle of Newcastle Brown in the back of a Transit coming home from a gig in a pub in Greenock, or getting too 'pished' and singing the complete works of Patsy Cline to assembled other drunks – whether they wanted it or not – and that's hardly Janis Joplin is it? But compared with where I came from, and where I was supposed to end up, it felt like I was Mrs Che Guevara.

Mine was a very small rebellion. I didn't actually reject the way I was brought up, or the people I loved, or the country I was brought up in. I didn't run away. In a way it would have been easier to do that to get out and 'find myself' in London, or New York, and be able to reinvent myself or simply obliterate who I was supposed to be and where I came from. Thousands before me have gone down that road. The truth is we never really get to run away, the past comes back and bites you on the bum just when you least expect it, as the demons and constraints we thought we had conquered haunt us until we face them. But I dare say I could have been free of all that responsibility for a while.

A great pal and wonderful performer and writer, Dave Anderson, once told me that I was the most responsible person he'd ever met, and I was only about 30! But I have always wanted to behave well and do the right thing. Be accepted. I didn't judge others and part of me really envied their ability to just behave badly, shout and turn up drunk or generally not give a toss about anything but themselves. I suppose I simply admired and loved rebels.

I didn't run away, mainly because being the dreamer and permanent optimist that I was, and still am, I hoped that in some way the perfect dream life of the showbiz/pop star/movie star would all just sort of happen to me eventually. That some West End or Hollywood producer would turn up and say 'Hey you! I'm gonna make you a star!' and whisk me off. In Newarthill that was probably a bit of a stretch even for the optimist.

I had watched too many movies when that small town girl made it all the way. I was trying to be different and the same all at once – never an easy thing to pull off. To have a showbiz career while staying close to the places and the people that I loved and respected was what I wanted. The drawback was that everything around me kept telling me that I couldn't do it and shouldn't even try.

In reality, we all know that even in the safest, most perfect of lives, things go terribly wrong. Those girls who played by the rules that have now changed, who conformed, who dieted for Scotland and kept their mouth shut must be raging now cos disaster still bloody happens, ladies! Divorce, affairs, cancer and sudden death turn up at the door anyway – life and death are random and no one is ever truly safe. But we all bought it, well, most of us did – and I certainly did for a while. The fantasy of the good life that was peddled throughout my early years, from the 1960s onwards. In every magazine, TV show, advert, by every political party or organisation and by every restrictive practice that existed in all the small villages and towns in Lanarkshire, in beautiful Scotland – land of my birth, my hame!!

Bonnie Scotland. A land with a psyche and soul made up of a heady cocktail that drives its population to drink. A toxic blend of Calvinist-Presbyterianism, severe Catholicism, massive ego, even bigger inferiority complex supported by insecurity, all settling within strict boundaries of conformity and general sexism. What a place, with of course a hell of a lot of rain to water it down and make it more palatable. You can get ice too if needs be!

Throw into that formula a city like Glasgow, with all its wonderful madness, violence, sectarianism and poverty – where a sense of humour is a necessity, as well as a great weapon, in the struggle to keep body and soul together. Where the wagging finger of the men in authority (from John Knox's statue over the city shouting 'Don't!' to all of us) that told women to 'shuttit!' Not an ideal world for a lippy woman like myself to thrive in, and if truth be told, not an easy world for anyone different – male or female – to thrive in.

There's a great line from one of my favourite songwriters, Michael Marra, in his song about 'Mother Glasgow':

In the second city of the Empire,
Mother Glasgow watches all her weans,
And trying hard to feed her little starlings,
Unconsciously she clips their little wings.

Even these days too many people's wings get clipped when they should be allowed to fly and flourish. Though the great irony in Scottish culture is that most women are pretty opinionated but we try our best to hide it, so as to maintain order, and to be accepted and play the game. Well, until we get pished and then the truth spills out and results in a 'rammy'. A favourite gag of mine is the one where the wee boy comes home from school all excited that he has got a part in the school show. When his mother asks what part he's playing, he says, 'I've got the part of the Scottish husband.' His mother is outraged and tells him to get back to the school and 'Tell that teacher to give you a speaking part!' The messages from authority however, and from the powers that be in the late '50s and early '60s, were very powerful about a woman's place, and what and where that should be.

The propaganda from the movies with my idols like Doris Day didn't help either. They sent a very strong message to women about who they were supposed to be. The '50s woman would ideally be beautiful, coiffed and even though she may have had a career, in reality she was just waiting for her man to come along, make her life complete and give all that nonsense up and have babies. Gone were the movies of the '30s and '40s with women like Bette Davis and Joan Crawford who were seen as strong and liberated, untameable and vibrant. In '70s Lanarkshire to me those messages felt just as strong. And in a way they drove women like myself out of our minds. On the one hand we wanted to have good jobs and independence, but on the other we were being told to just love our man.

My heroine was Billie Holiday. I loved what I have since dubbed 'victim songs'. The ones describing how much you love your man and how you will die if he leaves. Lady Day summed it up in the song 'My Man' with '. . . he isn't true, he beats me too, what can I do?' From my perspective now I would say 'Phone the "polis". If he hits you once, he'll hit you again.' But then it just seemed to be that if you sacrificed your very soul it meant you truly loved your man.

From Jack Jones with 'Wives and Lovers' to Sir Cliff with 'Living Doll', the messages were loud and clear. On the radio, the songs called us 'baby', 'sugar', 'doll', 'little girl', they told us to stay young and beautiful (as well as thin and blonde if you could manage it) and things would all be fine. The underlying message for a woman was that if you weren't all these things, you were unlovable. Not many songs for the 42 year old? Then try this:

Oh, you're 42,
and pretty heavy roon the hips,
You like your chips,
But I love you!

I wrote that one myself, could be a number one, I think . . . well maybe if Adele covered it! Unfortunately, women's lib had not hit the metropolis of Motherwell even by 1970. Mum was doing her personal bit for the movement and causing great changes in our house by going to work part time in an office and eventually going to night school to do her Highers, but there was no evidence of bra burning.

Amazingly now when I look back, I really disliked the girls who were rebels. Even when I watched Wimbledon, I liked the women in the pretty dresses and frilly pants, like Chris Evert. She was much more acceptable than Billie Jean King with her shorts and her specs and her muscled arms. Now I feel quite guilty because I judged one of the true heroes of the women's game – and one of the best woman players ever – on the way she looked, as well as the attitude towards her from the men who ruled the game. She didn't fit the allotted role or play the game the way a 'good woman' was supposed to. She lived her own life on her own terms, and that just wasn't right was it? It never ceases to amaze me that at times it's women themselves who are much more controlling and judgemental of other women's behaviour, it's a sort of self-policing.

Men were funny, from Eric Morecambe to Bob Hope, and even though Doris Day could deliver a great comedy performance she always had to get her man in the end. Women just weren't that visible in anything but the 'looks' department. Watching old Doris in *Calamity Jane* one night on telly changed my life. It gave me hope. My dad said, 'This is a great film, doll,' and I thought to myself, 'Aw naw, that means it'll be a cowboy or a war picture with John Wayne or Audie Murphy and I will have to listen to my dad's commentary all the way through telling me details about cowboy life or the war and explaining everything!' My mum maintained that during the '60s and '70s my dad watched so many of these movies that if we took the back off the telly all that would fall out would be horseshit and bullets! My heart sank. But then, there she was,

Doris on top of a stagecoach singing 'The Deadwood Stage' and that was it, I was hooked.

I have always had that dilemma within me: the desire to conform on the one hand and then to be irreverent, funny and rebellious. I was the feminist who wore make-up and thigh-length boots, I was the politico on every march from supporting the miners to anti-apartheid and women's rights, who didn't want to offend too much, who wanted to be liked, and who always saw the other point of view. Hopeless! I was the woman who wasn't supposed to have opinions about football, politics and comedy. I was supposed to sit and listen while the men talked – well, a pile of 'shite' – about football, politics and comedy. And God, I have endured hours listening to total 'balloons' talk rubbish about football while the other men all play along, pretending they agree. That assumption that a man is born with his brain genetically programmed to understand the offside rule and a women isn't drives me insane. It ain't rocket science and if an 8-year-old boy running about a park can understand it then why can't I? I demand the right to talk as much 'pish' about football as men do.

So, a big welcome to my world, welcome to the Scotland I grew up in and still am happy to live in. Caledonia, the land that I love but have argued, cried, sung, acted and thrived in . . . and it hasn't been bloody easy. Being a woman and funny with lots of opinions about, well, everything isn't easy anywhere. But it's twice as hard in the land of the macho funny man that is Bonnie Scotland.

CHAPTER 2

FUNNY GIRL

Funny women seem to be viewed with a sideways glance most of the time, mistrusted and, worst of all, not fancied. Yet most Scotsmen would tell you that the funniest person in their lives was their mum, who was hilarious – but you can't fancy a woman that's funnier than yourself can you? So in order to be accepted (and also to have a romantic sex life) I had to pretend and hang on their every 'hilarious' word. If I was funny then it had to be purely by accident of course and could cause many a fight. It was only just acceptable for me to sing in bands and possibly maybe act, but to be onstage being funny? Oh no, no, no!

I was always quite funny around the guys in the bands that I was in and they enjoyed all the banter, but we weren't ever romantically involved. But that proved difficult for one of my long-term boyfriends whom I loved, and whom I know loved me – the sight of me fronting my folk band and doing a funny routine – which actually was pretty rubbish admittedly, you could say a 'learning curve' for a performer like me. But my boyfriend couldn't see it that way, it just wasn't right even to try – men were funny and women weren't, end of story. So, instead I tried to become all Joni Mitchell and soulful, not a great plan I admit but I had to find an outlet to be creative.

I remember being at drama school and meeting this good-looking guy in a club. He asked me out, and when he asked me what I did, I told him about my acting classes, and singing in a band after school. He was quite perplexed by that and when we went out again, he asked if I would tell his pals that I was a hairdresser because he just couldn't explain an actress to them and he would be slagged for-ever about it. I actually agreed, because I fancied him and didn't want to embarrass him in any way. Of course I blew it by getting a bit pished, having a laugh and ultimately spilling the beans (in a very funny way, of course). Needless to say we never went out again – I think he married a hairdresser.

Throughout my life, whether working in bars, shops, hotels, a good career in teaching, bands, then theatre, TV and radio, I tried to be good and shut up – but eventually a girl can't help it! I wanted to be in control and have a petite figure (like actresses and singers are supposed to be). I wanted to play 'Camille' (though with the ample bosom I have been gifted, even I knew deep down that the frail, dying consumptive was a stretch). I wanted to do what I was told by the director, even when it was total 'pish' and I knew that he hadn't a clue. The hardest thing for an actor is to work with a director who knows less than you do and is convinced he knows so much more.

Now don't get me wrong, I don't mean that I was or am disruptive, as I'm not – too well brought up for that sort of behaviour. There will obviously be the disruptive element of the telling of theatrical anecdotes and gossip during rehearsals and that is only natural. What would be the point of life without them? But having a tantrum isn't my style – not back then, and certainly not now. Occasionally, I may be a pain in the arse, and talk too much, and have too many opinions for my own good. Women communicate differently. We interrupt each other all the time. We go off on tangents, we 'chew the fat', but this is seen in certain environments, especially working ones, as disruptive. I always want productions to turn out well and at least 90 per cent of the directors I have worked with – the wonderful Michael Boyd at the RSC; John Tiffany at NTS; Colin Gilbert at the Comedy Unit; or Hamish McColl on *Calendar Girls* and many, many more – will tell you that I work hard and do all I can to help a show succeed.

I don't do tantrums, or walk out, or indulge in histrionics. It's usually men who do that anyway; we women simply burst into tears, get sick, or use other attention-seeking behaviour. Violent shouting and bawling is always quite a shock for me in a rehearsal room. In fact, I can't bear those actors who stop rehearsals all the time to discuss their character, or throw their weight around like children when they don't get their own way. It's just ego and a lot of it is time-wasting. It does nothing for the production in the end, except that it lets the rest of the cast know that said actor is an arse!

But it's been a tough old road. OK, not as tough as the lives that women lead in the Third World but I am painting a picture here and hopefully you get my drift. Now, before I get the letters from Scots outraged that I am slagging them off or that I am besmirching the good name of my homeland and the males therein in a ridiculous manner, I would like to say, 'Ho, ho! Hawd on! Don't get me wrong, pal!'

I love Scotland. I live and work here; my children were born here; the man of my dreams was born and brought up here. I have been with my wonderful Bob for almost 30 years, and he is very much a strong male in opinions, activities (bloody fishing and football) and in his attitude to life. He has been known to tell me to 'shuttit!' with all that feminist claptrap and a fierce fight has then ensued. One of my closest pals in the world is the actor Andy Gray (a man who is not a born feminist). I work with men, enjoy working alongside them and it's made me the woman I am today – despite their best efforts.

I don't want to live anywhere else, and yes, that means even on the days when the rain is falling constantly sideways, when it's freezing and it's dark at three in the afternoon and you think that spring will never come, and some ranting, sexist, navel-gazing 'eejit' is talking rubbish on the TV or the radio, and I'm reading newspapers that are so insular, sneering and cringing that they make me want to scream.

Yes, even then, because in the darkness there is great discussion, bitterness, debate and argument that you don't get anywhere else. There are curries, kebabs and chips (sometimes on one plate) and songs from the honorary Scot that is Stevie Wonder sung at 2 a.m. on the karaoke, followed by a few tunes from the other great Scottish songstress Patsy Cline – because we as Scots are all black country singers in our hearts and souls. There are jokes that make me pee myself; a turn of phrase, a description, a song that lifts my heart; and every so often the sun comes out and it's the most beautiful place on earth – well, maybe not parts of Possil but that's the same the world over. And because there are voices that keep me sane, like those of Tom Leonard and Muriel Gray; journalists and writers like Ruth Wishart, Ian Pattison, Denise Mina, Iain McWhirter; paintings by

Ken Currie, June Redfern, Joan Eardley and Alison Watt; music from the late, great John Martyn, Michael Marra and singers like Pat Kane and Eddi Reader; people who make my heart soar (whom you will hear of later in this book); and because the light is magical, because of all that, there is hope.

For all the madness, there is hope in this wee land called Scotland. As the wonderful writer Peter Arnott said so aptly when asked to describe his native land, 'Scotland is basically an argument.' And I for one love a good argument – not one that ends up in violence, you understand, but a good 'barney' makes for an interesting night.

To those Scots who love to pretend that their country is *Brigadoon* or one big golf course where you might meet Ronnie Corbett loafing around in tartan trews of an afternoon; or that every decent Scot loves Jackie Stewart and wears a Pringle sweater and bonnet at a jaunty angle in bed at night; or even that there will 'always be a welcome in the hillside', this book ain't for you. It's about who I am; who I have ended up becoming; and taking a look at the life I have survived thus far and asking the major question of our time, a question asked by all the great philosophers down through the ages – from Nietzsche and Schopenhauer to Chic Murray: 'How the hell did I end up here?'

As I said at the start of this epistle, I was never meant to be an actor, or a stand-up, or a writer, or a political commentator; I was meant to be a good girl and simply shuttit! So where did it all go right?

CHAPTER 3

FOR STELLA

There's a part of me that wants to call this whole book *For Stella*. Ironically, when my mother was alive she would have loved the fact that I had named my book after her. She would have treasured it and dined out on it no doubt, as any proper showbiz mother would. And that would of course have driven me mad. She would have set up a wee stall in East Kilbride Shopping Centre with a sign saying, 'Elaine C. Smith is my daughter and she dedicated this book to me. I'm Stella. She is nothing without me!'

When she was alive, I was never able to give into that, her sentimental side – I was too embarrassed by it. Whenever she used the posh voice and said 'Yes, this is my daughter, the actress, you might know her from the telly,' I just wanted to crawl under a stone. She always told me that colleagues at work (she sold houses) just happened to guess that she was my mother. 'So,' I'd say 'They just walked into your sales office and asked you out of the blue if you were Elaine C. Smith's mother?' She would squirm for a bit and then reveal that they had just got talking and somehow it had simply come up in conversation. Got talking? How anyone got a word in was a miracle. People think I talk a lot, but they should have heard my mother – she could talk underwater!

Her ability to pass on useless information – and go off at tangents – could, and should, have been an Olympic sport. She would have been up on that podium with a gold medal every time. Her ability to start talking about one thing and move on to another without drawing breath was something to behold. No facts and a myriad of information that was no bloody use to man nor beast was imparted on a regular basis. She would arrive at the house laden with carrier bags (for a woman who lived on her own she never quite got the hang of buying for one). She would buy a multitude of things, especially if it was a bargain. 'I got these pork chops for you.'

'Thanks, Mum,' I'd reply, 'but I really don't like pork.'

'Och, ah know that, but they were only £1.99.'

She could shop for Scotland – another skill I have inherited. Then it would begin; pull the string and away she went – this all delivered in one breath by the way: 'Well, wait till I tell you . . . I was in Marks there . . . looking for a wee pair of *Pokémon* pyjamas for Hannah cos I'd seen them reduced the other day, and I know she loves that *Pokemon* doesn't she? But they only had the five to six [years of age] and I needed the seven to eight, and I met that woman Elspeth that used to live across the road in Bellshill from your gran, remember? Her husband had that terrible industrial accident, ended up in a wheelchair for a while but they got a lot of compensation . . . oh aye, built a conservatory, converted the loft and slabbed the front as well, but he never went back I don't think, though he was out the wheelchair as soon as the cash was through – but I'm saying nothing . . . and we were just gabbing and then I remembered that I had sold one of the flats in Hamilton to her daughter . . . she married an Egyptian doctor I think, and they'd lived out there for a while but she wanted home and he got a job at Monklands and they bought the flat, remember? Anyway she's doin' fine now, three kids, in quick succession too . . . but the Arabs are like that aren't they?

'So, anyway, Elspeth was telling me that her and her man had been out in Australia, aye, Melbourne, I think, well, two of her boys are out there and at least four grandchildren. I can't mind their ages but I think it's three boys and a girl . . . oh and they had a great time and she was looking well – could do wi' losing a few pounds, and I don't really think she's aged that well but then she wasn't from that great stock! Her father was workshy and that mother of hers had a tongue that could cut steel . . . but considering that, she was lookin' well. She was asking after you, says she remembers you as a baby and watches your career and is that pleased you're doin' well. Of course, I just said, "Well, I'm proud of all my girls", and told her about how well Louise and Diane were doin' with the hairdresser's and all that. It was lovely but she's a helluva gab, I couldn't get away . . . and then guess what? I went downstairs to the food hall for that chicken tikka masala that I love but they only had the low fat and I didn't want that – but I met her again! Isn't that funny?'

By this time I would have made a cup of tea, defrosted a chicken, loaded up the washing machine, answered a few calls and Dysoned the hall, she wouldn't even notice. But it was a great lesson for me to heed – if you are telling a story to an audience, have a bloody point!

Of course all that pointless gabbing makes me smile now and wish to God I could hear her say it all a million times. I would give almost anything and endure the embarrassment, to see her sitting at a wee stall in East Kilbride with this book. Stella died on 4 May 2005. My life, the lives of my sisters, her family, her grandchildren, her sons-in-law and all her extended family changed for ever. The knowledge that Stella was no longer walking on this planet changed everything.

I am reminded of a line in the film of Jane Austen's *Sense and Sensibility* about the death of the family's father. When an aunt complains that the daughters are taking a long time to get over their loss, their cousin replies 'Don't you understand? Their lives will never be the same again.' Never a truer line spoken.

Yes, life does go on and we laugh, cry, sing, dance and work – we get on with things, but life is never the same again. The heart finds a terrible place to reside, a place I didn't know existed until Stella died. Now when I think of my own daughters and how I feel about them, I realise that Stella was just so proud of me, and that I could simply never accept it. I felt it strangled me at times. I suppose maybe because she lived so vicariously through me and always seemed amazed and surprised at what I could do, due to her own lack of confidence and insecurity. But sadly, Stella lived her life never feeling that she was quite good enough or doing things properly, even though she was quite a snob and very pass-remarkable (in other words she said what she thought).

I would hear her talking to the TV to Lorraine Kelly or any other female presenter in her gaze, saying things like 'Well, hen, I don't know who dressed you the day but they should be shot.' This from a woman sitting in her dressing gown, with tea stains on the front and her bottom set of teeth out. But the world never got to see Stella looking like that. Oh no. She was always dressed, as a neighbour once remarked, like something out of a bandbox. And matching? Always matching! A blue bag and brown shoes was the ultimate sin and no hairdo and lipstick were hanging offences. She worried far too much about what other people thought and I followed her example, becoming a people-pleaser if ever there was one, a trait that's taken me a long time to drop, and then learn to live life on my own terms.

I think because of her unhappy childhood and her subsequent struggles with being a mother at such a young age, which evolved into an unhappy marriage, she slowly went down the path of melancholy and depression. As a consequence, she didn't really know, or love, the real her, or me. So, when I started my career and she shared my enjoyment of it, I felt that it was the only part of me that she really loved, and that the real me was much more difficult to love. Part of me knows that I became an actress in an attempt to separate properly from her. Maybe, I reasoned, if I was on the stage, under the lights with Mum sitting in the audience, she would at last hear me say, 'Look, Stella, I'm not you!'

Looking back I realise that she was growing up at the same time as I was myself. All the love that I wished she had demonstrated to me as a child she was able to do when I was an adult, but by then I didn't believe it. I was suspicious of it. I watched her grow to be a fabulous grandmother to my own daughters, and much as I loved the fact that my girls were on the receiving end of it, I did think, well, who is this? This isn't the woman that brought me up! All the cuddles and kisses and open demonstrations of love, I never got any of that. But it wasn't her fault, she was so young, had never had much love and affection in her own life and didn't really know how to show it. She was very emotional and could be moved to tears easily by everything from *Coronation Street* to a song on the radio. When she felt happy, or sad, or even proud or pleased, her first reaction was tears.

I was the oldest too, so I think I was more of an experiment as far as the 'weans' were concerned. That I loved her is not in question, even four years on as I write this, a well of grief surfaces, to the point where water runs down my face. This reaction, I have to say, is far less frequent than it was at that time, but when it comes it's so painful and so real that I feel I can't breathe. It happens when I hear a piece of music, hear a daft joke, see something that reminds me of her – and it's not the usual soppy stuff that it's supposed to be. It's the little sayings she had, like 'don't have medicines on an empty stomach'; remembering that she thought that LA and Los Angeles were two different places; it's seeing myself start to buy two-for-one offers in Tesco, even though I don't need them (but it's a bargain); and realising that I am, after all, my mother's daughter.

I suppose I spent a great deal of my life trying to deny that. There's something about mothers that drives daughters to distraction and forces us to do all we can just not to be like them. But over time, when they're no longer here, being like my mother doesn't seem like such a terrible thing. If I end up half as kind, daft, thoughtful, opinionated, emotional and caring as she was, I think I will be all right. The things that drove me crazy then are the things that, now she's gone, I miss the most. They are the things that make me smile the most. The things that only I, my sisters and my daughters can laugh about with a 'That's Stella talking!'

So to understand, how the hell I ended up here, I have to tell you all a bit about her because therein lies the key to my own journey. My mum, the daughter, the sister, the grandmother, the mum-in-law, the friend, the saleswoman, the gab . . . that was Stella.

CHAPTER 4

WHO DO I THINK I AM?

Stella was born in a tenement flat above the Co-op on Clydesdale Road, Mossend, in Bellshill, Lanarkshire on 17 January 1934. The flat was one of two above the store and they were relatively posh in that they had an inside toilet and bathroom – a rarity for families in the 1930s. The house had two bedrooms, the smaller for her parents and the larger room with the bay window for the girls. Joan and Eileen in the double bed in the window, Stella, Margaret and Magda in the other. The only boy, Jim, slept in a bed in the living room. She was the fourth child of John and Elizabeth McGarry.

John McGarry, my grandfather, was a bright Irishman who landed in Scotland at the age of seven from Magherafelt in Derry. Originally he and his family lived in Govan and then moved to Craigneuk in Motherwell in the early 1900s. His father, who was both illegitimate and illiterate, came over to find work and found it in Lanarkshire in the steelworks. His sense of shame and humiliation at a father who couldn't read and of dubious parentage seems to me to have been the driving force in John's life. His desire for betterment, education, and a sense of suspicion and mistrust started very early in his life, and he never lost it.

He was an intelligent man without formal education and worked hard to end up as works manager in Smith and MacLean's in Mossend, Bellshill, hence the decision to settle with the family close by. But his journey to that position had been a difficult one, full of a sense of betrayal (he only got the job three years before the works closed and when there was no one else left, according to family legend, with a Masonic handshake).

He met Elizabeth Robertson (or 'Betty') when they were at school together. She was extremely bright and I think would have gone on to university had she been given the chance. But she was a girl in the Victorian era in a steel town with no money, so that dream or ambition would never be realised. Given John's own background, he must have been so attracted to this tall girl who was top of the class in everything and that sense of awe about her was always present. I think he envied her intelligence.

Gran was born in Dalkeith, the oldest of three children, where her mother ran a shop, a general store I think. She, along with her brother Jimmy and sister Kate, moved to the area of Craigneuk in Motherwell, presumably to also find work in the steel mills. She was relatively old by the standards of the 1920s when she married. She was in her late 20s and had, I think, assumed that she would never marry. She may have possibly thought marriage wasn't for her. She actually had a great life, with well-paid work from various sources including the library, and had a good social life attending evening classes, and had a great circle of women friends too.

It must have been quite a shock for her when John McGarry walked back into her life and within the space of ten years she had married this twinkling, bright Irishman and ended up with six kids! Betty was tall (she was 5 ft 8 in.), elegant, quiet, intelligent and bookish. She was never seen without a book, and in fact legend has it that the kids would be running riot through the house and Betty would just be sitting there with a book, lost in a story as mayhem occurred all around her. But I think that my papa must have swept her away from the life she had planned.

I can only piece together bits of her own parents' lives and why she didn't marry but I think it may have been to do with her mother. It seems that my great-grandmother had a history of depression and mental illness and spent a lot of time in and out of hospitals. In those days that would have meant that, as the oldest, Betty would have had to maintain the family home. At 17, her brother Jimmy, joined the Royal Navy during the First World War, and her sister Kate got a job in service and was on a boat to the United States as quick as she could. She ended up living in the USA for the rest of her life.

By all accounts John McGarrry was charming, handsome and, above all, funny, which is always fatal for a woman. Even through all my mother's loathing of him, her one area of forgiveness was always about how funny he was. He must have swept Betty off her feet and he absolutely adored her. They shared a love of theatre and would make trips into Glasgow to see plays at the Citizens Theatre, the Citz, but I don't think they were big Music Hall fans.

Their first daughter was named Joan after they made the trip to see Sybil Thorndyke in *Saint Joan* at the Citz alongside her husband, Lewis Casson. My mother and all the family talk fondly of the nights when they all sat around the radio and listened to plays from beginning to end in rapt silence. Radio remained a great source of comfort and calm throughout Stella's life and a daily dose of *Woman's Hour* kept her sane when her own kids were small. Betty was a product of the Victorian era, as she was born in 1896, and this was evident in the way she carried herself in life. Manners, grace and elegance were second nature to her and also meant a great deal to her.

Betty may have been bringing up six kids in a flat above the Co-op, but she appeared to manage and retain a sense of quiet elegance and was always seen as a bit of a lady. She wore a hat every day in life, even to the Co-op it wasn't unusual to see her sitting reading in front of the fire with her hat still on her head and a nice scarf around her neck. When she became a pensioner she refused to go on any of the church outings or bus runs – she hated being treated as an OAP and herded around on a coach trip.

At Gran's house, meals were always served on a fully set table, with tablecloth, tablemats and silver cutlery (no eating on your lap or in the kitchen – EVER). We had a proper breakfast, followed by lunch and finally dinner, all served at the dining table. She was a deeply religious woman, though you'd never know to speak to her, but she was at mass every morning at Sacred Heart Church in Bellshill and took the St Vincent de Paul trolley round the local hospitals for 25 years.

Papa's own religious beliefs altered apparently when it suited him. When he was hung-over and refusing to go to mass he was a Trotskyist and non-believer, and when he thought he was being persecuted in any way he was a Catholic. He rarely went to mass himself and when his other daughter Eileen told of her decision to become a nun, he was appalled and furious that this bright, sporty girl was throwing her life away, and in bouts of drunkenness threatened to burn down every convent in the country to stop her.

The fact that her daughter, Stella, left the religion to marry my dad, along with the fact that her grandchildren (the three of us) were never christened, must have hurt the devout Betty deeply. It's a testament to her, and her true belief in a tolerant form of Christianity, that she never let us know. Her love and care for us were always present. There was a time, apparently, just after Stella and Jim married (and before I was born), when relations were so strained that there was no contact between my mum and her family at all. Most of this was due to my mother's relationship with her father and his desire to control everything in his children's lives.

When Stella was going out with my dad and they decided to marry, her father went as far as trying to get my dad sacked from his work as a turner in Clyde Crane Engineering. Bellshill, and the villages surrounding it, was a relatively small community and therefore most people knew each other, or at least knew of each other. The story goes that John (as a works manager himself) had a talk with one of the managers at Clyde Crane Engineering. It would have taken place in the pub, where Papa did most of his deals and scheming, he too was a believer that anyone could be bought. His wife and kids scrimped and saved but he was always flashing the cash and buying friendship and entertaining the men in the boozer. So he tried to have Jim dismissed, but it didn't work.

Ironically, my dad was saved because of religion. His foreman and shop steward were Orangemen and my dad's sister was in the local Orange band so it was assumed that he was one of them (even though he'd no religion at all). They determined to protect him from this Catholic boss (and overbearing father-in-law), who didn't want a good Protestant man to marry his daughter on the grounds that he came from a poor family and wasn't good enough for her and that he wasn't a Catholic into the bargain. So, in a way, I owe my very existence to sectarianism and the Orange Order. Never thought I would ever write that sentence. God bless King Billy!

My mum's view of herself was that she was quiet, shy and submissive. In actual fact she was the rebel. She was the one who rebelled at school, gave 'cheek' up to the hated nuns (she thought them cruel, violent, vicious and jealous of the girls in their charge, with a few exceptions). I don't think her academic career was helped by the fact that her two older sisters – Joan and Eileen – had excelled there, and so she was constantly being compared to the ex-school captain, and the captain of the hockey team! In short I think she was bored; the family route of academia was not for her. She wanted romance and love and adventure. She wanted another life. She was constantly getting into trouble with the priest for being caught with boys and going off and not telling people where she was going.

So at only 19 she was determined to start a new life and just forget about her family. It was a classic reaction to pain and anger in a young, headstrong woman, I suppose. I think basically she was in a very big huff.

Stella regretted to the day she died the hurt she caused her mother and never forgave herself for one particular incident. She was on a bus a few weeks before the wedding and saw her mother. She stood to get off the bus and her mum tried to speak to her. My mother stuck her nose in the air, walked past her as if she didn't know who she was and got off the bus. Awful. It says a lot for my father that he made her return home to her family and make up. He must have known that if left to fester over time these wounds can never truly heal. After they had been married a few months he felt that she should attempt to make peace. Stella resisted, but was missing her family very much and relented. The visit was difficult but broke the ice and there was never a fall-out again. There were the stresses and strains, rivalries and slights that exist in all families, but never anything as major and painful.

I was born in 1958 and the healing was greatly helped with the birth of the first grandchild, so I was incredibly spoiled as a result by all the attention. I've never got over it – becoming an actor seems to be all part of the pursuit of that same, adoring attention that I got for just arriving and being – any decent therapist would tell you that, I'm sure.

My grandmother was a huge influence on my early life. I spent many days and weeks with her, as did my sisters, in our early years. In summer it was wonderful. I loved being at their house and she loved our being there, she had a huge garden (in the days when council houses were built with lots of room inside and out). She took us to mass with her even though we weren't Catholics. I think my mum felt it made up for her desertion and my dad was a non-believer so he didn't mind, I think he saw it as part of our education in life, as well as a way of healing any rifts.

Gran never forced her religion on us. We went with her because that's what she did every day. We hadn't a clue about the procedures so she put up with our attempts to douse ourselves in holy water and sitting backwards on the wee platforms meant for you to kneel and pray (as we thought they were special seats for kids) or my curtseying as I went in and out of the pews. I thought that's what others were doing too. It was a long time before I worked out they were making the sign of the cross with their hands and not actually curtseying. And then after mass we would go to the Bellshill Road Co-op for sweets (the start of another addiction). Happy days!

Gran taught me to knit, to set a table (which I do really well by the way – a work of art on a special occasion, as my daughters will testify, and I am the only one allowed to do it). More importantly, she passed on her love of learning and reading, which I have to this day. She has been a constant presence in my life and although she died when I was 15 she has never really left me.

Stella talked of a feeling that her father found the family too much for him. Apparently he coped fine with the first three kids and enjoyed them but tragedy struck as his second son Kevin died after only a few weeks of life. They were all devastated. It was into this situation that Stella was born. She was the child that arrived after Kevin died. For Betty there could have been a sense of relief, alongside her grief, I think, given that she had more breathing space before the next child.

When Stella did come along, it seems to have been to a very tired mother and a father who was rapidly losing interest in the family. She wasn't a boy, which may have been a disappointment to Papa, and she was obviously very over-protected because of what had happened with Kevin. She talked often of how fearful and at times melancholy she was as a child. I think it must have given her the desire to escape.

Another two children came around pretty quickly (Magda and Margaret), which seems to have been a bit much for Papa. His wife was always busy and tired, and it appears that he spent more and more time in the pub. It appears also that Gran spent more time in the church, where she found great solace.

Stella's sense of shame about her father and his behaviour never left her. It may have come at a very difficult time for her – her early adolescence coincided with his escalating drunkenness. Although Stella had gone the family route, dux at primary and a place at Elmwood, she hated it. She wanted to be out in the world and live. She loved boys and wanted to be at the dancing, wear make-up and marry Cary Grant – well, a girl can dream. All of it was a desire to escape what she perceived as the oppressive life she was living.

John McGarry was not your typical wee west-of-Scotland drunk. No, no, he seems to have been a gentleman drunk. This was your actual suited, respectable church-going works manager. Always with a shirt and tie (the old wing collars, too), pinstripe suit, fedora, posh overcoat and a fob watch – the works. Not an easy look to carry, I would imagine, in 1940s Bellshill, but that's who it appears he was. He was a man with a big ego (and related to Irish royalty in the form of his being related to the 'Papal Count' that was the world famous Irish tenor John McCormack). He had, it seemed, many insecurities and demons and a great deal of anger that would only surface when he'd had a drink – pubs the length and breadth of Scotland were unfortunately full of very similar men. Like all tyrants, he had a hugely sentimental side and with a drink could be in tears as quickly as he could be in a rage.

When I got to know him in his later years he looked like Winston Churchill, which was a shame as he had been a very handsome younger man. I adored him. He was funny, cuddled me, let me look and play with his beautiful fob watch, which I thought was the most fascinating thing I'd ever seen, bought me sweets all the time and generally made me feel like the centre of the universe.

He got another black mark from my mother when I was born. He was so thrilled to have his first grandchild that he turned up at the house a bit the worse for wear one night with a huge bag full of sweets for me. He had obviously forgotten that, at five weeks old and with no teeth as yet, it might be a bit tough for me to eat five shillings' worth of Fry's Chocolate Cream. Well, it was the thought wasn't it? It just confirmed to her what an 'eejit' he was. As he got older, his Irish roots meant more and more to him, but being an avid Celtic fan was as far as his Catholicism went. As a kid I didn't understand the whole football Rangers versus Celtic thing, so never got his teasing of me about football.

I didn't go to Catholic school, I had been sent to the local primary, which was a supposed non-denominational school (though we sang Protestant hymns, said Protestant prayers and the Church of Scotland minister visited every Friday – how that was non-denominational I don't know). Anyway, all my pals and the boys in class supported Rangers or Motherwell and therefore so did I. I didn't actually know what it was all about and when I asked my parents they were vague and dismissive.

My dad had never been the least bit interested in football and still isn't, and we were all girls so there was never even any talk of football in the house. But I did glean from the chants in school that supporting Celtic was bad and that only Catholics (also bad for some reason) supported Celtic. At seven years of age I knew nothing of football or sectarianism; on one side of the family I had avid mass-goers and on the other my dad's sisters played in a Protestant Orange band. I had yet to learn the line of loathing and bitterness that existed between these groups.

So Papa enjoyed winding me up when I said I supported Rangers and after a few whiskies he would get into the Irish songs. As soon as the John McCormack records were on I knew the tears would flow: 'The Kerry Dancing', 'I'll Take You Home Again Kathleen' – I enjoyed these little pieces of theatre, I didn't understand them but they were fun and dangerous and full of emotion and he always gave me half a crown (a lot of money) at the end of it all. Talk about a captive audience.

One afternoon I did get distressed when he came back from the pub. I didn't know where he went of an afternoon because he always said the same thing. He was 'going a wee message', as they say in Lanarkshire, or 'going to see a man about a dog'. I was confused that this dog never, ever appeared – he must have seen a helluva lot of whippets in his time.

Anyway, he'd obviously had a lot more than usual and the records went on and I sat on his knee, but his weeping became quite uncontrollable. I ran out to the garden where Gran was hanging out a washing and said: 'Papa's crying!' She looked at me with a very careworn expression and said: 'Just leave him, go and play,' which I did. I think I saw him again the next day when he'd slept it off. When I told Mum she took on the same expression as Gran, slightly angry, hard, but resigned – a look I have seen since on many people's faces who share the same bond of living with someone with alcohol addiction. So the man that rolled up pissed when Stella was a young girl was usually in a taxi and very well dressed. But that didn't stop him falling off the garden wall and being carried into the house by his children.

On one occasion, burned into the young Stella's brain, he was left on the hall floor to sleep it off. They had carried him in from the garden, (where he had tipped off the wall), tried to rouse him but eventually Betty told them to leave him. His children had to step over him to get to bed – an incident that filled my mother with disgust and shame which she never got over. It seemed that all his ambition was put into his kids and particularly his only son Jim. Fortunately he had very bright children who really benefited from the state education available at the time and the progress that had been made to help working-class children to achieve.

Joan was the first to get to Glasgow University to study English. Joan adored her father and she was the apple of his eye. Joan didn't marry till she was 39, and stayed at home till her late 20s where she helped a great deal with the family finances. I think Papa thought she would never leave, so when she did marry he was pretty much against it. She married another Irishman in Séamas, a lieutenant in the Royal Navy and a lovely man.

We later found out that Papa's objection was more about finances than any real objection to Séamas. He had gone behind Gran's back and cashed in a huge chunk of his pension to give him a substantial amount of drinking vouchers to flash around. He'd assumed that Joan would always be there to look after Gran and Aunt Magda financially. It was a real act of selfishness and betrayal.

Eileen was offered a place too, but held firm and just after her 17th birthday was admitted to a convent in Glasgow, where the family watched and wept from behind a gate as her beautiful dark hair was cut off. She went on to get a degree and became a teacher and ended up as a headmistress of a school in Nigeria. Her smile was magical and she was truly a holy person if ever there was one. And, of course, my mother thought she looked much better in the white habit that nuns wore in Africa, saying, 'The black is too depressing and does nothing for her.'

Eileen was diagnosed with breast cancer at the age of thirty-nine and died three years later after terrible suffering, never quite accepting that God had forsaken her. A couple of days before she died she was found trying to crawl to mass. I was 12 when she died and the family were utterly devastated, I don't think my mother ever got over the loss.

The pressure on Jim – the only son – must have been immense. He was amazingly bright, studying Greek and Latin while at Our Lady's High in Motherwell, but he was also really sporty, always playing football. My mother talked of her amazement at his ability to stand at the sideboard with a sandwich in one hand, football boots over his shoulder while doing his Latin homework, and then going on to score a goal as well as coming top of the class. Jim was Stella's hero, everything a man should be, and her protector against the cruel jibes and control of their father.

But although Jim's real love was literature, he had a father who wanted a doctor in the family and he wasn't going to settle for anything else. So Jim opted for medicine at Glasgow University. He must have struggled a great deal in his first couple of years but managed to fit in sports, the debating society, clubs, girls and a job to keep him going financially. He overcame all the hurdles of religion and class to go on to become head of obstetrics at the Southern General Hospital in Glasgow. He was a wonderful and dedicated doctor.

Stella told me that she watched all this pressure, all the competition to be the best and come first in the eyes of her father and just rebelled and rejected it out of hand. By all accounts the pressure on the younger girls, Magda and Margaret, was not as tough. Magda had learning difficulties so luckily would never feel the academic pressure that the others did and would remain living with her parents well into her adulthood.

Margaret, as the youngest, must have been very hurt by Stella leaving and all the upset that caused. She was actually the one my mother was closest to and most envied. Margaret was born beautiful and bright, with the look of the moment (very Audrey Hepburn), hair cropped very short, little make-up applied and slim. Stella recounted often an episode of her walking with a 20-year-old Margaret along Argyll Street in Glasgow on a summer's day. Margaret had been on holiday in Cornwall and had a tan and was wearing a coral-coloured dress with a matching lipstick. My mum was pregnant with me and felt huge as she watched men falling off the pavement to turn and look at her beautiful sister, who was totally unaware of the effect she was having.

Margaret finished her training as a nurse at the Royal in Glasgow, after being pursued by many a doctor. She transferred to Bart's Hospital in London simply, as she said, to get away. To have a different life, a life away from the pressure of her family, the drinking and the oppressive culture of sectarianism – that was her goal.

It wasn't apartheid by any means but to be a Roman Catholic in the west of Scotland in the '50s and '60s was far from an easy path to walk. It was insidious in its execution. Margaret tells of the fact that all her friends as nurses and doctors were non-Catholics, they had all come to her home, but she was never invited to theirs – ever. That was the culture; being a Catholic, even an educated, middle-class one, marked you out as different.

She endured a lot of poverty as a young nurse in London, going years without a winter coat because she couldn't afford one. She met and married an English naval officer, Chris Edwards, whom she'd met through Jim, who was in the navy as a doctor doing his national service at the time. They moved further south to Plymouth and went on to have three wonderful daughters, Claire, Ann and Siobhan, our only cousins on the McGarry side. Margaret never came back to live in Scotland, though at one point all three of her daughters did.

So, at the ripe old age of 15, much to her father's distress, Stella announced that she was leaving school to get a job. In a highly academic family, her announcement was a bit of a bombshell. But she carried it through and thanks to a letter written by her father she got a job as a trainee cashier in a furniture shop in Motherwell and worked at a succession of office jobs until and during her marriage.

There were too many arguments with her father and she left home eventually after one final fight – with her brother Jim holding on to her father and telling him to let her go. I think she stayed with a friend and their family because these were the days when there was a shortage of housing and a young woman could never have got a flat on her own.

She met my dad, Jimmy Smith, when she was only 17 years old. She was at a party in Wishaw and was supposed to pair off with my dad's brother Bill but there was a mix up and she ended up with my dad walking her all the way home. They started going out and although they were from quite different backgrounds, against all odds they married in February 1953.

CHAPTER 5

JIMMY SMITH ('DOLL')

So what about my dad? The 'doll' reference is because that's what Dad always called us – or in fact most women in his life. We maintained it was because he couldn't remember our names and that was easier, just in the way that actors call each other 'darling' because they can't be bothered remembering each other's names. Ironic I think that I also ended up playing a role, for the best part of ten years of my life, called 'Mary Doll'. To this day when I phone he says, 'Hiya, doll', or 'Hiya, angel'. For a while the feminist in me hated it, but now it makes me weep because I know that to him we were these wee magical girls, and it's a way of keeping us there – back in time. He did the same with his sisters too.

Jimmy Smith was the oldest son of ten children (Rena, Mary, Jimmy, Bill, Andy, Isabel, John, Cissy, Rita and Fred) born to Isobel and Jimmy Smith of Holytown. Unlike my mum's family, who were relatively middle class in their outlook and wealth, the Smiths were pretty poor. Stella often said that she thought she was poor until she went to my father's family home. In fact the first time he took her home, he had gone to a second-hand store to buy a new set of living room furniture to replace the stuff they had (the second-hand furniture was better than the stuff they were living with!). He obviously thought that my mum was posh – actually it was just more educated than anything else.

The McGarry house wasn't wealthy but it was full of books; they had a writing bureau, and a piano; they listened to the radio; they went to mass and Gran had a woman who helped clean and do the washing. So pretty posh in a way I suppose to some folk. The Smith household had none of that. They were all hard-working, good people – just victims of the poverty that many suffered in the pre- and post-war years in working-class Scotland.

Papa Smith had been a miner and a railway worker but silicosis (and a pack of Capstan Full Strength every day) led to many periods of unemployment and ill health. Dad used to take us up to see his parents every Saturday afternoon. Some of my aunts and uncles still lived at home (Dad was away in the RAF when his younger brother Fred was born, so they were like two families), and they would be handing out bowls of soup from the big pot in the kitchen.

The house was always jumping with kids and relatives. There was Aunt Rena and my cousin Kate – who was the oldest grandchild, but actually older than my Uncle Fred! This was all too common in many families, with mothers still having their own children when their oldest was having their first! There was Aunt Mary and Uncle George Reid – he was the jolliest man on the planet who loved kids and laughed and chortled at his own jokes constantly. He was a great kidder and all the weans loved him. Their own kids were Isobel and Charles, who were great fun to play with.

Aunt Frances and Uncle Andy, and their two oldest – Jim and John (Andrea and Drew came later) – were my closest cousins. We were very close in age and my parents socialised a lot with them. We went on holidays to resorts in Bridlington and Rhyll; in convoy with them on many a fair fortnight, where our cars overheated on Shap Fell and the legendary traffic jams went for miles. Family folklore has it my Aunt Rena got out of their car, went into the shops for her shopping and was able to catch my Uncle Nick 500 yards up the road an hour later!

Aunt Ruby and Uncle Bill, with my cousin David, were always at the Smiths on a Saturday early on in my life, but they moved to South Wales when Bill got a job at the steelworks in Llanwern in the mid '60s. It was a really big day when we all met on the platform at Motherwell station to say goodbye. It felt like they were going to the other side of the world. I was confused and couldn't understand why the adults were hugging and so sad, although I did feel a wrench when told that I wouldn't see David, or my laughing, joking Auntie Ruby for a long time. Little did we know that we would end up driving to Caldicot and Newport for many a holiday with them throughout the '60s and early '70s.

That long, long journey south through England was quite an undertaking – the packing, the cleaning, the endless checking of locks; the bins emptied; the arguments about who was or wasn't doing what; the picnic; the juice; the comics for the journey; and the three weans in the back of the Vauxhall Victor, roof-rack piled high with the snake clips and polythene covering it. It's a wonder that the car ever bloody moved, it was so weighed down, and I'm sure we hit 40 mph at least twice on the journey! But I think it gave my dad a sense of adventure and achievement. I mean, this is a man who spent most of his working life in steelworks or engineering works, covered in oil or grease, going to work in the dark and coming home in it too. The sense of light and hope must have been fantastic, and I must admit that even now driving south when I get on the M74 and head towards the border I feel that same sense of anticipation and excitement.

I still like the fact that I can stop at the service stations that we could never go into as kids because they were too expensive. We thought they were exotic palaces, the big one with the mushroom restaurant on the M6 seemed like a magical place – but we only ever got in to use the loo. I still have a vivid picture of the scene. Dad cooking his sausages on his wee Primus stove, the yellow folding chairs and picnic table, all set for breakfast, as we all disappeared into a field to have a pee (which I hated or cos I always seemed to manage to wet one of my socks and then spent the rest of the journey wondering what the 'ming' was). There we all were at the side of the road with traffic flying past, holding our plates or our hair as the big lorries approached. It was like Brands bloody Hatch, but my dad sat there surveying his achievements and going into interminable detail about the journey ahead and what the route would be, which was of no interest to three girls under the age of ten. It seemed endless, but when we drove through the beautiful Wye Valley we knew we were almost there.

Anyway, back to his early days.

My Smith grandparents' home was as chaotic, loud, lively and full of smoke as it sounds and to me at the age of four was a place of wonder. It was just full of life, with a park – which meant freedom for us kids – at the end of the road. I think I have sought out that 'life' ever since, that notion of family. Yet as I grew up I realised that much of it was a veneer, as the truth of the home emerged in more detail. But back then it was brilliant and I loved going there.

Much as I loved the McGarry household and being the centre of attention there, I was the only child, surrounded by adults. So being with all my cousins and all this life was fantastic. I hated going to the Smiths if all the relatives weren't there, it was far less exciting. Gran Smith (Isobel Sommers) was a cold, rather remote figure, probably just overwhelmed by what life had thrown at her (ten children with a couple of miscarriages in between). I don't think I ever saw her smile. I never received a card, a present or anything from her and I have no memory of her ever speaking directly to me.

I have tried to piece her life together and know that she was from a relatively well-off family with one brother (Frederick) and one sister (Cissy – 'Cis'). Her father died in an industrial accident in Stuart and Lloyds factory in Bellshill and I think they must have got some compensation that allowed them to have a relatively comfortable life. Frederick was killed in the First World War (six weeks before the Armistice in 1918) and the two sisters were left with Gran Sommers, who went on to live till she was 94 and resembled Queen Mary apparently.

Cissy married Andrew Brown and to her sadness was never able to have any children. Isobel married Jim Smith (I'm not sure whether she was pregnant or not, but it seems odd that she married someone from a totally poverty-stricken background when she was so young). The relationship between the sisters was never easy, Isobel envying the freedom, money and holidays that Cis could have, and in her turn Cis envying the children that she would have loved. Neither woman ever seemed happy and had a terrible melancholy about both of them.

My dad remembers his gran coming every week on a Tuesday and giving them a penny each (which was a fortune to them), and it indicates the level of poverty that their mum would take it from them as soon as Gran left. If their dad was working then they would occasionally get the penny back on a Saturday, which was then spent on an afternoon at the pictures in Bellshill (a ha'penny to get in) and topped off by a roll from the bakers and then filled up with chips at the chippy for another ha'penny.

I now think that she was just very unfulfilled and unhappy. Unfortunately that was transferred onto her kid; my dad remembers no kindness or warmth or even encouragement from her in his entire life. She had such a hard time and I think she must have constantly wondered how her life had turned out as it did, for women in those days there was nowhere else to go. So her upset, exhaustion and frustration were there for all to see; by the time it got to the younger children it seems to me that they were left to their own devices. Fred and Rita (who was a really stunning-looking girl) suffered greatly from that neglect. Rita was pregnant at fifteen, and would have four kids in quick succession, tragically dying of cervical cancer at only thirty-four years of age. Fred fought with the demon drink through his life and died in his 50s – how he lasted that long none of us know.

The older members of the family all lived into their 70s and 80s (at the time of writing this my dad is still ballroom dancing four nights a week at eighty-one) but the younger ones suffered more after their father died and the older kids had left home.

Gran Smith would take herself and her knitting (legend has it that she could knit a pair of socks on four needles while sitting in the dark and never drop a stitch) off to the pictures every Thursday afternoon. This was viewed by some at that time as being a bit of a selfish act towards her family. These were the days, of course, when a man going off to the pub every night for a beer was his right, but a woman knitting through a Thursday matinee was selfish – I ask you! I now think it was probably the only thing that kept her sane and am glad she had a wee bit of escapism in otherwise difficult times. But my sadness is that I never knew her, as she died when I was in my early 20s.

I know my dad found her cold and remote and that led, understandably, to a mistrust of women in later years. As the oldest son he had a lot of pressure to leave school and earn money. He recounts a tale of his mother's coldness when he was off work with a poisoned throat. He was really ill, unable to lift his head for the sweat and the pain in his throat as well as the poison floating around his system. His mother was so angry that he was losing wages that she refused to go up and see how he was. He kept trying to shout for help to get some water but eventually gave up and attempted to go downstairs himself. He passed out on the stairs and a doctor was eventually called. I don't think she spoke to him even then.

My Papa Smith was another remote figure to me. My dad called him 'Pop' but I only remember him as a wee, wizened, toothless, silver-haired figure in a pale-blue cable-knit jumper sitting next to the fire with a box of Capstan Full Strength (brought by the family) but my dad worshipped him.

The RAF and the Second World War saved my dad's life and gave him a sense of order and discipline. From as early as 1940 he was in the RAF Cadets and always wanted to join up. He went diligently for the next four years and then enlisted at only 17 (he forged his age so he could join) and did his basic training as an aircraft gunner before he was 18 and was headed on a ship to Fayed in Egypt when the Armistice was signed. But there was still a job to do, particularly in the Middle East, and he was part of the Photographic Reconnaissance Squadron who helped remap the countries of that region.

He was free and living his own life, though still sending his money home for the family in Holytown. He didn't care where he was headed, in fact on the form all servicemen were given to say where they would prefer to go he said that he just wrote in big letters across it 'OVERSEAS'. He just wanted out, to see the world, and for many young men like him this was the only way to escape from a life of poverty and limited horizons. He was an ideal recruit and he said that he never complained about the food because he had never had three square meals a day and a bed of his own to sleep in in his life. In a way, the services took care of him and made him feel of value to his country and in general in a way that he'd never had as a child.

CHAPTER 6

EARLY DAYS

Out of these families came Jim and Stella. They married in 1953, when she was 19 and he was 24. There they were, my mum and dad, this young, hopeful, happy, somewhat naïve, emotionally starved couple. They were very dapper dressers too, and it's easy to see why Stella thought my dad was a bit like Cary Grant, with his dark hair, black overcoat, white scarf and good manners. And he had got someone very unlike his mother, educated, bright and from a middle-class family, maybe the life his mother should have had. I like to think that they were full of optimism, starting out on a road they hoped would bring them fulfilment and happiness.

It was a difficult start, because my dad was not a Catholic and in the 1950s that was very shameful in the eyes of the Church. A Catholic could not marry anyone who was not of the same religion or who wasn't willing to become a Catholic. I think my dad was prepared to do that for Stella but then looked into it further and felt that he couldn't. He wasn't a believer in God himself and at the time the Catholic Church also had a ruling that if there was a choice in a complicated birth of saving the child or the mother, then the baby (an innocent) was to be saved. Dad vehemently disagreed with this, especially as he knew that he had a really rare blood group and this was a possibility (he had always been a blood donor and was on an emergency register because of this, so knew the risks to a new baby). He refused to become a Catholic.

Anyway, their first house in Motherwell was in Watson Street. Stella described a feeling of absolute elation and hope when they got the keys to that wee room and kitchen in a tenement (having given the 'key' money as it was called, i.e. a bribe, to the councillor – a drinking buddy of Papa's, I think). Those first years were very happy, though Stella and Jim were keen to have kids. But I didn't come along for five years, though Stella miscarried in between.

But they were relatively well off with Dad so they could afford a car, meals out, holidays. Dad has never smoked or drunk in his entire life (maybe why he has made it to be a very fit 81 year old), so there was no drain on the finances. He was a man who handed his wage packet unopened to my mum on the Friday – an act seen as saintly at the time.

He finished early on a Saturday and would go home and wash and change and then walk up to the Odeon or the Rex Cinema to queue for tickets for the latest films and then meet Mum from her work, have something to eat and then go on to the movies. They also would think nothing of driving down the coast to Ayr on a nice summer's night for a fish tea if they got finished from work early enough.

They also went cycling, as for years before he had met Stella, Dad had gone with his pals on the bikes up to Loch Lomond, so it was something they did together until the weans came along. It always seemed such a contented happy time for them. They were young and free, with enough money to enjoy life and no real ties. They had holidays too, though they were few and far between in those days, but life did get better as the years went on. It wasn't until I was born that my dad got Christmas Day as an official holiday, before that it was New Year's Day that was the holiday and it was common across Scotland for men to work on 25 December until the late 1950s. They drove to Fort William and Fort Augustus and down into Bridlington in England. There they were, like millions of others in the post-war world, with everything to live for – being of that generation, that had survived all the horror, greeting the future with open arms and full of hope.

Stella had a great sense of style and always wanted to look like Grace Kelly or Audrey Hepburn (well, who didn't?). She actually looked a bit like Judy Garland, with the dark hair and the turned-up nose – which she never liked (she had no faults, she would often say, until one day 'it turned up'). But Judy wasn't classy enough. The others oozed breeding and taste to her, and that's what she always aspired to.

Around the time I was born she bought herself a red 'swagger' coat and paid 21 guineas for it. That was a fortune when a week's wage was about £8. She saved and saved for it and told us she bought it for the fleur-de-lis satin lining. It was beautiful, and a good piece of 'schmutter', as 20 years later when it came back into fashion I wore it to drama school all the time (over jeans though) to many admiring comments, followed by my sister Louise, who wore it for years too.

I have to admit that the way Mum dressed had a big influence on me. She was meticulous about her accessories, for example. 'Miss Matching', as an old friend always called me, observing each day, 'Oh, is it a pink day today?' when all my accessories matched up. I've eased off a bit, but the ultimate sin for my mother was a brown bag and black shoes or gloves that didn't match. Well, there really was no need for that was there, in her opinion. It showed a lack of breeding as far as she was concerned and people should have been forcibly taught to match their outfits. Unlike her mother, she hated hats of any kind because they would spoil the 'do'. The 'hairdo' was of vital importance; if she had the do she could face the world. My mother was a woman who had a shampoo and set every Friday in Jayne's Hairstylist at the end of our street. She had the blond streaks put in there, the perm for a bit of body and always a bouffant (or 'a bit of height', as she called it). Above all her hair had to have height, she hated flat hair. The only time I ever saw her with flat hair was when tragedy or illness struck. Seeing Mum with flat hair or a headscarf on and without lipstick was a bewildering experience for me.

The first time I can remember is when I was only about five years old, I came home one day to find my grandmother in the house (complete with scarf around the neck and hat still on). Initially I was delighted but soon realised that something was wrong and that Gran was there because my mum was sick. Dad was also home from work early and the doctor was there and I could hear talk of 'waiting for an ambulance'. I didn't feel scared, I was just a bit excited at the thought of an ambulance outside our house (see, typical of my sense of drama, already loving the thought of the attention it would bring and the stories I could tell at school the next day!) I did get alarmed though when I walked into my parents' bedroom to see Mum in bed in the darkened room with a basin in front of her and coughing blood into it. No one knew I was there and it was only when I said 'Mummy' that they realised I was in the room. I was ushered out quickly with a 'Don't worry, your mum is fine she just has to go into hospital for a wee rest.' The next few hours and days are a blur, but somehow I was ushered off to stay with my Aunt Frances and Uncle Andy in Motherwell and was enrolled and started at my cousins' school, Glencairn Primary, with John and Jim.

I was there for around six weeks and I loved it. I was in the flash maisonette house that I loved (more of that later) with my favourite cousins and my Aunt Frances, who was so kind and warm to me. As with most kids, you adore the person who isn't your parents, and gives you attention. At this point I had my new sister to contend with and wasn't enjoying being ignored so there I was, the only girl again, with all the attention coming to me.

I loved the school too, because I was the new girl and therefore slightly exotic. They obviously knew that my mum was ill and the teachers were lovely, I had a ball. In fact six weeks later when Mum got out of hospital I was devastated at the thought of going home. I hadn't even seen her in hospital (those were the days when kids weren't allowed in).

My mother's illness turned out to be tuberculosis. Apparently she had had the disease in her teens but according to the doctors had fought it off herself, which was very unusual at a time when many children her age were dying or being shipped off to sanatoriums across the country to recover. Hard for us now to realise what a killer the disease was. My husband Bob had it in the early 1960s and was on antibiotics for a year, but by then it wasn't the killer it had been.

Another couple of occasions stand out for me, one of which was when Dad lost his job. I came home from school to find my mum with her hair in a scarf with rollers in – she had washed her hair herself – what? Basically it was because things were so tight financially that a hairdo was too expensive. For a few weeks we didn't have our usual food either and a lot of cheaper food was on the table, with few treats around.

Dad had always had low blood pressure, though early in his life we didn't know that and therefore we always got a real fright when he got something like a sore throat with a temperature because he tended to pass out. An early memory of this is seeing him actually hallucinating, his temperature was that high. He was sitting in our hall having been in bed ill with flu, and he was talking what I thought was complete gibberish but then we realised that he thought he was in the plane that he crashed in when he was in the RAF. He was giving the coordinates, altitude, the lot, and was very panicked because he was there! He was reliving it all, with my mum trying to get through to him saying, 'Jim, Jim, it's me, Stella. You're all right.' But he couldn't focus, and for a child, it was a very scary thing and though eventually we got the doctor in and got him back to bed it was pretty weird for me at ten years of age to watch.

These episodes also seemed to happen at times of extreme worry and stress. Money, compared to some folks, was never a real worry, but as the breadwinner, Dad needed to work full time, and for any person, no matter how much you enjoy your work, only the weekend free, plus a couple of weeks' holiday a year, is not a lot for anyone to relax. We were all young, so it was impossible at that time for Mum to get out to work and it was still kind of frowned upon too.

So Dad's first stroke when I was in my teens should have been no real surprise. He had been 'head hunted' by another firm and given a promotion that meant that he would have to actually be in charge of a section in a plant. As I said, my dad was, and is, a great worker – never happier than when he is building something or taking an engine apart, and his knowledge is remarkable. If you were a boss looking for someone with a work ethic and an extensive knowledge of everything from ball-bearings to general engineering, then you would pick Jimmy any time. However, I think that because of his lack of formal education, he found the thought of any responsibility that involved a lot of paperwork, or even dealing with the formality of management, very difficult and the source of a lot of internal struggle.

Of course, Stella had always wanted him to get a job in an office and go to work in a suit instead of a pair of overalls, but not for him, for her. In her eyes it would have improved her standing no end and she equated class, respectability and intelligence with a man in a suit.

We only have to look at the recent banking crisis or parliamentary expenses debacle to realise that a suit means very little!

He went for the interview, got the job and everyone was delighted, telling him he deserved it, well, except for his employers who had counted on him and were less than pleased to see him go. I think that was a source of stress to Dad too. But this job was more money, more responsibility and a step up. The day before he was due to start the job we heard the car come into the drive, and then a long blast of the horn and for some reason Dad didn't appear. After about 15 minutes Mum went down to see where he was and found him slumped over the steering wheel. He was barely conscious but as she brought him round it became evident that his speech was slurred and that he couldn't move down one side.

The next few weeks are a blur for me; well, I was a teenager and only really interested in myself, boys and pop music. In that order! I don't know whether I was much of a help, but I do remember a round of doctors, hospitals, upset and worry over losing the new job, hardship financially because for the first time we were living on sickness benefit, and, gradually, watching my father recover. Stella's hair was very rarely done for a few weeks so I knew things were bad. Dad now tells me that it wasn't a full stroke but a TIA (a mini-stroke) but for many months he went to rehabilitation almost every day and he worked so hard to get back to fitness. He would sit watching TV holding little springs that would exercise his hands and strengthen the muscles in his arm.

This inevitably put a strain on the marriage. Three kids, no work, and a marriage of many years by this time; as they say, when money worries come in the door, love and romance go out the window. Stella was a woman who was coming to terms with her own life, having survived her past family life, her life as a young mother and generally growing up. She wanted more from life, and like many women in the late '60s and '70s was enjoying changes that the feminist movement had brought and was fighting her own little battles domestically. She was back at night school doing her Highers – which would enable her to do further courses or get a better job. She'd also been working part time as a cashier in a bingo hall and in offices to try and bring in some much-needed cash.

Dad on the other hand, having escaped his past, was happy to simply do all he could to support his wife and kids. Like many men of that time, he was confused as to why his wife was unhappy and unsettled – why want more than what they had? At this point he must have just been focused on getting back to fitness.

Writing this now, I realise my desire for a big 'do' is no accident. A good hairdo gives me a sense that all is well in myself. I know that if my girls see me with flat hair they wonder what is wrong and usually laugh. Psychologically, I think it must make me feel secure. If the do is fine, then life is all right. You only have to look at me to see the same traits as my mother, Stella, never knowingly underdressed, matching accessories and colours and of course, big hair. Yes, I am my mother's daughter after all.

CHAPTER 7

THE MESSIAH . . . WELL, ME!

I was viewed as a bit of a miracle. First child, and first grandchild, a baby they had waited five and a half years for. They were overjoyed to become parents and I think Stella certainly felt that it would make her life better and more complete – a mistake that many young women make. She loved being pregnant and the centre of attention, she felt a sense of purpose and belonging that she hadn't felt before.

It was a hard and difficult labour for her, as Stella reminded me on every birthday. When the day came round she would launch into the 'Well, 15, 25, 30, 36 years ago today I was just starting a 35-hour labour, there were no drugs in those days, just get on with it, and that wee midwife she was a horror wouldn't even give me gas and air. Thank God when that lovely Sister came on she was an angel and held my hand, well you were on your own in those days, none of this husbands in with you malarkey. I went through three shifts of the nurses till you decided to make an appearance.'

My Auntie Maureen was the best at the telling of tales – funny, warm and a delivery that any comedy turn would kill for. 'Well, girls, as you know I had a hellish time with oor Alexander and then to top it all the afterbirth wouldnae come away.' This said sotto voce in case any men could hear. (I was actually hiding behind the couch about 12 years of age listening to the women talking and gossiping.) 'So this lovely wee Asian doctor said to me, "Maureen, we need to get this oot, hen."' (They always seemed to call her by her first name too.) 'And he went oot and came back in with what I can only describe as a hubcap. I just looked at him but he took a run and jump with that

59

in his hands and landed on my belly, and I have to tell you, girls, it worked. All shipshape with a cup of tea and toast, no bother. There was a helluva draft for about a fortnight but I was fine!'

So, Stella's labour was drug-free and hellish according to her, with some cruel nurses who gave her little comfort in Calder Bank House (strangely enough only about half a mile from where I live now in Glasgow). But she did also say that she had never felt better about herself and what she had done. It gave her a fantastic sense of achievement and for the first time in her life she felt she'd done something right. I confess I felt the same when my first daughter Katie was born, the sense of elation and knowing what I'd brought into the world far outweighed anything that I have achieved before or since. That feeling when I woke in the middle of the night after she was born and saying the words 'I've got a daughter,' was the best feeling in the world.

Stella opted for that particular hospital because she had such a terrible experience at Motherwell Maternity when she'd miscarried two years before I was born and vowed she would never let a certain doctor near her again. It made it difficult for visiting for Jimmy, as it was miles from Motherwell and they had no car at the time, but Dad made it every visiting session after work, in fact the day after I was born he was so excited that he arrived unannounced and was not allowed in before visiting. So he left a message to say that he was just passing, and wanted to see the baby. Just passing was ten miles out of his way by public transport. Mum told me she had never seen him so happy. On the way home in a car he had borrowed to collect us (with me in a carrycot in the back) he pulled over to just look at me. He then turned to Mum and simply took her hand and said, 'Thanks Stella.'

I was taken home to their room and kitchen in Watson Street. I don't remember much of those days obviously, except falling off my cousin's bed and splitting my eye open, but after that trauma very little else except that I was happy, content and the centre of the universe. In 1960 they moved to the upmarket two-room and kitchen in Thorn Street in Motherwell, Lanarkshire. For me, at that age, the Motherwell of the late '50s and early '60s was a paradise, when in reality it was just a large steel town. When I look at photographs now I can see it for the industrial town that it was, a dark place with lots of soot-covered tenements and buildings.

This industrial town supplied the steel for all the shipyards on the Clyde and beyond, dominated by the massive Colville's steelworks and foundries. There were huge chimneys in the distance belching out smoke and God knows what else, as worries about pollution and its effects on the environment weren't really thought about back then. Being in work was what mattered, and providing a decent life for your family was the dream, especially if you had just returned from, or survived a war. At only three years old, I just assumed that the bricks on the buildings were meant to be black, not realising, like most people, until the 1980s when they started to clean the buildings after the Clean Air Act, that at one point the buildings had actually been a sandstone colour.

We had a ground floor flat with a front door opening out onto the street and a back door looking onto a big common courtyard with drying greens and the bin store. It seemed huge to me, with the other side of the greens feeling like the other side of the world. To get around to them and our back door you had to enter through a 'close' and Dad had built a little picket fence around our 'bit' and it was painted in a black gloss, as were the door and the coal bunker, which I always thought was very *Little House on the Prairie*.

I started to discover a bit of independence as I was allowed out to play, but never to the other side of the tenements or too far away from the door at the back, and never out onto the street, that was *verboten*! I was very protected and Dad had me on a pedestal, where I was viewed as a complete genius and a miracle rolled into one. He obviously didn't realise that he was sowing the seeds for a life of attention-seeking (perfect for an actor) and a belief that whatever I had to say or do was special. It was a pretty big shock to me when I discovered early on that everyone wasn't as keen to hear and see me as Dad was.

Mum was a great leveller, being less impressed by my shenanigans as she had to deal with this trumped-up three year old on a daily basis, but in later years did admit that I had been a great baby. She could always bring me down to earth with a bump, and frequently did, usually after a show, when she would make the supposedly innocent comment about my outfit, or constant praising of how much weight I'd lost (implying of course that I'd been a fat git beforehand!). She would be found, even when I was 40, with her hand up my dress pulling down my underskirt because it was ruffled, or telling me that I should have worn 'the other dress', because that was nicer and I looked thinner in it, just as I was heading out to a big do. She loved recounting tales to my sisters and boyfriends about my desire to be the centre of attention and that she had always known that I had delusions of grandeur.

Apparently I had a problem with constipation as a child and therefore a great fuss was always made when I did my business in the potty, so I naturally assumed (well, you would; wouldn't you?) that everyone else would be as fascinated and delighted as my parents usually were. So one night, we had a house full of aunties, uncles and weans, all sitting around chatting and drinking. I felt the urge (probably due to all the excitement and exhaustion from lots of attention-seeking behaviour) to empty my bowels. I disappeared into the bedroom, did the deed, and then walked proudly back into the living room with potty in hand going around the said company to show them this magical, steaming turd that I'd made. Awaiting the usual applause and screams of delight I was therefore very confused when instead of 'good girl', and 'well done', I was met with silence, some muffled laughter and then lifted bodily out of the room with potty in hand. What could have gone wrong? No applause or anything! I was shattered, my first lousy review.

My competitive streak emerged then too. I had got a beautiful pram for my dolls, a miniature Silver Cross just like my mum's pram. She loved that pram and she kept it for the three of us, polished to perfection. It was a magnificent specimen of a pram, if I do say so myself. Huge, white with a maroon hood and rain cover, with all her matching frilly pram sets (everything had to match) and the Silver Cross badge along the side to prove it was the real deal. It cost an arm and a leg but Stella wanted the best (I think some of the royal babies' prams had a Silver Cross so she had to as well) and she loved it. The covers were always spotless and matching, with the little baby ornaments dangling.

So when she was pregnant with Louise they decided that I would get a wee miniature one from Santa so that I didn't feel left out. Mine was white and green and I did love it, but when one of the other girls got a trendy pushchair that folded up, I was so jealous I could have spit. Why could mine not fold up? Rather than show my envy, I decided that I would tell her how inferior hers was to mine. I started showing her all the ways that my pram was better than hers and was doing a good selling job until her big brother came over and said 'Can it do this?' and topped me completely as he pulled the back of the seat forward to show that it could fold away. Not to be outdone I grabbed the lining of my pram and pulled for dear life, ripping the whole thing apart in the process. Realising what I had done, I burst into tears and tried to convince my mum that 'it'd just happened', anything but accept responsibility. I got 'kept in', (or 'snibbed') for that, accompanied by a 'skelp' around the legs into the bargain and even got a very rare row from Dad. I was suitably ashamed and devastated by the whole affair. Then, they had the bare-faced cheek, as seems to be the way of all adults, they laughed uproariously while recounting the story to all the relatives. I was very confused, but did realise that bad deeds and mistakes could end up being used to get some laughs and keep you as the centre of attention too – even if they didn't laugh at the bloody time!

The top of the bill tale was always the one where my mother claimed that she always knew that I was destined for a life of luxury and great things. This was always told to embarrass me in later years. Apparently she had looked out of the window one day onto the back court where I was playing with the other kids on my bin bike (all the rage they were: a three-wheeled pedal bike with a little bin at the back, it was cream with blue piping and I loved it). Anyway, she looked out to see me sitting on it, legs up off the pedals, while two of the boys were pulling me along like my servants. 'I knew it then,' she'd say, 'Too bloody lady-like and grand even to pedal.' I think we were playing 'Queens and Slaves' (a game I made up) and naturally I was the Queen.

Going 'up the street' in Motherwell was an event that took place almost every day, as this was a period when people shopped for their supplies on a daily basis. This meant that I got scrubbed and dressed and walked out to Merry Street and then up to Brandon Street, where there was a lot of traffic and all the shops. Motherwell was a thriving, busy community and my mother would never have been seen dead without her hair 'done' and the lippy on, with matching pram set. And, of course, I had to match too. So it was on with the good, clean gear for me before we ever ventured outside to go shopping. She was always very proud that I was able to keep my clothes clean and tidy, but I think it was fear of the reprisals from old Stella (or Mrs Danvers, as she became if I spilled a drop of something down my dress).

For daily stuff we always ended up in Ross's fruit shop. It smelled brilliant, fruit, vegetables and flowers and the cheery women always gave the wee ones a lolly. They were friendly and Mum thought it a better class of greengrocer. We would wander up to get other 'messages' (shopping), butchers, bakers, etc. but Ross's was the most memorable.

The big shop was the Co-op and I loved it. I loved the smell, as it was a proper department store where Mum would get her dividend – or 'divvy' – and there was a tearoom, though it was always deemed too pricey for us and Mum preferred Robb's tearoom above the bakers on Merry Street. But the Co-op had those magical glass cases with all the displays in them, from gloves to perfume, and lots of wood panelling, but best of all it had those amazing brass tubes where the money and paperwork were all wrapped together, shoved in a wee brass capsule and as if by magic was sucked through this maze of tubes into the ether. You then had to wait ages for your receipt and change to come back in the same way. I loved it, though at only three years of age I couldn't really work out where the money had gone or come back from. It was like a fantastic magic trick and I just couldn't grasp that there were people sitting in a boring accounts office at the other end counting the money. In my mind this was a giant machine with a mad professor working it at the top of the building.

You could get everything in the Co-op, I got my first school blazer there, coats, dresses, shoes. The school shoes were the bane of my life. I hated them. My first pair of hellish lace-up black Tuff shoes. I've never been a sensible shoes sort of a gal and have been known to be out walking along rivers and hillsides in a pair of attractive mules (well, they matched my outfit!) and I think it all derives from this time in my life when as a five year old I was forced into the Tuff black lace-ups. Why couldn't I get nice petite black shoes with straps and a wee heel, why did I end up with the sensible black lace-ups that weighed a ton and did little for a well-turned ankle? I was only five, but a girl has to look her best. But I was forced to wear them with those words every fashion-conscious girl never wants to hear. 'These are far better for you and they will last for years.' Aaagh, I didn't want them to last for years, I wanted to grow out of them in a week!

The Co-op dividend was icing on the cake. Now, sadly, the building lies derelict, ironically only yards from my sister Louise's first flat and from the hairdressing shop that both my sisters used to own; their first-ever salon, 'The Workshop'. Hairdressing seems a natural progression for my sisters, given that my mother spent half her life in a hairdresser's and it was great for Stella as she got free hairdos for the rest of her life. The Co-op building became lots of things; from bars to nightclubs, but was really badly damaged in a fire some years agoand has never been repaired – a shame for a building that was once the centre of the town.

Those days in Motherwell were happy and settled for me. My time was made up of playing with the other kids in the back court – though always warned about never going near the dustbin store in the centre of the drying greens for fear of catching scarlet fever. I never understood what that was and got myself many a row after being found on top of the bins shouting, 'I'm the king of the castle' (queen, surely) to the minions below. It was an early form of a stage for me (and in some theatres I've played, the backstage area is not unlike that old tenement bin store!). The only other real row I remember getting (apart from the pram-ripping incident) was the day I went off to hear the big band and didn't tell anyone.

There was a lot of talk and excitement about something called the 'Walk' and some of the other kids were saying that they were going to watch it because there were flags and bands and it was great. And it was passing along the end of the street. I asked Mum if I could go and she said an emphatic no, that I was too young. I asked if she would take me and she gave another no. I couldn't understand it, my parents were always up for fun, the shows, the beach, so why couldn't I go on this? Other parents were taking their kids, why couldn't mine? What I didn't know was that these bands were on the Orange Walk and that they were marching to proudly show their Protestant heritage, and God help any Catholic that got in their way.

This was a day to stay indoors and keep your head down and was a day that Catholics tried to disappear. I knew nothing of all this because I didn't go to church at all and religion was something that was never discussed. I had been to mass with Gran in Bellshill but that was just something that Gran did. We also got sweets from the Co-op on the way home – a necessary means to an end for a kid – so it was all Greek to me (well, Latin actually). But that parade and hearing the band were my first introduction to the happy land of sectarianism.

Looking back, what amazes me is that all these people who lived so well side-by-side, looking after their kids, working hard and socialising together would then stand at the side of the road and cheer bands playing songs about being up to their knees in Fenian blood. Was hatred really lying underneath? But I had no idea about that at the time. I just wanted to see the bands.

So I snuck along to the end of the road even though I knew I would be in trouble. I had never been that far away on my own before and remember feeling a great sense of fear and adventure. There were hundreds of people lining the street and I could see very little. And then we heard them, the bands, and the noise was unbelievable. The accordions, flutes, the flags, the uniforms, the crowds cheered and clapped and at first it seemed so exciting, but the louder it got the more menacing it became and I became afraid. It was the drums, especially the big drum pounding away. I don't know whether we were near a Catholic chapel or not, because tradition dictates that as they approach a Catholic church the bands get louder and more intimidating. As Billy Connolly so brilliantly put it, the guy on the big drum turns into Buddy Rich at the mere sight of the home of Papishness!

Well, Buddy or not, I was terrified. The drums were banging so loud and my heart started to pound with it. I just wanted to cry and run, and that's exactly what I did, only to be met by a deranged mother who hugged and smacked me in alternate strokes, such was her relief that I hadn't been spirited away by the Orange Walk! I had never seen her so upset. We were due to walk to my Gran's for tea and we tended to walk through the scheme at the back, onto Muir

Street and out to the Bellshill Road. It was a long walk for a wee one but I always liked it because when we were nearly there and past Forgewood at the bottom of the hill there was the waterfall. I always thought it was magical and where fairies lived. That and walking with my hand in Mum's, her in the red swagger coat with the hair done and lippy on had, until then, been a favourite journey.

But not on this day. Mum became a tyrant, who refused to take my hand or speak to me or even stop at the waterfall. She was so angry and scared over my desertion and disobedience that she refused to speak to me. I didn't understand then, although I do now. Having since experienced panic and fear over a child wandering off in a supermarket I can now understand her terror. I know the feeling of that near heart attack. However, my punishment continued as she then went on to recount the tale of my misdemeanours to my aunts and Gran and Papa. How could she humiliate me like that? It was a major public shaming and I hated it. To my mind I felt that she should just have been pleased and delighted that I'd come back. But no, her punishment was her silence, a weapon I myself have adopted and used to good effect over the years – and generally it works. If I am ranting and raving there is nothing to fear' if I am silent you are in big, big trouble.

Then to cap it all, my idyll was shattered. My mother announced that she was pregnant and my life was rudely interrupted by the arrival of a new baby, my sister Louise. Life would never be the same again for me, the Princess in the ivory tower had to make room for a new centre of attention, the baby. There was a new kid on the block and I didn't take it well. It was all a bit of a shock, it was the days when no one really explained what was happening with pregnancy and I was so wrapped up in myself I don't really remember much talk of the new baby except at a family wedding when my mum was about seven months pregnant and all the relatives kept asking me if I wanted a brother or a sister. My answer of 'no' was greeted with much hilarity by them all, but I bloody meant it.

Stella went into labour very quickly and Louise was delivered in minutes into the arms of Mrs McKee from upstairs (apparently there was a request from Stella to take her pyjama bottoms off and as this was done Louise landed in Chrissie's arms). It all took about half an hour, apparently. I had been whisked out the front door (it must have been an emergency if we used the front door) and taken to Gran's and I arrived home three days later to a brand-new baby. For weeks I ignored her and wanted life to go on as before but it just wasn't the same, my parents were preoccupied with this little crying thing who was basically just an inconvenience for me. And I was so jealous.

It took about six weeks for me to get the notion that the baby belonged to me as well. Our neighbour's teenage daughter (Margaret McKee, who was our babysitter for years) came and took the new baby for a walk in the pram. As she left she teased me that she was taking the baby and going to keep her for herself. Until this point I had been apparently giving her away willingly to anyone who asked. But on this occasion I went crazy, running after her shouting, 'You can't take her, bring my baby back!' She did, thankfully, and the bond between the sisters was sealed after that. My cover was blown and I allowed her to stay and share my life – much as it was still a bit of an inconvenience to have a usurper in my royal household.

Louise was born in 1961 and our little flat was too small for a family so my parents set about finding a bigger house with a garden. They found a woman who was looking for a smaller house in Motherwell and did a house swap and the deal was done. So followed the big move to a house in Mosshall Street in Newarthill, which was really four flats in a steel-framed block. It was a three-bedroom, 'Scottish Special Family' home. It was absolutely freezing and I mean Baltic (not helped by the fact that we moved in December). It was so cold that the water in the toilet pan froze. I go and visit my dad, who still lives there now, and it is a lovely double-glazed, centrally-heated home with fitted kitchen and all that. It was very different in 1962.

Fortunately my dad was 'Mr Handy' and he set about quickly decorating and rebuilding the house. Louise and I shared a bedroom eventually and we even had a room as a playroom (though it was a storeroom for everything for many, many months so there wasn't much room for toys). The family stayed in Newarthill for the next 25 years or more. Stella then gave birth to another daughter (my wee 'sis'), Diane, on her very own birthday (17 January) in 1966. Family legend has it that my father turned up at Bellshill Maternity with a pack of nappies and split them – half for my mum and half for the baby – on their joint birthday, or so Dad loved joking to everyone. He said it had saved on flowers!

CHAPTER 8

NEWARTHILL

From the metropolis of Motherwell, Newarthill felt like we were in the heart of rural Scotland. It was only three miles away but could have been a hundred because the difference was especially huge in the early '60s. The Newarthill I grew up in had been a small mining village, nowadays it's more like a suburb of Motherwell, which is in turn like a suburb of Glasgow, given that it's only 12 miles away from the city. But then it was a world away, a trip to Glasgow was a whole day affair, leaving early in the morning and returning after tea.

The high street of the village was a mixture of small tenements, miners' rows and '50s-style council houses. The original village was still there in 1962 when we moved there. It felt quite strange and exotic to us, as if we had moved to the country. We could see the massive steel plants from our back windows. The village was built on the hill or high rim of Lanarkshire's 'steel basin' as it was known. Those massive steelworks down in the valley glowed a vibrant red at night and the lights sparkled in the distance; to me as a child they looked magical. Up close it was quite gothic, dirty and frightening.

When we lived in Motherwell, I remember that we used to walk with the pram with my baby sister Louise in it along the road that divided the huge Colvilles steel plant. We used it as a short cut to get to my aunt's house and I will never forget how dark, imposing and gigantic it all seemed. We always rushed to get home before the works came out because the men poured out like ants in their hundreds at the end of a shift. I remember getting caught there one day on the road home with my mum all dressed up (red coat and matching everything). It was so vivid, this attractive woman with her pram and small child in full Technicolor surrounded by all these men in dark clothes and dark, dirty faces rushing past us. The noise of the horn going off at the end of a shift on a Friday was amazing. Seeing all those men running out was terrifying but really exciting and full of life, a life I would never know.

Our house was in what was locally known as the 'Top Scheme'. They were all Scottish Special steel-framed houses (as I said before, freezing with ice on the insides of the steel windows until we got the storage heaters put in). We were top right. The house had a garage, a driveway and a big back garden and we even had a swing. At the end of the street was the local butcher's, the grocer's, and Jayne's hairdresser's. There was also the baker's shop attached to the large Muir's Bakery with all the noise and bustle of the delivery vans every day. The sweet smell of bread and biscuits baking was fantastic as we passed on the way back home from school.

The view from our front window was over several fields looking up towards Cleland and beyond. There were still a few farms there and it was common for us to walk up to get food from Watson's Farm. We hated it because it involved a fifteen-minute walk through the scheme, which felt like a hike through the jungle to an eight year old, and all to get fresh eggs.

I hated the smell of the farm from the muck spreading and couldn't believe anyone would want to live in this muddy, smelly place. The daughters, Margaret and Jean, were at the primary school with me though we were never close. I liked them but they seemed odd to the rest of us, as they lived on a farm, though they were very bright. At the farm I would say a shy hello and then Mrs Watson would literally go out to the chicken shed and pick the eggs up and put them in a box. The job I really hated was going to the farm for a chicken. The reason being that the farmer basically walked out to the hen house and wrung the chicken's neck and then handed it to you, feathers and all!

We then had to walk back holding it by the neck. Disgusting, though I still enjoyed my dinner and it would have taken more than a few feathers to put me off my mum's roast chicken. Dad would pluck the chicken before cleaning it and cooking it for Sunday dinner. Much to our relief as kids, once we got the phone installed Mum would phone up the farm in advance and order it 'plucked' before we picked it up. We could get about three meals out of it – the roast, then the next day a bit of chicken in gravy, or chicken 'sannies' (sandwiches), and then a pot of soup from the stock.

The village shops could charge what they wanted because they had a captive market. We were always aware of what shops to go into based on price or overcharging. You never saw a poor greengrocer in those days and they always had the bought houses in the area. A bought house was really posh as far as we were concerned, as everyone we knew was in council or Scottish Special Housing Association, so owning your house meant you were really rich.

There was the paper shop (run by the Prentices), the Post Office – which was run by the Mulders (though no connection to *The X-Files*) and a Dutch family whose son David was in my class at school. There was also Wullie Kane's General Grocers, where items like butter were cut in front of you from a big slab, to whatever size you wanted. Wullie also held the magic ingredient of the whole shop, sweeties, so kids loved going in there. An MB bar (that tasted fab and was huge, not like the ones I have tasted since) or a Ruffle bar were bought with the 3d. a day we were given, or from saving from 6d. on a Saturday. It had a real sense of a village, a community.

Our downstairs neighbour was Mrs Maxwell, who was great to our family. I don't think I ever really knew her age because she was always a 'grannie' and deaf as a post. She was one of the original villagers and still spoke (or shouted) in what we called 'Old Scots'. The church was 'the Kirk'; tonight was 'the nicht', though we were never allowed to speak like that. We were taught that it wasn't proper and was common too. There was a sense of shame, as well as a bit of snobbery, in Mother about the way we had to speak. She had the polite telephone voice, as well as the 'good voice' for speaking to people like the doctor or anyone in perceived authority. Slang was never allowed.

Mrs Maxwell had three daughters who were all married with kids who also lived around the corner. Those girls became our great pals for many years. Margaret, Christine and Barbara were great playmates and were also great performers too – we always had a concert going in their garage or our back gardens in the good weather. A blanket over a washing rope for a curtain and off we went with our MC of the day and various chaotic singing and dancing routines. They introduced me to my first notion of a show and acting to an audience, and I think they generally got that sense of theatre from their family.

The Maxwells' house was always busy. Their granny would be shouting at everyone, and they'd be shouting back as she couldn't hear very well. There was lots of life, bustle and passion along with the singing and comedy of Margaret and Christine's dad, Donald Watson. He was a real laugh and a total character and would give you a rendition of a Frank Sinatra at the drop of a hat, and after several pints of the 'laughing ginger' (complete with golf trews and bunnet) you had little choice but to watch and learn from a master entertainer (complete with his build-up of 'In a minute, in a minute!' which generally took about 15 till he gathered himself).

Their grandpa, Mr Maxwell, was what is known in Scotland as a great 'Burns Man', meaning he loved the works of Robert Burns and he would be often reciting the bard at family parties. I never really understood all the Burns stuff until much later and I love the fact that our national hero is not a warrior or a politician, but a poet, which says much about the Scottish psyche and soul. Grandpa Maxwell was quite a severe man to my mind but this ex-miner came alive when reciting Robert Burns. He was like a different person. Mr Maxwell doing 'Tam O' Shanter', or 'Holy Willie's Prayer', was a marvel. Always really appreciated and with huge applause and respect from everyone listening. Respect was always afforded to people who could recite poetry properly, sing really well or do a bit of Mario Lanza (proper singing) and the best of order was demanded.

The Maxwells also took in lodgers, which was quite a common thing then. General Motors and Euclid had a huge tractor plant about a mile away and they had foreign workers who needed lodgings ('digs'). So Mrs Maxwell rented out two rooms all the time. She was a wonderful baker and cook so it is no surprise that her digs were always full. It's how I came to meet Per and Gunther from Sweden and many from down south who were introduced to Scottish hospitality – good grub, clean digs and when house parties happened (which was more usual then as folks didn't have the cash to go out for meals or entertainment) there was also much drink, humour and a sing-song.

I started Newarthill Primary School in August 1963 shortly after my fifth birthday. I actually do remember being walked down to the school in my uniform by Mum on that first day. She took me there and back for the first week and then I was left to my own devices. I was quite happy as all the other kids were left there too. We didn't want our parents treating us like babies and being the only kid with their mum would have been a source of shame, the group was all, even at five. What a difference from how I treated my own daughters, whom I finally allowed to walk on their own to school – only around the corner from where we lived – when they were nine years old. The thought of letting Katie or Hannah walk the same distance as I had to do all those years ago at the age of five would never have occurred to me. But I know that I learned more about life on those walks to and from school.

The school was a Victorian building on the High Street and about a 15-minute walk from our house. I thought nothing of that walk, where I would meet the likes of Anna Dow en route at the bottom of the road and make my way to school (sometimes via Kane's grocery shop if I had the cash). Initially the school had outside toilets next to proverbial bike sheds (though there were never any bikes in there). The smell was awful, 'minging' as we called it, and I would go the whole day holding in my wee trying to avoid having to use them.

We were taught by the Infant Mistress – Mrs Graham. I remember little except that she wore a dark overall over her dresses, had grey hair and glasses and was quite stern. My favourite things were the books we got to look at and the different coloured blocks that we got to count with. I can still picture them in my mind and to this day numbers are associated with colours for me. I did have quite an imagination even then and a desire to seem a bit more exciting than I actually was. I think I inherited that from both my parents: Mum with her desire to better herself and Dad with his amazing ability to tell stories. He used to tell stories before we went to sleep. Versions of *Dick Whittington* or *Snow White* that had little relation to the real stories, but they were full of magic and light – so much so that I argued blind as a six year old with my teacher that Dick Whittington had a giant sports car at the end when he got all the riches! The real version of course was a total disappointment.

Having been spoiled I found it difficult to be one of the pack so I found a way of getting attention, and that was to make stories up. As a five or six year old, I convinced my pals and myself that the Beatles came to my door for a drink of water (they were just passing through Newarthill and were thirsty according to my story, and just happened to stop and ask. Well, why not?) The other tall-tale was that my wee cousin had been stabbed up a close at the weekend (obviously some news story overheard and recycled to make me look in the know). I had an actor's imagination and an ability to convince even myself that it was all the honest truth. I loved the sense of power, the one-upmanship, being the centre of attention, with the other kids believing every false word.

I had my mother's ability to talk non-stop and my father's overactive imagination. He could talk on his chosen subjects for hours. Unfortunately, his chosen subjects were not always the desire of everyone else – an hour on the construction of the Forth Road Bridge or the revolutionary nature of the ball-bearing, 'Which in effect was more important in the war against the Germans than the Spitfire. Without the ball-bearing, doll, the war could have been lost!' This to an eight year old was not the most interesting of topics but if he wanted to talk about it then he did.

Growing up in the village, as with everyone's childhood, the summers seemed to last for ever. The park in the middle of the scheme was great for kids: a big green space with tennis courts, bowling greens, football pitches and of course the chute and the swings. There was also a maypole and a large bandstand in the middle, though I don't think I ever saw a band or an instrument played on it – obviously a throwback to far-off days when the park was used for public performances. However, the bandstand was great for games we invented; it became a castle, a stage for pop groups we imagined we were performing with. It was great too for shelter on rainy days (well, those days when the rain wasn't falling sideways and knocking us over!)

There were the picnics up the Metal Raw burn (don't ask where the name came from). A picnic being a packet of crisps, a cream soda, or a badly made sandwich stolen from the house – unless we planned it properly and our mums made an effort for us. The arranging was always the best bit, the anticipation and much planning, because once you got there it was just a wee stream between two fields about 500 yards from the house, but we thought the walk took an eternity. We were all adventurers – the Secret Seven or the Famous Five (I had to be George of course, though secretly I wanted to be the pretty, girly one but I couldn't help myself and had to take charge). We had bicycles, as traffic was nothing like it is now, so it felt very safe to just cycle around to your pals or go off for an adventure.

There was the Gala Day and the Robert Burns competition, usually centring on the Miners' Welfare Club. There was also a preoccupation with parades, from the Church Hall in the aptly named Church Street, to the newer Church of Scotland in the middle scheme (facing the Catholic Church in a defiant face-off). In the Girl Guides, the Brownies and the Girls' Brigade, I marched up and down with the Union Jack flying proudly with the others. I don't really remember a Scottish flag being there, this was pretty soon after the war and a sense of 'Britishness' was still the order of the day. But I do remember being very bored with all the marching.

What was the point? Little girls between six and twelve marching in step around a hall on a wet Tuesday did little for the creative mind. And all the militaristic stuff with captains and lieutenants was a bit much. But on parade days the church was packed and the sight of all the flags at the altar gave the church a great sense of theatre.

Again I was desperate to belong so joined everything and as a young teenager read my Bible religiously, went to church and even helped out at Sunday School but God didn't ever appear. Not that I wasn't good and well behaved, but the absence of fun and humour and life bored me rigid. I tried to believe so much through the Youth Fellowship and other religious social groups, and even convinced myself that there 'had' to be a God looking after us all. But in the end, I'm afraid, my brain switched on and I realised that for me it was like believing in Santa Claus or fairies, all very lovely and comforting, but basically made up to stave off the fear of the unknown and death. For many, religion brings great solace and comfort and that is wonderful, but for me now at 50 I'm afraid it just doesn't fit. But I did try very hard for many years to believe.

I was introduced to good singing and performing by the family next door, the Grahams. Their dad, Tom, was a really effusive and funny man who loved kids and was a great singer and musician. His own children, Ross, Valerie and Janet, were great at harmonising and Ross played the guitar. I loved it when they came to our parties and the stuff they sang and played introduced me to another Scotland. The music was that of Hamish Imlach and contemporary folk music, which was really taking off in the late '60s and early '70s. Bands like Gaberlunzie, the Tannahill Weavers were all the rage, and represented a real resurgence in owning our own musical history, that didn't always look to the past but actually looked forward. Up until then I thought that 'Ten Guitars' and 'Crazy' and 'He'll Have to Go' were the real quaint Scottish folk songs because that's all the family sang. Singing was a huge part of my upbringing and it brought attention and admiration if you could do it. As a kid you were never allowed to join in, that ritual was for the adults.

When I was younger, I loved the gatherings of the family and friends that would result in a 'show'. There was the cleaning. My mother cleaning for Scotland and everywhere had to be spotless, just in case. Just in case someone opened the hall cupboard and found out that we were slovenly, filthy 'gits'. No one ever did search in that cupboard or under the bathroom sink but it had to be spotless just in case. My kids would tell you now that I am the same. When people are coming to stay, or for dinner, or a party, my utility room gleams – even though no one goes in there. Always 'just in case' the tidy police turn up and I am shamed. Of course folk are usually too pished at a party to notice.

Another trait inherited from these times is that my sisters and I always have a tin of John West Salmon in the cupboard just in case folk arrive and we need to feed them. In the '60s and '70s a 'salmon sandwich' was a real treat and giving that to any visitors showed that you were many steps from the poorhouse, so we were never allowed to eat it 'just in case' Mum was caught short.

Then came the cooking (Dad's curry being a truly exotic way-out dish of the era). All any of us had tasted up until that time as far as curry was concerned was of the Vesta packet variety. When we had our first taste of this new Vesta food, we were all running for glasses of water because it seemed so hot and nippy to us. Come to think of it, I remember when they brought out cheese and onion crisps for the first time and we thought they were miraculous. Such flavours! Until then we had the plain crisps with the little blue bag of salt (and how rubbish was it when you opened them up and found that it was missing?) Anyway, we thought that Vesta was 'out there' in the spicy stakes.

So Dad thought he would have a go himself. His curry was based on the Vesta model, with raisins and currants and God knows what else in there (probably a few ball-bearings in there too) and everyone loved it. The folks would arrive to a very tidy house about 7 p.m. with the bowls of crisps and nuts on the coffee table and all the furniture pushed back against the walls. Dining-room chairs brought in for this special occasion, 'poofies' (yes, that's what they were called) and occasionally kids' seats from the bedrooms too.

In they'd come. Rena and Nick, May and Tommy, Kate and Jim, Forbes and Margaret, Fred, Vicki and Jim, wonderful Maureen and 'Ma' Alec. Everyone would bring booze (and those who brought beer and drank whisky or vodka all night were remarked upon greatly – mean bastards!). So the conversation and the drinking would start things off, with some music in the background (a Burt Bacharach, or Jim Reeves) and there would be a laugh and a joke and a gossip. Then it would be time for the grub (mainly to stop people getting too pished before 9 p.m.). After the food things were more jovial, with the women in the living room discussing various medical procedures from hysterectomies to piles and childbirth. The men were in the kitchen at the temporary bar, discussing everything from cars to work – but never football, religion or politics; they were to be avoided as they usually ended up causing a fight.

But the focus of the evening was always the sing-song. I didn't find my voice until I was a teenager but I had listened and learned from an early age and saw what it was like to 'stop the room'. That was where I learned a sense of showbiz and theatre. Respect and rapt silence was for the good singers, laughter was for the ones you liked, and you joined in with those who were too pished to remember the words. And there was always a sense that this was a show and there was billing, too. The duff singers (or the ones who were just having a laugh with comedy songs and generally poking fun) would go first. Next would be a bit of variety, maybe a poem, or recitation or a bit on the piano, or a Mario Lanza-type song. The end of this section of the evening was always the top of the bill, and that was the good singer. And of course that's where I wanted to be because the good singers had this fantastic effect on the room, it was as if everything stopped, people listened and they were moved. Our living room wasn't our living room any more as the singing transported everyone and lifted their hearts with the words.

Top of the bill in our family was always my cousin Kate, who had a deep, strong and powerful singing voice with a great sense of drama. She was a serious singer, always doing the dramatic songs such as Shirley Bassey's 'I Who Have Nothing'. Weirdly, the favourite of everyone was her rendition of Don McLean's 'Vincent'. I don't know whether most of my aunts and uncles even knew who Vincent Van Gogh was except from the Kirk Douglas movie of his life, but Kate sang that song and you could hear a pin drop.

The Grahams from next door would occasionally come in and they brought a bit of class with them too. They played songs that were from the contemporary folk movement that was so popular around Scotland, a more modern take on folk and not pop songs. It was brilliant to see the reaction of the room to them, a mixture of intrigue and surprise that Scots could sing in their own accent and be funny and moving too. Until then all efforts had been made by singers to get rid of their accent and sound as American as possible. They did songs by Hamish Imlach like 'Cod Liver Oil and the Orange Juice'.

At one memorable party, I heard Billy Connolly for the first time. An uncle had brought a copy of an early album of this hippy-looking folk singer that was recorded at the Tudor Hotel in Airdrie. There was a very prevalent attitude around at that time that anything recorded locally, or in our own accents, must be rubbish but the folk scene in the early '70s in Scotland was burgeoning and new stars were being born who had a different sense of themselves and their culture. Connolly had started to get a reputation as a really funny guy, although he was still seen basically as an 'all right' folk singer and banjo player, but gradually the talk between his songs became much more popular than the songs themselves and an album was recorded. It was taken around and played in houses up and down the country and was like some sort of a bootleg album (well, not many had been made so they became a bit like gold dust). We played a bit early on and I thought he was wonderful; Mum thought he was a genius but Dad thought he was too rude.

I started to listen to it all the time and learned his famous routine 'The Crucifixion' off by heart and did a bit at one family gathering. My Uncle Tommy was blown away by what I did and kept on about how good I was and how good my timing was (ach, he knew a thing or two did Uncle Tommy). Again, I loved the effect of having all those people listening to me. My confidence grew as I got more laughs but I was eventually told to 'shuttit' as my parents didn't want me to get too full of myself.

Eventually, as I started singing with my cousins (John and Jim) in their band, I got more confidence in my voice and that in itself was a strange feeling. I had a good voice but I was aware of the billing issue and knew that Cousin Kate always had to be top of the bill and too much fuss over me wasn't a good thing. I loved her and her singing, so the day that I ended up as top of the bill in my own right was quite a sad one for me. She was lovely to me but was aware of the competition when we went out to family events at Hastie's Farm, and the like, where Dad had me up to sing in a flash. But I learned it all from watching her.

Along the road from us lived the Tyrrell family and their dad Joe was a wonderful professional piano player, who occasionally would pop in if there was a party. I had never heard our piano played so beautifully. He was classically trained and a music teacher, as well as playing in pubs and clubs. His only problem was that he liked a drink too much and of course to keep him playing everyone handed him drink – not a good mixture.

One of the lodgers with Mrs Maxwell downstairs became a very close member of our family and his name was Forbes Campbell and came from beautiful Portpatrick (a place that I would know well in my later years as *Two Thousand Acres of Sky* was filmed there and I adore it). He was a great busking piano player and was the person who made me want to play. He eventually fell in love with and married our babysitter Margaret McKee, and they had two sons. He tragically died in his early 30s when they were involved in a car crash in Ayrshire. But I will always see him sitting at that piano in our living room.

This was my first real introduction to poetry. It was the poetry of our lives – country songs, folk songs and Irish songs; from 'How's The World Treatin' You' and 'Help Me Make It Through the Night', to 'Crazy', 'Blue Moon of Kentucky', 'Bandiera Rosa' or 'Singin' in the Rain'.

After the singing came the dancing. The Trini Lopez and Joe Loss records were put on and the dancing (full ballroom or otherwise) commenced. Many of the men ended up in the kitchen arguing about football and the women who weren't dancing were in the kitchen having the fight about who should clean up.

'No, Stella, I'll do the dishes.'

'No, Rena, it's my house.'

'Yes, I know, but you've had all this work to do.'

'No, honestly!'

And on and on and on. There was occasionally a fight too, either a 'domestic' between husband and wife who disagreed on levels of permitted drink, or if the football banter had gone a bit too far. It's weird how things change in life. As I was growing up this was a source initially of wonder and I loved becoming old enough to be allowed to stay up and watch. To be tickled and kidded by my uncles, and to listen and watch my parents be different; to see what they were like when they really laughed, or danced or enjoyed themselves. By 16, of course, they became a complete embarrassment. At 19, I would walk into that living room and think, 'Aw naw, they're singing,' and leg it!

There I was, Ms Superior, cool in my platforms, velvet jumpsuit and Afghan coat after a gig with my band, dreaming of being Joni Mitchell or Stevie Nicks. All the wonderful music I was listening to, Stevie Wonder, Aretha Franklin, Crosby, Stills, Nash and Young, Bowie and Marc Bolan was what I really wanted. So the family singing the same old songs was so lame to me.

Yet, at 50, I see that same look on my own kids' faces when we 'have a night' in the house with family and friends. I see them with that same look that says, 'Aw naw, they're singing' and it makes me laugh. I know that they think we are the least cool, weirdest bunch of people and that parties should be about drinking, listening to music and getting off with folk. They don't need the focus. They don't need the show. But 30 years from now they will. And, like me, the songs they will want to sing won't be hip-hop classics from Jay-Z, or tracks from Adele, or even the goddess Joni. They'll be the songs that their drunk, old folks sang, like 'Put Your Sweet Lips', or 'Secret Love'. The songs that have stories and melodies and are a part of the culture they were brought up around. There is no better poetry for me than a rendition of Robert Burns' 'Ae Fond Kiss', a Shakespeare sonnet, or a Yeats poem. But I can also be reduced to tears by a Willie Nelson classic or a version of Kris Kristofferson's 'Help Me Make It Through the Night', or 'For the Good Times'. It was our poetry, which of course you never appreciate until you reach a certain age. But in those moments, when everyone is singing in our living room, I can see the ghosts of all my family, my aunties, uncles, cousins and grannies. They're alive again. All our ancestors are in that room singing alongside us. I know that both my girls will have those memories of us when we are gone and that's a great thing – to be remembered through a song, even if it is fuelled by several Bacardis.

CHAPTER 9

SATURDAYS AND SUNDAYS

For as many years as I can remember the weekend began in the same way. We got to sleep late, or if we got up early we played in our rooms so as not to wake Mum and Dad. The most exciting times were if we got to go to the Saturday Club at either the Rex or the Odeon in Motherwell. From around the age of ten I was allowed to go with my friends by bus to the pictures, where they showed films for kids. Old black and whites like the Three Stooges, Abbott and Costello as fillers, then a serial like *The Famous Five* with 'lashings of ginger beer' (I never knew what that was but it sounded great, and I was always desperate to be one of them and speak with that accent too because it was proper!)

It's only when I think about it now that I realise that as a kid I never saw anything with a Scottish accent at the pictures. We never watched kids like ourselves. The nearest we got to it was watching working-class American kids whom we could relate to. Generally they were street-wise and working-class and we felt we knew who they were. All the British pictures (well, English pictures really) were boring, concerned with posh people who bore no relation to the lives that we were living.

When they came on you could count the minutes until the chaos started, throwing sweets, or rotten fruit (my cousin John loved that and used to go to the fruit shop across the road and buy thruppence-worth of rotten fruit on his way in and wait for the kids to get bored and start the mayhem. He was chucked out the pictures many a time). Yet with some of the American films with the likes of Hayley Mills or

Judy Garland and Mickey Rooney, you could have heard a pin drop. This lack of our own accents and culture (apart from an occasional patronising accent or kilt on show) was the same on TV, but it was so subliminal that we just accepted it, there was no other option. Like black children having to accept that all the actors were white.

Sometimes Dad got up early (around 7 a.m.) and went into work to do a short Saturday shift of overtime (generally the hope was that two nights until 7 p.m. and a Saturday morning, as well as all day Sunday, would give him a good wage so he did that whenever he could). If he was working then this meant he was home by noon and then had to have the big fry-up (the traditional Scottish 'heart attack on a plate'), with everything fried, even the bread. He would then get washed and changed and off for the weekly shop in Motherwell or Wishaw. If he wasn't working then his brothers – always Andy, sometimes Fred or Bill – came up and entered into the world of 'the garage', a dark and mysterious place that we girls rarely went into. For years, Dad was just a voice in the garage to us all.

Dad loved restoring cars. He never, ever, had a new car in his life. It was always one from a scrap yard that he and his brothers spent weeks and weeks welding together; fitting new bits to it, new engines, re-spraying. I knew what a MacPherson strut was by the age of six because that was the conversation at the dinner table, as well as tungsten being the hardest metal known to mankind, that only a diamond could cut. The garage was an obsession which we supported because it meant that we could watch what we wanted on the TV. When he came in it was his choice, there were no televisions in our rooms in those days so we dreaded him coming in to watch *Tomorrow's World* and then turning the channel over to something else when *Top of the Pops* came on. Watching *TOTP* was essential for any girl to be cool at school and if you went in on a Friday not having seen it then you were out the loop all day, and it was terrible. But Dad always thought it was 'rubbish' and not proper music. Stella, on the other hand, loved pop music, from Pink Floyd to the Beatles. She was always very moved by music, either to dance to or simply to get into. Not Dad, however. So we loved the voice in the garage. He had installed gas and electric welding, spray-painting compressors, chains to lift out engines – the whole works. It was his little empire of engineering.

On a Saturday morning it was Stella's job to have the full-cooked breakfast (eggs, bacon, square sausage, mushrooms, potato-scones and tinned plum tomatoes) ready when the shout came up, 'Tell your mum 20 minutes to breakfast!' I'd like to say that she was all a-flutter and happy to do it but she absolutely hated it, being treated like a skivvy and making the breakfast for the men to sit at the table and eat and chat, then leave the dishes for her to wash. She would moan and mumble all the way through preparing it and would slink off and leave them to their riveting *après* breakfast chat of cylinder head gaskets. Not a happy bunny.

Ironically, when he first met Mum she couldn't boil an egg, literally. He always loved telling the tale of Stella putting a pot on to boil an egg, forgetting about it and coming back to find a melted pot and a bit of a handle (along with an exploded egg) on the cooker! So he taught her to cook and she ended up becoming a great baker too. Though every Saturday I think she regretted the fact that she had ever learned as she was reduced to cook and bottle-washer. That was a source of many arguments between them at the time and the start really of a seething resentment that came to a head many years later.

Eventually, the men would emerge from the garage around one o'clock, and Dad would wash and change, and get ready to drive Mum and the rest of us to Motherwell for the weekly shop. They took our formerly 'collision-damaged' Ford Cortina (later a Vauxhall Victor) to Galbraith's in Bellshill, or Cochrane's supermarket in Motherwell. Occasionally, we'd embark on an even bigger jaunt to exotic Wishaw.

This weekly shop was seen as a great advance for humankind. No longer did women have to buy their groceries and meat on a daily basis, they could get the bulk of it done in a 'wunner' and it was cheaper than the prices charged by the local grocer and butcher too. I hated going on the weekly shop as it seemed to take for ever and was so boring so when I was old enough I was allowed to stay at home on my own, as long as I did some housework. But the real treat for me was that I got to sit on my own and watch a double bill of Hollywood musicals on BBC2 and I couldn't wait for my parents to get out, take my sisters and leave me on my own. My jobs, while they were at the shops, were the usual cleaning, ironing, peeling potatoes, hanging up washing, etc. and they were all done ASAP so that I could sit down and watch my idols like Doris Day.

I watched all the Margie films, with Jeanne Crain, whom I thought was just the most beautiful girl. I empathised with her teenage struggles. Those films were set in a time when life seemed so simple and easy. I adored the *Moonlight Bay* films with Doris Day and Gordon McCrae, *Carousel*, *Alexander's Ragtime Band*, *Meet Me in St Louis*, *Yankee Doodle Dandy*, *The Seven Little Foys* – the lot.

Occasionally, there were the *Road To . . .* films (deemed musicals because of old Bing Crosby and Dorothy Lamour) but it was the comedy that got me. Bob Hope was, well, just the funniest man. Shame I couldn't agree with his politics, but God he was a bloody funny man. Then came the 'God' of musicals – Gene Kelly. I just adored him and *Singin' in the Rain* still makes me weep and gets better with every viewing. I couldn't get enough and I was always one of 'those' girls in the stories; my head full of songs and romance (well, 'shite' if I'm honest). I truly believed life would and could turn out like that – always with a happy ending.

It was there, on that chair as close to the colour TV as my eyesight would allow, that the whole showbiz bug was born. Like most kids, I was in front of the mirror with the hairbrush singing my heart out but for me it went deeper because I could actually sing. Of course I did dream that Florenz Ziegfeld (usually played by Walter Pidgeon) would turn up at my school when I was in the middle of a Gilbert and Sullivan operetta and shout from the back of the hall in a mid-Atlantic accent, 'I want her, yeah, the wee dumpy wan at the end – I'm gonna make her a star!' It never happened, and as I grew to become a teenager who moved on to other idols and fell in love with Rod Stewart, James Taylor and Joni Mitchell, my ambitions changed from the musicals to becoming a singer-songwriter. But deep down that desire to entertain and a love of that type of vaudeville-variety never left me.

The musicals were only ever allowed to be interrupted by the tennis from Wimbledon, and I owe my love of the sport to Mum. In the early summer, tennis took over my life – as a spectator – and I adored the whole thing and it was something Mum and I shared all our lives. The tennis club was across from our house and I would go for a game of doubles only to look up and see Stella sitting at the bedroom window shaking her head, obviously realising that her daughter was no Margaret Court. It is a great regret that I never managed to take her to Wimbledon, as she thought it was the height of class and glamour, though having been to the venue now, I was a bit disappointed actually. I took up the game as a player in my 30s and loved it, but was rubbish to begin with and am now a bit better but don't play enough to really improve.

Anyway, my Saturday afternoons meant that I got around three hours to myself before Dad came back from the shopping to sit and watch the wrestling. That was another ritual – the wrestling – the hours I spent with him and my sisters watching the Royal Brothers tag-team, Jackie Palo and Mick McManus and that long-haired camp guy Adrian Street (whom Dad instantly disliked, as anything a bit camp or too showbiz brought a bit of a frown to his face and we knew he didn't approve).

We girls (well, not Mum, it was all a bit beneath her so she would be at the hairdresser's for her weekly 'do', especially if they were going to a dinner dance that night at the Coltness Hotel with a band and chicken in a basket) loved the wrestling when it was fun and clearly staged for the comic value, though at the time we thought it was all authentic. It was even better if a rammy broke out and fists and tempers flew. But Dad always liked the proper wrestling and good, clean fights. He only sat down to watch it when the steak was on. Because of Dad's upbringing and a lack of good food, he always insisted on decent cuts of meat and top-quality food. So it was sirloin or Popeye steak for all of us every Saturday, nothing less.

So every Saturday night 'he' cooked. Dad was, and still is, a great cook because he had to be in his early life. Steak with onions, mushrooms and chips, I can still smell it to this day – that smell coming from the kitchen – it went 'roon' yer heart like a hairy worm. And then, and only if we ate it all up, were we allowed the *pièce de résistance*, the cream cookie (synthetic cream of course – real cream was too expensive) from Galbraith's. Happy, happy days! The rest of the night was spent watching TV before bed.

The rosy glow picture I have in my head is of us kids in our pyjamas, sitting with roasted cheese, watching the *Morecambe and Wise Show*,

Cilla Black, *The Lulu Show*, Cliff Richard, *Take Your Pick* and of course *Sunday Night at the London Palladium* – all those variety shows, and I think to a certain extent it was a true picture. So my life was certainly not *Angela's Ashes*, I was fortunate to be born at a time when the working classes were able to enjoy an affluence that generations before could only dream about.

Sundays were the dreariest day of the week. I don't know whether it's the same now, but when I was a kid, Sundays went on for ever and NOTHING happened. Everywhere was shut, the buses hardly ran and everyone went to church, or was supposed to. It was stifling and oppressive and seemed unending. Around about seven o'clock in the evening the fog tended to lift and the day started to feel normal again, coupled with the realisation that it was back to school on Monday, but even that was a relief compared to the awfulness of Sunday.

Our village felt like it had a big cloud over it on a Sunday. The churches in that area were a huge influence and a lot to do with the feeling of gloom. Going to one of the churches, the big Church of Scotland, the R.C. Church of St Theresa, the Brethren Hall or even Mr McGibbon's morning meeting was the only game in town. So we went to the lot, mainly because we were told to but also because all our pals went and it was seen as the proper thing to do.

We started off at Mr McGibbon's morning meeting about 10 a.m. He was a character, a lay preacher who took services for kids on a Sunday morning in the British Legion on the High Street – complete with his speciality of bad organ playing, which would generally include a rendition of 'Silent Night' in the middle of July, still, I might add, in his bicycle clips. Even at eight I knew this was odd and a comic scene but he got very upset if you giggled and to be barred from Mr McGibbon's morning meeting would have brought huge shame on us so we stifled our laughs for as long as we could and sang at the top of our wee lungs.

We then went to the Church of Scotland for the big church service. A weekly dose of hell, fire and brimstone – well, not quite, but it was pretty austere fare for an eight-year-old girl. But the church was where it was noted, by the village's self-appointed elders, exactly who had turned up, what teachers and villagers were there and who wasn't, who had a nice chat to the minister (Mr Morris, who was also the school chaplain) and who wore the biggest hats.

We went to all of the churches, including the Brethren Hall, but not to the Catholic St Theresa's, which we as 'Proddies' were never allowed to set foot in. Given the situation with my parents' religion, or lack of it, Dad's atheism and my mother's guilt, the Catholic church felt like a mysterious place to me – except when I was with Gran – where we would not be welcome. But Stella wanted us to get a bit of God and religion and particularly when we were at school, our social scene revolved around our pals and inevitably the church. We went because our pals went, and it took years for us to understand why Mum always dressed us up so carefully for church but couldn't tell us why she couldn't come with us like the other parents. She felt a terrible sense of shame.

CHAPTER 10

COMEDY

So my love of showbiz, musicals and comedy started in that living room and I can safely say that if it wasn't for TV I wouldn't be in the business today. I would have definitely gone the 'good girl' conventional route, maybe stayed as a teacher and got my fix of entertaining folk in a sing-song at New Year as my cousin Kate did. A further irony of my ending up as a theatre star in particular is that until the age of 12, I had never been in a theatre. Cinema and TV provided me with all the showbiz that I knew. We lived 15 miles from Glasgow – where our nearest theatres were – and this was before the Motherwell Civic Theatre was built. Many of the old theatres had been turned into cinemas or dance halls, as the touring variety shows were dying out.

So with the 1st Newarthill Girl Guides I boarded a hired coach to go to the King's Theatre in Glasgow to see the then huge Alexander Brothers in their *Alexander Brothers Show*. Hard to believe now I suppose, but they were huge Scottish variety stars. They played in theatres and clubs all over Scotland and were on TV regularly on shows like *Thingummyjig* and especially at New Year. They travelled all over the world in their kilts. Playing to 'ex pats' yearning for a bit of the old country and singing the guid old Scots songs like 'Nobody's Child'. Yes, you are right, that isn't a Scots song, but they had a big hit with it. They did songs like 'Dark Lochnagar', 'My Ain Folk', 'Scots Wha Hae', all with accordion solos in the middle too.

We had to be in our uniform, which was a bit embarrassing for fashion-conscious girls like us and we climbed the hundreds of stairs to the 'gods' (gallery) in the King's. I was a bit miffed because we were so far away from the stage, very different from the cinema or the TV where you could get a great view. And I felt a bit sick too because we were so high up and I couldn't work out how we managed not to come crashing to the ground. The gods in the King's is huge – 500 seats – and was mainly used by the workers from the shipyards in Glasgow when they came straight from work to see a show. They used to have bench seating and were all tiled. It always smelled of oranges because the workers were given them to eat during the shows and the whole gallery was then hosed down (hence the tiles) to clean it between the shows.

A bit of magic happened onstage during the show. There were comedy sketches between the acts and in them were some of our finest actors and performers. Duncan Macrae, John Grieve, Walter Carr – and I can still to this day see Roddy McMillan doing a sketch about a drunk man coming home and trying to get in his house. It was a masterful piece of acting. The complete hysterics and appreciation of 1,750 people in the hall was just magical. This was the only piece of theatre I had ever seen before I entered the hallowed halls of the Royal Scottish Academy of Music and Drama in 1975.

My adoration of Eric Morecambe started with TV in my childhood. I still can be reduced to tears when watching an old Morecambe and Wise programme, not just for the great routines but because it evokes such a powerful memory in me and I know that it's gone for ever, so it mixes with a terrible sense of sadness and loss. Safe to say, I think that goes for millions of us who were brought up around that era.

I loved seeing the change in my dad when he watched Eric Morecambe. Generally Dad was quite a serious and at times stern man but he had, and still does have, a great fun-loving side and this was brought out by big Eric. My dad's whole face changed, creased into laughter lines and at times left him helpless with the giggles. It was wonderful to see, and I suppose the urge in me started then when I saw how laughter changes people. Their burdens lighten and the light comes in for just a few seconds and it's wonderful. The night Eric did the sketch where he pretended to be a ventriloquist with a puppet on his hand that had unbeknownst to him fallen off and all that was left were his two fingers, had my dad literally falling about, and he had to get up and go into the kitchen to stop laughing.

I wish I could remember the first time I was thought to be funny but I can't, it was sort of gradual. But one day I said something in class that the teacher started laughing at, as well as the other kids. I'm sure it was an innocent comment or something I'd overheard from the TV, but I was as surprised as anyone else at the response. And the boys took to me because I was quite cheeky and, as they said, a good laugh. I became 'Wee Smithy', and though I got it wrong many times in my attempts to be a comedy genius, I suppose I started to work on the act around the age of eight.

I liked the feeling of being the one in control of the laughter. It brought me a bit of popularity and gave me a role. The problem was that my ebullience tended to spill over into the classroom and I have to admit that I spent many an hour in the 'chatterbox corner' or outside Miss Robertson's classroom door. The internal struggle was always there in me, between trying to be the good, studious, academic girl, as I was quite bright and always in the top three in the class (which received the usual response of 'Why weren't you first?' from my parents of course – and you wonder where I get any drive that I have?) and the class clown. This struggle started early.

I loved making my mum laugh, as she was a great giggler and even when she was in a bad mood I could make her laugh, so she was my guinea pig. She had good comedy taste and loved Chic Murray, Billy Connolly, Rikki Fulton and Jack Milroy. She was also a huge fan of *Rowan and Martin's Laugh-In*, and as I got older I was allowed to stay up with her and watch it. It was so colourful and weird and educational for me to actually see women like Goldie Hawn and Lily Tomlin being allowed to be funny in their own right and not just as the butt of the gag. Let's remember that we were still in an era of *On The Buses* where women were the 'nag' or 'ugly' (or both) or the 'pretty one' who was stupid and never got to say anything, so it was brilliant to see women being funny.

But Stella's real favourite was Dave Allen. I think his particular sense of humour and his storytelling as opposed to gag-telling, along with the Irish twinkle, reminded her of her dad though she would never have admitted it. She just adored Dave Allen and had a secret fancy for him too I think – he and Jack Jones (the singer not the TUC leader!) were her pin-ups.

Looking back, I realise that we were at such an important time socially and culturally. We weren't rich but we were part of an emerging working class that had hope and some security after years of war, poverty and rationing.

My parents must have felt incredibly lucky.

CHAPTER 11

THE GOOD LIFE

Our house was rented but we had a car, a phone (with a party line, but it worked) and a colour TV. As described earlier, we also had holidays in, for example, Morecambe – not Blackpool, though, as it was too common for Mum, 'full of drunk Glaswegians'. In fact she didn't like going to the Glasgow Fair holidays because there were too many Scots and they were always a bit common in her eyes and didn't behave like the genteel woman she aspired to be. So, for the Smiths, it was Bridlington, Morecambe, Whitley Bay and Rhyl.

Each new gadget brought into our house was greeted with wonder and amazement: the hoover, the front-loading washing machine, the tumble dryer, the colour TV – all these things confirmed to us all that life was on the up and up. A favourite gadget for me was my Aunt Frances and Uncle Andy's tall American Frigidaire, in their wee kitchen in a modern maisonette in Motherwell. It was brand-new, and one wall had just big glass windows onto a balcony/veranda, which believe it or not looked over the lily pond (or paddling pool) in a communal garden space for the kids. This was the first of the new housing projects in Motherwell after they pulled down the tenements and if you got one of them then you felt as if you'd won the Pools. My relatives had waited in a cramped tenement for years with three young kids to get one and we were all pleased, but secretly jealous, when they did.

I loved that house. They had a modern corner-unit-type sofa with little coffee tables joining it together which I thought was just divine. But the fridge, the fridge! Ooooh it was huge and had a sort of red-pink light inside that came on when it opened. I thought it was the coolest thing on the planet. And they had a radiogram too! This huge piece of furniture could play records as well as tune into the radio and it lit up when it was played – surely a piece of engineering worthy of the NASA space programme. They also had a cocktail cabinet: it was so chic that going into their house felt like being on the set of *Bewitched*.

As a couple, my Aunt Frances and Uncle Andy always seemed like the couples you saw on TV too. They genuinely loved one another and were openly affectionate and cuddled and kissed but not in a sloppy, embarrassing way. It seemed that they both felt really lucky to have found one another, I don't think I have ever met anyone as content with her life as my Aunt Frances. She loved her husband and thought she was the luckiest woman in the world, loved her kids, loved being a housewife and was always so delighted to see me. Always called me 'Chicken', or 'Pet'. Nothing was ever too much bother for her.

In stark contrast to this role model of domestic bliss, my mum, much as I loved her, was always discontented, melancholy and unhappy. I don't think it was anyone's fault and nowadays I think it would be helped by counselling for mild depression. I think her early life left her with many scars that she didn't know how to deal with as a young woman in her 20s. As her oldest daughter I bore a lot of that angst and upset with her. A story that made me cry and still does was one that she told me a few years before she died. By this time my parents had divorced (after 35 years together) and Stella was living in her own flat, had a job she loved, grandchildren, holidays with her pals and generally gadded about the place in her wee car.

In the early years of their marriage, my parents and Aunt Frances and Uncle Andy went everywhere together. They went out together for meals, went on holidays, had kids at the same time, got their houses, cars, you name it. As the years passed they drifted apart, the kids grew up and went their separate ways and when my parents' marriage broke up, there was even more of a distance. So one lovely, sunny day Mum was sitting at traffic lights at the entrance to Strathclyde Park when she spotted a white-haired couple in their

'60s walking across the road laughing, hand in hand. She said she couldn't stop watching them and thinking, why isn't that me? It was all I ever wanted, to be in a happy, loving marriage with one man that I could share my life with, who would adore me and I would adore him. It was only as the couple got closer that she realised that it was Frances and Andy. She dissolved into tears and realised that any envy she had felt was never about their radiogram or cocktail cabinet but that they had found each other and were still so happy, even after all those years.

Dad felt lucky in his job and genuinely loved it. We were lucky in many ways because my dad was a hard worker and had a real determination to provide for his family. We had a swing in the garden (well, it was homemade by him from steel tubes that he'd welded together and painted for us, but it survived for about 20 years). He built me a doll's house from scratch, an amazing bungalow with a roof that detached and decorated with wallpaper the same as our house, and furniture to match. He built a set of cubes that could be used as chairs, tables, put together to become a couch – all made from wood and painted pale blue. I loved them and we had all our friends the street playing with them for years. For a young kid he really was a dream dad.

Our family life wasn't perfect by any means, but it was similar to most of the other families in our scheme. Solid, with two parents, a dad who worked and a mum at home, both striving to do the best they could. Extended families were everywhere, so grandparents, aunts, uncles and cousins were close at hand and very much part of all our lives. Dad never smoked or drank in his whole life and my mother, though never a smoker, was a social drinker (two Cinzanos and she'd be singing). Her early life did nothing to add to her love of the drink – or of drinkers – yet on the flipside she loved the lifestyle, and the freedom and laughs that it brought. It was when the atmosphere or the drunk turned nasty that she loathed it. No accident then that she married the opposite of her father, teetotal too, though Dad wasn't anti-drink (he actually would occasionally have a sweet stout). But I think he had seen too many lives destroyed by it, at home and in the RAF, to ever be in its thrall. As a kid I wished that my dad was like other men and felt odd that he never went to the pub for a pint like other dads did.

My father's own drug of choice was work, followed by his hobby of doing up cars when back at home. To call it an obsession was at times not an understatement. It was the cause of much tension between my parents. As so often happens in life, we think we have gone for the opposite of our parents and we end up with a different version sitting in front of us.

CHAPTER 12

SCHOOL

School always seemed a bit of an odd place to me. I liked playing with my friends and I did actually enjoy learning and was fortunate enough to do quite well. I didn't have problems with reading and counting and was therefore seen as a good pupil. I was enthusiastic too as I wanted to be liked and to be praised, as just like most kids I reacted well to praise.

Our only real creative outlets were sessions of gymnastics – i.e. running around the school hall until dizzy, and throwing and catching a bean bag. Yes, not much equipment in our school in those days. We had singing lessons with Ms Buchan. God love her but she wasn't a 'looker', as my mother was heard to remark. She had buck teeth, glasses with those very '60s-styled tails at the edge, and a very ruddy complexion. She was a bit of a 'sensible shoe' wearer with a nice kilt and blouse, not quite the height of fashion even in Newarthill. But she did have musical ability and taught us all our Robert Burns songs from 'Ye Banks and Braes', to 'Let Us Haste to Kelvingrove', and did her best to get these kids from a small mining village in Lanarkshire to sound like the Orpheus Choir.

Personally, I love choirs that have regional vowels as well as the top choirs that can do the *Messiah* note-perfect. There is room for all types, and neither is right or wrong. But to try and get kids in Birkenhead or Glasgow to sing without a trace of their natural accent was just another bit of cultural imperialism to my mind. Of course, at six years of age, I did my utmost to try and sing posh. Poor Miss Buchan, she had her work cut out for her.

I loved singing, as it had always been such a part of happy times in my life so I would give it my all and was fortunate in that I could learn quickly and hold a tune. So I was put in the choir from an early age and would use any opportunity to give the class a song. Not just classical, or seasonal tunes, but pop songs as well.

At the age of eight I started piano lessons with a lovely woman in the High Street in the village. She was young and kind, and lessons took place in the front room of her council house. I loved going there and learning because she made it fun and I developed quickly. Unfortunately after about a year she went off and got married and moved away and I moved to another woman in the village and I hated it. It was boring; she was crabby and managed to make the whole thing uninteresting. My enthusiasm waned. Thankfully, my parents noted this and set about finding me a new teacher.

My Papa McGarry heard of their enquiries and fortunately knew of a great teacher in Motherwell. Her name was Mrs Hughes and I think that they had known each other before they both were married, and I could still see that Mrs Hughes had a lot of affection for him when they met again when I went for my first lesson. She was all coquettish and girly in his presence and I saw the effect he must have had on Gran, as well as a few other women, when he was a young man.

Mrs Hughes was a great pianist herself and was a good teacher. Her house was unlike any I had ever been in in my life. Most of my family and friends lived in council houses with similar furniture and fittings. Mrs Hughes' house was in a lovely, leafy, wealthy area of the town. It was lined with trees and the old Victorian houses had driveways. Hers was a semi-detached with beautiful bay windows and a lovely double entrance. It is still there to this day, still a lovely house and around the corner from where my sister Louise now lives.

In the bay window of the front room sat a baby grand piano, something I had only ever seen in the movies or on television. Pupils were only ever allowed to play on it if they reached a certain standard – the lucky pupil at that time was Graham McNaught, who was fantastic. I turned up early one day and followed him into my lesson and was invited by Mrs Hughes to listen to Graham play his pieces for his audition to get into the Royal Academy. He was only about a year older than me but when he played I couldn't believe it. It was beautiful, magical, and the look on Mrs Hughes' face was that of complete rapture. No wonder, it must have been wonderful to see one of her pupils play so wonderfully, especially when most of her days were full of pupils plonking up and down the piano and murdering tunes the way I did. Hearing him play that day, I realised that the piano was not where my future lay. I hope that Graham went on to have a fabulous career.

To this day I honestly have no envy or jealousy when I hear people who can really play or sing much better than myself. I just feel a sense of wonder and privilege and it lifts my heart. Being able to sing with some of the musicians I have performed with is just joyous – Kennedy Aitchison, Irvin Duguid, Gordon Wilson, Simon Niblock, Paul Newton – all wonderful people at the top of their game.

Until I was about 14 and the boredom and drudgery of practising every night had finally got to me, I enjoyed piano. But eventually it took a back seat to a desire to sing in bands and go out with boys. I managed Grade 5 and did OK and ended up at the Royal Scottish Academy of Music and Drama (the RSAMD) in Glasgow for my exams and those hours of boredom did end up being of huge benefit in my career. My ability to read music, as well as play, helped my singing and let me be part of the band occasionally in the theatre company Wildcat – and of course I've just had an incredible role as Cora the church organist in *Calendar Girls*. Little did I know when I dragged myself to lessons for years that I would eventually use it so often, maybe I would have stuck in a bit more instead of listening to Marc Bolan. My basic knowledge did allow me to write songs and dream of a being a singer-songwriter, to learn and play the chords and songs that I love from James Taylor, Carole King, Joni Mitchell and Crosby, Stills and Nash – but more of that later.

I only played piano in school once for the school service. I had to play for them to sing along with the hymns and I was pretty rubbish. God help those who were trying to sing along with me and it served me right for bragging that I was going to piano lessons. An early lesson in not blowing your own trumpet – or piano for that matter. School shows were pretty formal and boring affairs: the choir with 'Ye Banks and Braes', then a poem or a nativity play. I don't remember any drama or anything truly creative with input from the kids themselves. It was all quite conservative and nothing different happened in shows in the school until I was about ten, when the new headmaster arrived.

My love of reading really kicked off around Primary 3 when a temporary teacher arrived. Her name was Mrs Kitchen and I really liked her. She was old in my opinion which probably meant she was about 50, and had flame-coloured hair and dark glasses and wore a lot of heavily powdered make-up with bright lipstick which gave her a sort of crazy look. She always wore an overall too – brightly coloured, or blue, it was designed to keep her clothes free from chalk. But if we had been good as a class then at the end of each day around 3 p.m. she would get us to put all our books away and she would read to us; it was liberating. The book I remember transporting me to another land was *The Lion, the Witch and the Wardrobe*.

The threat of not getting our story at the end of the day was enough to make me shut up (sadly the same didn't go for some of the boys) and if Mrs Kitchen refused to read because of our behaviour I was devastated. Even now I can recreate that feeling of complete peace that came over me when she read to us and I have been an avid reader all my life because of that feeling. For her, it must have been rewarding too and not only because the class was quiet. We all quietened down and we left her class calm and were less likely to start a fight with each other on the way home.

She was an interesting woman who had spent much of her time in India and Africa. She chatted to us about her life and the way other children lived, which opened a whole new world to us, and her tales were as good as the books at times. She liked kids too and found our ideas and comments funny and interesting – rare for a teacher in the early '60s – and for some reason found herself back in this wee village teaching. She had contracted malaria in Africa and was frequently absent because she would have relapses, much to my selfish annoyance because we didn't get the next chapter of the book.

All that cosiness was unfortunately blown away by our next teacher, Ms Robertson. She was what was termed a 'spinster of the parish', and I think lived with her sister and mother in a house on the main street. She wore glasses and had a neat curly perm (I think she wore a hat when she was outside, as if she was going to church) and she also wore an overall of the Hackett flowery variety that tended to give you a headache if you stared at it for too long. She went to church every Sunday and was a Sunday School teacher, no surprises there. If I were to draw a cartoon of a typical Scottish teacher of the period it would probably look like Ms Robertson.

She was a tough, permanent fixture of the school and everyone dreaded going into P5. She was seen as a good teacher, in that you learned a lot by force and by rote (i.e. continued repetition of tables and spelling which were drummed into you by a mixture of boredom and fear) but she was also very strict, with a tendency to shout a lot. But I do owe my knowledge of the times tables and being able to count to her. That and the hugely important ability to make a lap bag and a peaked scarf – skills I have used frequently since I was ten, NOT! I owe Ms Robertson all that and I thank her, but there were very few smiles and laughs in her class.

Totally the opposite of the atmosphere in her class was the one encountered when we went into the classroom of the wonderful Mrs Rhind. She was in her 50s by the time we got there but we all loved her, and you learned a lot too. She was a great storyteller, loved teaching kids who were chatty and had something to say for themselves, and she laughed a lot. I felt like she was a special auntie. She told stories of Canada, a country she'd lived in for a while. Years later when I was on a family trip through the majestic and breathtaking Rockies from Lake Louise to Vancouver, it was Mrs Rhind's voice that I heard describing the views and also when I spotted the Canadian Pacific Railroad and the trains passing us. She had instilled that sense of wonderment into me about the beauty of that place and it never left me.

She did what all good teachers should do: created an environment where learning felt like fun and something interesting. I looked forward to going to school when I was in her class and I know the other kids did too. She was disciplined too – though she could be knocked off her stride too easily by a question about Canada, which we kids cottoned on to quite quickly. Fortunately she liked me, and even though I was put into the 'chatterboxes' group – go figure – she was a teacher who actually liked what the kids had to say, and we made her laugh.

Until this point I had been a chatty, bright pupil who did well, always in the top five in the class and like most children, I was thriving in an environment which encouraged and nurtured. That all changed with a new headmaster, 'heedie'. Up until his arrival, the school had been run by Mr Ritchie, a man the kids and staff all loved. He was quite a kindly, benign presence and the atmosphere in the school was generally bright and welcoming. Primary 7 were always taught by the head teacher, usually a man in those days, in preparation for high school I suppose, so we got the new guy.

I had come from a warm, caring, environment with Mrs Rhind to a cold, severe classroom with a man who thought children should be seen and not heard and punished if they were not. My ability to listen and learn slumped in this man's class – basically, I was bored rigid. Now I realise he was just a bad teacher for me. Sadly, it came at a vital time in my learning and I dropped to about twelfth in the class because by the middle of the term I couldn't actually give a toss. I was bored, uninterested and demotivated. I didn't want to do anything for this man and his approval meant little or nothing to me.

It was still a time when teachers were not questioned and a parent ostracised for daring to question the quality of the teaching or what went on in schools. Many think nowadays that it has gone too far the other way and that schools and teachers can't function properly because of the interference of parents or fear of what may happen if they discipline a child. But give me that any day over the verbally and physically abusive treatment that was meted out to kids of my generation and before. Kids were caned and belted as routine and no one gave a monkey's.

One of the worst days of my life (well, I was only ten) was coming home from school to find Mum in tears and Dad furious with me. Mum had been called to the school for the meeting with the headmaster about me leaving and going to high school. These were still the days when kids were sent to different high schools depending on their academic ability. The dream school in our area was Dalziel High in Motherwell, as the really 'brainy' kids went there. The Grahams, next door, all went there and they had the blue blazers and uniform of success in my eyes. The other option was Bellshill Academy, which was also a good school and many bright kids emerged from there, but it didn't have the snobby kudos that Dalziel High enjoyed. The kids with no hope were sent to Braidhurst High in Forgewood – seen as a very tough area of Motherwell, where tales of gang fights in the playground at lunchtime were rife.

As I'd always done well at school, winning prizes, etc., my parents assumed that I would get to Dalziel. Their shock when the headmaster told her that my work had slumped and I was in the middle of the class and wouldn't get there, added to the fact that I was the most disobedient and insolent child he had ever had the misfortune to teach, was all a bit too much for Mum. She was devastated and I got a bollocking and told I would be lucky if I ended up a bus conductress. Actually that was a job I had always coveted, oh to be a conductor ('clippie') on the buses with a beehive, loads of make-up, a fitted uniform and chewing gum shouting, 'Comeoangettaff' to the masses. A dream job for me but not where my parents wanted me to end up.

It was on that day that I first really felt the weight of expectation on my shoulders, especially from Mum. First child, first grandchild, loved, adored but with all of that came a lot of responsibility and to be honest it's taken until now, at the ripe old age of 50, to shake free of that weight.

My success was her success, in the eyes of her family and the world, and I had to do well for her more than anything else. I dare say that feeling of entwining, or what therapists call 'enmeshment', took hold of me then and that's why separating from my mother has been so difficult for me since her death. She died and I didn't know who I was supposed to be. The roles got a bit confused and I became the responsible adult as I watched my mother crumpled and crying over what her daughter had done, or not done. It was all about her grief, her humiliation and her upset at being spoken to by this headmaster like that. The shame of it.

I couldn't fail because I had to make her life a success. It was a heavy weight to bear. I don't think my sisters ever felt that way, because my subsequent success allowed them to have an easier passage and to choose a bit more of what they wanted to do in life, as is usually the case for the younger kids. The oldest gets most of the pressure to do well, gets the stricter rules to live by. My sisters' curfews were always much more lax than mine – I was always amazed when my young sis Diane – as a teenager – was allowed to turn up at 1 a.m.

half pished with her pals when I would have been kept in for a month if it had been me. But it's like one of my favourite lines from the Steve Martin film *Parenthood* when they confess that they were too protective of their oldest son and caused him problems because of it. Their explanation ends with 'Well, you are more relaxed with later kids, by the time you get to four you let them juggle knives.' How true!

Anyway, I went into school the next day, chastened, shamed and with the weight of the world on my shoulders. I had to buckle down, work hard, shut up and improve my work. Generally throughout my life I have always been able to do that and it all stems from this time. Screw the nut, stop the carry-on, sacrifice the fun and games even if it is under the tutelage of a pillock and get what you need out of the situation. The Heedie did have a creative side and we would always be assured of a nap if we got him onto his favourite subject of songs, poetry and all that. He would talk endlessly about Robert Burns ages and recite poetry that hovered above the heads of us ten year olds. My saving grace in his eyes was that I could sing, and I was needed for his choir and school concerts.

I auditioned for the school show and we had to go and sing for him in front of the class, which was pretty scary. Because of my love of pop music and our neighbours the Grahams, my references were all from the likes of the Beatles and not Burns. So I chose the Beatles' 'Norwegian Wood' as my audition song (not really that appropriate for a girl aged ten). The lyrics were a trifle risqué – and I did wonder at the giggling and the look of bemusement on the face of the teacher. But I loved the tune and made the choir.

My marks improved and I moved up the class, much to the relief of my mother, and the heedie's views softened, but years later Mum confessed that she had never really believed him and that she was so upset because he was such a prat and spoke to her as if she was an idiot. She also told me that she had been really angry with him and defended me, saying that she found his comments hard to believe as no one had ever found me difficult before. I wish she'd bloody told me at the time. But I was saved the agony of whether I would get to Dalziel High or not anyway, because a new school system came into being – comprehensives.

Our year (1970) was the first school year in Scotland to be educated in this new school system. Instead of dividing kids up into 'bright' and 'not bright', which in effect told two thirds of the population to go off and weave baskets, children were to be sent together from one area to be taught in the same schools in an effort to give those kids who were effectively branded as failures at 11 a better chance of a good education. As we now accept, children develop at different times and condemning kids to struggle because of an IQ test that they weren't ready for was failing too many children. By the old system, because of my headmaster's bias, I could have been sent to junior secondary and thus never have been given the chance to work and develop academically. The comprehensive experiment was a lifeline for me, and many children like me.

'Zoning' meant that you were sent to high school based on where you lived and not based on your academic abilities. It meant that the really bright kids went to the school too and it was hoped this would prevent schools being 'ghetto schools' – although Margaret Thatcher's 'parental choice' in the '80s tipped the balance again. All the kids in Newarthill were to be bussed to Forgewood and to Braidhurst High. We were disappointed that we wouldn't get to the hallowed Dalziel High and we were terrified about what would await us in the supposed killing fields of Braidhurst, but at least we would all be together and the whole class would be on the bus of a morning.

CHAPTER 13

HIGH SCHOOL

I loved high school. I desperately wanted away from my primary school and all the negativity I had suffered. When someone has a negative view of you it's very difficult to change it and in some ways it gets into your core and my sense of self-belief was fragile, to say the least. It was confusing to be adored on the one hand, but with 'conditions' applied in that it seemed to me that I had to be a good girl, attractive and succeed in order to be loved. I know it wasn't what my parents thought they were doing but it was the messages that I was receiving. Given their own backgrounds and the lack of love in them, they probably thought they were the most demonstrative people ever. But shows of affection or approval or emotion were not the stuff of life around us so the only way to show approval was if someone was doing well at school or sport or music, for example.

Not for us the stuff of sitcoms and nice English middle-class families coming through the door and shouting, 'Darling, I'm home', before kissing the wife and children. American sitcoms were even worse for us because they kissed even more and cuddled and played with their kids too. I remember asking Mum and Dad one evening why we weren't like the families on TV and why didn't they kiss each other when they got home? Dad was on nightshift and my sister Louise and I were usually in our 'jammies', sitting on the floor watching TV and the usual routine was that he would say cheerio to us all before going out the door and that was that. So when I asked that question they both flushed, burst out laughing, and as Dad moved towards the front door to leave, they gave each other a kiss. 'Ah, so we were a wee bit normal after all', I thought, but it was their reaction that stayed with me. It obviously never occurred to them to do it as a natural everyday thing. In those days, love, approval and affection for me and almost everyone else I knew seemed to be a conditional thing and only given if you were good, and not just because you were loved. I've always wanted my own girls to feel that they were loved simply for being here – for existing – not because they were ours, or because of what they achieved in life, but simply for being in our lives because that was something I had never really felt. You'll have to ask them if it's worked but it was certainly my aim.

So, I got to start over again at a new school and try and do a bit better. The sense of shame and of failure still hung over me and I knew I had to work hard. Due to my 'slip in the ratings' I didn't make it into the top class in the first year but I was in the top stream of children they thought were bright and would go on to do O grades and Highers. Even though this was a comprehensive school (very modern, with a relatively new main glass building, a tower block and playing fields around it), it was still run like an old-fashioned public school. We had a house system, I think named after rivers in Scotland (I was in Rannoch). We were put into houses on our first day and points were accrued through sports days and other activities.

Many of the heads of department still wore gowns over their suits, shirts and ties; the female teachers weren't allowed to wear trousers (not until the '90s, actually) and we were sent home if we didn't have the full uniform: a black or grey skirt, white blouse, tie, black blazer with school badge, and appropriate socks or tights and shoes. No coloured tights, no kinky boots and no trousers for the girls, and positively no make-up.

We were marched into the main hall for assembly every morning and I could hear the 'Woman Advisor' as she was called – complete in her gown of authority – checking for skirts that were too short, or the wrong colour of tights, and she'd be shouting to some girl, 'Catherine Welsh, get out of that line and into the toilet now and scrub that massacre off your face.' Eh?

At 9 a.m. we had prayers and a hymn, followed by any school information. These were of course Church of Scotland prayers and hymns, though it was supposed to be a non-denominational school. Unfortunately, in practice, in Lanarkshire, that made no difference, because once you were in there it was 'Proddie' hymns and prayers the whole way.

Much as I hated my school uniform and did everything I could to deviate from it (wee ties, big fat ties, huge knots, skirts rolled up, skirts rolled down, platform shoes, kinky boots, weird hairdos, hairbands and ribbons, make-up, the lot) I am actually a fan of the uniform. I can still see the kids in my year who were from really poor backgrounds, with their slightly grey or yellowing shirts, the blazers and skirts that were too big or too small, and the scabby shoes and socks. But that uniform saved them from even more ridicule. Had they had to compete with the 'fashionistas' even in the early '70s they would have been humiliated – the school uniform is a great leveller. I am also a fan of the morning assembly, as I think it pulls a school together to give it a greater sense of itself. It's one of the disappointments of my daughter's high school that it was designed and built without a hall big enough to house the entire school all at the same time. It means that the staff have to work extra hard to get a sense of cohesiveness amongst the pupils.

Not being in the top class in the first year meant that I didn't do Latin, and bang went my mother's dream of 'her daughter the doctor'. Latin was a prerequisite for medical school and my mother at her convent school had been a keen Latin scholar, well, according to her anyway. But this was actually all about her brother the doctor, as success in life was always measured against her brother, my Uncle Jim – her hero and protector, the bright, good-looking one.

So things were a bit frosty when I came home to tell her that I was in the third from the top class and I do have to admit that my ego took a bit of a battering when I realised that girls who were not as bright as I was in primary were in the top class and doing the beloved Latin and I wasn't. I adopted a plan which was that I would work ten times as hard and try to get moved up a class so that I could do Latin. I even used to copy Latin exercises out of my friend's book to learn the old '*mo, amas*', etc. but trying to teach myself Latin wasn't a good idea and I abandoned it after about a month.

I did, however, do well in 1A3 (my class) and after exams was back in the top three so by the time I got to the third year and choosing subjects for O grades I was in the top group again. First and second year weren't always easy though. We had the usual smattering of good teachers – Ms Kelly in English, whom I adored; Ms Adams in history and French; and later Norrie Bissell and Mr Hunter. But we also had the' old guard', the teachers who for the life of me I couldn't understand why they had been let near a classroom. And worst of all were those who employed the 'dark sarcasm of the classroom', as Pink Floyd so rightly called it. Who used their age and experience to belittle and humiliate kids who were trapped in a system that gave them no say or right to defend themselves.

There were teachers who were worn out, in it for the pay, and others who were just complete idiots, who threw tables, chalk or dusters, or who had a 'Lochgelly' (a leather strap that was fashioned in the Fife town of Lochgelly, with two leather prongs that were agony when hit with power and force onto your hands). Some male teachers carried them under their suits to be brought out at any time to beat a child's hand into a black-and-blue mess.

I was belted occasionally, usually for 'gabbing' in class ('no way', I hear you say) but never to that extent. The things that always hurt me more were the things that were said anyway. I was told by Mr Kerr (then a young maths teacher, who went on strangely enough to teach my oldest daughter as a head of department in her school) as a young 12 year old after I'd been put out the door for asking a question about maths, in that I didn't know why a $'2 + B^2 = C^2$'. To this day I don't know what I did wrong except to take it literally and not understand that it was a formula for solving mathematical problems. I genuinely wanted to know why and he couldn't tell me, so he put me out the class and told me that I had far too much extrovert energy. When I asked him what that was he said: 'Ask your parents!' I duly went home and asked Mum, who said, 'It means you're a bloody show-off,' so give him his due, he was right. And when I met him years later at my daughter's school (where I am reliably informed that his teaching style and dry wit had not diminished) he congratulated me (in a tone that only an old teacher can employ) in choosing the correct profession.

I had always known that I could sing and at primary there were a couple of other girls who were better than me too, and that is always the lesson for any performer. No matter how good you are, there is always someone better, either round the corner or snapping at your heels. But in my room, singing into my hairbrush along with the pop stars of the day, I knew that I had a decent range and that I could detect the right note, I could hear harmonies easily, and sing them too. I loved harmonising better than the lead vocal actually and would annoy my pals with constantly singing along with anything but the tune.

I knew I could sing, though, I just knew it! I could feel when I unleashed the power of it that it would work. I never really let it go because it would have been seen as showing off and that didn't go down well with my pals in school. Drawing attention to yourself wasn't seen as a good thing and frequently you were put down for it. Success in the choir was fine but don't bloody brag about it or dare to say you wanted to be a singer. What is it that they say about familiarity and contempt?

It was in Mrs Johnstone's music class in that first year that I realised that it's much easier to perform in front of strangers than in front of those that know you and take any ability you have for granted. To this day I would rather play to 2,000 strangers in an auditorium than a few folk who know me well and are quietly thinking, 'Aw, not that again, I've heard it.'

In order for the teacher to find out the range of our voices we had to sing a few lines of a song around the class. It was just the girls in our section as the boys were done separately. The song chosen for us was luckily a favourite of mine called 'The Four Marys' and was about the last night of Mary, Queen of Scots' life before she was executed by Elizabeth I. What wasn't known was that her maid, also called Mary, was executed alongside her for God knows what but that was the deal. I loved history and loved this period of history too and was always and still am moved by the song.

> Yestere'en the Queen had four Marys,
> The nicht she'll hae but three,
> There was Mary Seaton and Mary Beaton and Mary Carmichael
> and me

It has a really haunting melody too. So we started singing a couple of lines each. I was in a class of girls I barely knew – who had all been at other primary schools throughout the area. Here was my chance to make an impact, so it got to me and I did it full blast and it was in my key too. 'Sing out Louise.' Mrs Johnstone stopped at the end of the phrase as the other girls all turned and looked at me and smiled and said, 'Well done, Elaine, a good strong alto.' I'd done it, I'd stopped the room and I loved it. On the way out all the girls were saying things like, 'Heh, you were really good, you can really sing.' Though I loved it, I managed to look suitably surprised and display some humility – I'd learned by then never to get too big for my boots even if inside I felt brilliant.

The boys were taught by the male music teacher, and head of department, Cameron P. Merriweather (yes, honestly, that was his name). I mentioned him in a book a few years ago and after his name I had put in as a joke that his name was a 'Proddie' name if ever I heard one. What was brilliant was that he wrote to me when I was appearing in pantomime at the King's in Glasgow, thanked me for the mention and signed his name, and underneath put 'Proddie and Proud!' Hilarious. For those not from, or familiar with, the religious divide of the west of Scotland and the humour and 'slagging' that comes out of it, I should explain. The humour side is the best bit about it, the bitterness and violence that come from it is the ugly and depressing side. Far too many lives have been marred by it. The only positive thing is that the west of Scotland has found a way of laughing at it (always the most powerful weapon, I feel, in the fight against ignorance) so a lot of good-natured ribbing does take place.

Mr Merriweather and Mrs Johnstone were to play a big role in the start of my road to show business because they put all the shows on in school at the time, and the only ones permitted were Gilbert and Sullivan operettas like *The Pirates of Penzance* and *The Mikado*. I remember Mum coming to one of the shows and heard her remarking to someone that she didn't really like Gilbert and Sullivan, she preferred opera to operetta (this announced in quite a pan-loaf voice of course). Eh? Opera? This was news to me as I had never heard any opera played in our house and I know for a fact that the closest she got to seeing it onstage was a production of the musical *Hair* at the Metropole. She probably heard it on *Woman's Hour* on Radio 4, which she listened to avidly, and must have decided to chuck it into a conversation with someone she thought she had to show her class and breeding to.

It was just a sign of my mother's snobbery and she never liked any of the shows I did at school, and Dad rarely made it to concerts either, because he was always working, so Mum would occasionally come but always under sufferance. This was of course in the days before video cameras and a parental presence for all little Johnnie or Emily's achievements. Parents who came to see things at the school were the rare ones. I always felt really jealous of the kids whose mum came to see them in the choir because mine didn't, and when Mum did she moaned about how bad the show was and how poorly turned out the teachers were. 'I mean, you would think that they would at least make an effort, some of those women teachers didn't even have a bag to match their shoes – what kind of example is that?' I would sit there listening and try to get her to speak about what I had done but that was glossed over in favour of handbag-slagging.

To give Mum her due, she had been brought up in a home where classical music was played and Radio 4 was the order of the day. She did love Mozart's *Eine Kleine Nachtmusik* and Beethoven's *Pastoral Symphony*, but it was hardly an extensive knowledge and in reality she tended to prefer the Beatles or the Beach Boys. When I was practising my complex classical pieces (like Bartók), she would be the one shouting in from the kitchen for me to, 'Shut that rammy up and play something with a tune!' But as soon as any of the family dropped by, I was wheeled in to play a bit of classical, with 'Für Elise by Beethoven being the big favourite, thus demonstrating that she was bringing her kids up properly.

Anyway, I settled into Braidhurst quite quickly. There were no gang fights or running battles in the playground as had been predicted to terrify us. The people, and area, of Forgewood, although suffering from poverty and neglect, were welcoming and friendly. I became great pals with loads of girls from the area and their families were terrific. There was the usual problem of bullying, but not at the level we are led to believe it is at today. Bullying can be a horrible thing to witness or be on the sharp end of and too many young lives have been ruined by it. I'd had a bit of it at primary and the relief when the bullying stops is fabulous, but it leaves a lot of fear. Thankfully, high school provided me with a new, wider group of friends and I was able to avoid those who had any power over my well-being. What amazes me is that the girls who were the worst bullies seem to have no memory of it in later life. A couple of my friends now who were badly bullied at school say the same.

I was at a big lunch when a very attractive woman came up and introduced herself to me and told me that she was at school with me. When she told me her name I nearly dropped my fork here was this respectable mother and wife of a doctor or something, standing in front of me smiling, when I remembered the terror that she put in most girls' hearts all the way through early school. She was a real loudmouth, a violent girl who was always fighting on the school bus or threatening both boys and girls and generally terrified us all for years and was someone to avoid. The relief when she got off the bus at Carfin was wonderful. So I laughed when this lovely woman told me who she was and I said, 'God, you used to terrify me and my pals.' She looked at me as if I was speaking German and said, 'Me?' and I said 'Yes, you were terrifying, always fighting and bossing people around, we used to quake in our boots.' She laughed and dismissed what I was saying with a, 'Don't be daft,' and I realised that she had no memory of what she had done or the effect she had had on all of us.

I got my nickname at school early on from the boys and I was always seen as a bit of a laugh. 'Get "wee Smithy" to do it' was the cry when they wanted a teacher distracted and to get them off lessons, and I was quite good at it too. One day I was standing outside the dining hall with another girl from my class and two older boys behind started pushing us and put their hand up her skirt. She was really upset and we went to get Mr Hunter, who was the teacher in charge of the queue. We told him what happened and he asked who the boys were and we said we didn't know. He told my friend that next time she had to just hit them back or shout and he turned to me and said, 'What would you have done?'

'I would have bashed them, sir.' He laughed loudly and from that day I was 'Basher'. Fine in second year, but he was still calling me it in fifth year when my image was in question. But he was behind my becoming a prefect too. There was a bit of resistance about my having this role as I was a bit too lippy for some teachers and certainly not a sports team captain or top of the class. But I was in the school shows, the choir, the netball team (not really for my skills as a player but more for the psychological advantage of my shouting at opponents and team-mates). So, he championed me and I was eventually made a prefect with a warning from him to 'not let him down'. I don't think I did.

My first foray into the 'business of show', apart from the choir, was, as I mentioned earlier, *The Pirates of Penzance* by Gilbert and Sullivan. I was in third year by this time and a strong alto singer. I was in the chorus and hated singing the songs that the girls had, all that 'Gaily tripping, lightly skipping' malarkey and so I kept getting into trouble for being disruptive, i.e. 'gabbing'. Mr Hunter was doing set-building and stage management, and really helped produce the whole thing, and one day while we were hanging around I said to him, 'Sir, why do all the girls have to do all that stupid singing? Why is there not a woman policeman, they have got the best song too with the old "Tarantara, Tarantara" song? Can I not be a policeman cos my voice is lower and suits that better?' He just laughed, but a couple of days later he pulled me out of the dinner queue and said he had discussed it with the music department and they thought it was a good idea. Eh?

So I was taken to sing with the boys and given the WPC uniform and sang the 'Tarantara' song with them (though I did have to sing in the female chorus at other times). But there I was as a singing WPC but with a new recruit (a wee tiny boy from first year who was actually too cute and funny by far in my opinion and stole a bit of my thunder). Looking back it was a classic variety sketch. A 'maw, paw and wean' routine with me constantly trying to keep control of the child while singing and maintaining order. It was groundbreaking for our school and brought the house down.

I even got my first good review in the *Motherwell Times*, but the highest praise came from my mother, whom I had begged to come to the show and she actually turned up. She told me I was very good on the way home, and even added that I was funny. Yes, I'd found a way to make my mother laugh. Dad was very encouraging of anything musical or entertaining and had actually got Louise, my younger sister, to play the organ. She went to a very different kind of piano teacher from me, though, he didn't teach the traditional way with scales and exams and Louise had a good ear and learnt much more quickly to play tunes that my dad loved. Well, her teacher had 'taught the Alexander Brothers you know, doll'.

So Dad bought her the organ, which she was a whiz at and could handle all the foot pedals too, so for a while any talent I had was pushed to the back burner, which I actually enjoyed as the pressure to succeed wasn't all focused on myself. Poor Louise though, at the age of ten she'd be wheeled out at every occasion to perform, and the sight of this wee skinny lassie with her bowl-cut hair and legs a blur on the organ brought much applause and amazement. Dad also had got in tow with a wonderful man who ran the St Andrew's Ambulance concert party which went around old folks' homes and hospitals entertaining (or punishing, depending on your viewpoint) the residents and Louise was a huge hit. I occasionally went along and sang with her – yes, the 'Singing Smith Sisters', and we did 'Banks of the Ohio' and 'Jambalaya' to great applause. Well, some applause anyway. But Louise was the star. But more importantly so was Dad as he found his niche out there onstage when Alex couldn't make it. He introduced and then compèred the show and told several bad gags into the bargain, and he loved it.

I continued to do school shows, or an occasional PTA (parents and teacher association) concert where Louise and I did our act. As Louise got increasingly better and got more attention I started looking for other ways to be creative whilst singing. I started going to my cousins – Jim and John – on a Friday after school and they had loads of pals who could play a bit as well as sing. Jim played the electric accordion, and John sang and played bass, but their pals from Dalziel High who lived in the posh houses in Orchard Street had the ultimate – a garage. So there we all were rehearsing in the garage, doing everything from 'Smoke on the Water' to 'Diana'. OK, we were a bit confused but suddenly Saturday afternoons were all about the band and I was allowed to be a backing singer as I was good at harmonies and danced about a bit, as girls were supposed to. I brought along my pal Catherine Reid who was also a terrific singer and eventually we got a couple of songs to do together.

Our first gig was at Motherwell Trades and Labour Club on Airbles Road and we were paid 50 pence each, a princely sum, especially as we were rubbish. The band had to do backing for some of the singers in the audience too and they didn't read music, and trying to follow singers whilst they are singing songs you yourself don't know is never easy. Amazingly, we were asked back (I think because we were cheap) and gradually over the weeks we got better and the punters liked us – a nice group of 14 year olds doing old tunes for bugger-all money in a half-empty club wasn't exactly Las Vegas but it was great experience and the locals were so good to all of us.

Eventually we got an evening gig, so we must have been doing OK, but again I saw what nerves can do to people with great talent. I was nervous as hell but once I was on the stage I felt great and just got on with it, but Catherine was so scared the nerves really betrayed her voice. I remember being in the ladies toilet afterwards where a punter gave us her opinion (don't they always?). She turned to Catherine and said, 'Aye yeez were no' bad, too bloody loud mind you, but you, hen, you need a bit more of what yer pal's got [she pointed to me], she's got the confidence, hen, you need more of that.'

Until then I had thought that a great voice was all you needed but I realised then that the performance matters just as much, as well as whether the audience likes you. You can be the most talented person on the planet but you won't make it if you can't win the audience over – a big lesson, and one I have had to learn again and again. We continued to play for a while but it all sort of fizzled out as we all got on with other bits of our lives, so the world tour and chart domination never happened but it was great fun, if it was sometimes a bit bruising.

All of this got in the way of any schoolwork or studying for my O grades. I basically pretended to myself and my parents that I was studying – though how you do that when listening to Radio 1 ('My Brother Jake' by Free being a particular favourite remains a mystery). The shock when I got my exam results was pretty awful. I sat seven and got four and again I got the lecture about the ruining of my mother's life as well as my own thrown at me. I was allowed to stay on for my fifth year as long as I got rid of all that nonsense with the bands and concentrated on my studies. In my defence, I did knuckle down, especially given the humiliation of knowing that girls who weren't as bright as me got better results, it was primary school all over again and just when I thought I had it covered and knew what I was doing I got too cocky and caught up in dreams, boys and music and took my eye off the ball. A lesson I still continue to learn I have to say.

I had a pen pal from Canada called Glen whom I started writing to and we had lots of music in common and of course, like all 15 year olds, I thought he was gorgeous and I was madly in love with him. He was coming to the UK and asked if he could come and see me, which he did. He of course didn't look at all like his photos, or the guy I had built up in my head, so love was not on the horizon. I had to entertain him, though, and I ended up taking him to the local folk club in the Silverburn Hotel.

Folk music was really hip at the time, so every James Taylor lookalike was on the circuit, as well as some fantastic bands. Although I was underage I got in and ended up as a regular there (in the audience). I got to know lots of the guys (had a few romances too) and eventually started another wee band with Martin and Billy, who were great guys. We even did a couple of gigs together and though we were all right it was hardly Crosby, Stills and Nash. I learned a harsh lesson too with the band while performing, and that is that all the material you think is funny when you are all rehearsing is not necessarily funny for an audience. I had the guys in stitches doing some daft song and we decided to do it at our gig in a Hamilton folk club – and it of course died on its arse! The silence was deafening as I went out into the audience and tried to gee them up to join in; they didn't and it was the loneliest place in the world. The look on the face of my then boyfriend Jeff, as he watched us and tried to slink down in his seat, was the stuff of performers' nightmares.

Jeff was very honest and basically told me that he thought that we weren't good enough and that basically I should just give up. I was really hurt but I respected him for being so honest. I think he just feared for me and my silly pipe dream that would come to nothing and I'd make a fool of myself in the process. My husband Bob is as brutally honest as this even now – but his is the voice I trust the most.

So with all this experience (good and bad), I started writing songs on the piano and learning songs by Carole King, Joni Mitchell and James Taylor. Somewhere inside, though, despite the knocks, I did feel I had some talent and enjoyed singing so much. Again I daydreamed that I would be sitting playing and singing and some record A&R man would just discover me, though I don't think Motherwell was on their route. Acting, or becoming an actor, didn't even figure in my mind. It was something so remote from what I thought possible that I didn't even dream about it.

We had another PTA concert to do and Ms Adams was despairing about how boring it was going to be with one act trailing on after the other as usual and I came up with the idea that we could make it less boring by tying it all together like a play. Tom Wright, who was a pal (also a brain-box, talented and the school captain) got fired up by the idea too and we came up with *The Rehearsal*. Basically we wrote a play about auditions for the school show which let us have all the acts coming on but also let us have an audition panel and a wee play too. It was the first time I got to say realistic, naturalistic lines too and I really loved that. I of course got to audition too, with that fantastically written line, 'Well, come on then, you've been desperate to sing your sad song for us to get into the show too, so let's hear it.' I think it's an Ibsen line actually.

I had asked Mrs Johnstone if she would accompany me on the piano and I chose James Taylor's 'Fire and Rain' as I loved the song and always sang it well. Once again I got that feeling of having an audience in the palm of my hand and when I finished I won a huge round of applause as well as lots of praise from the other pupils and teachers. It was fab and I knew I was onto something but didn't know what to do with it, it just felt so great. I started to get a real sense of myself, and I got myself together after that. I had matured, was working hard, was getting a really positive response from teachers and felt that I had something to offer the school.

It was my last year though, as I didn't want to stay on for sixth year and it would have been financially difficult for my parents if I had. If I didn't do well in my Highers then I would have to find a job, though I had no idea what I wanted to do. Every time the careers officer mentioned a career in something I would say, 'Oh, I'd like that.'

Everything from civil servant to air hostess seemed like great ideas, but now I realise that it was the actor in me – I just fancied playing the role for a bit and not actually doing the job. I did tell them that I was auditioning for drama school to try to become a teacher and he eventually said, 'Look, you stick to the drama idea,' just to shut me up.

I had taken up Higher modern studies as well as Higher history and both subjects really opened my eyes to what was going on in the world and my opinion was actually encouraged by teachers for the first time. I remember that magical feeling when Norrie Bissell arrived as the new head of history and actually asked us what we thought when we were doing the First World War and the League of Nations. All the very academic kids sat silently and tried to give the right answer but he said, 'No, what do you think?' Well, never having been asked that they were stumped – I thought I'd died and gone to heaven. I gave an opinion, he liked what I said and carried on the discussion. I'd never had an adult do that before.

I loved his classes and learnt so much and I think I got an A in my Higher actually. Modern studies was the same; I loved the discussions about world events, talking about the Middle East, the USA and Africa. It was the '70s so we were in the middle of the Three-Day Week under Ted Heath's government so there was a lot going on politically – not that I'd really noticed except that there were nights when the TV was off and we sat with candles and a coal fire. It also meant that Dad's work was out so money was scarce, but generally my parents were in support of the workers and thought that Heath was a bit of a buffoon, but there were no huge political discussions – not like the ones my own kids have to suffer now. My oldest girl walks in to hear Bob and me arguing about the government, or discussing Israel and Gaza, and raises her eyes and says, 'Youse are freaks!' Charming!

But there was some sort of a go-slow, or work to rule, at the school with the janitors and staff, which meant that in our last year we weren't allowed to have a school disco for the leavers, which we all felt was really unfair. I sort of became one of the spokesmen for our group when we asked to speak to the headmaster about it, and I found out that I was quite good at putting my point across. It was nerve-racking, but it felt good, particularly because I felt the situation was unfair on us. All my politics come from a feeling of what is unfair or unjust to this day. Anyway, we were told that we couldn't have a disco in the school and that was that.

So I, and a few of the others (Elaine Porter, Yvonne Eadie and Tom Wright) decided to find out if there were other halls available. We went to the Masonic Hall on the Bellshill Road not far from the school and asked how much it was to hire it. We went back to the school and had a meeting with the pupils and some sympathetic teachers and decided to print tickets, charge folks 50 pence entry, and we would give any profit to the *Blue Peter* Fund and set about finding out things like hiring a disco and buying crisps and juice. We even went to the police and informed them about the event so that if anything happened (drunk boys fighting was the obvious fear) they would have knowledge of the whole thing. The stewards in the hall were great too.

When the news got out about what we were doing we were warned by the school not to go ahead, but we did. The tickets sold out. A couple of days beforehand Dad got a phone call from the Headmaster (which was really unusual and quite scary) asking him if he knew what I was up to and that it was a very risky venture which he wanted Dad to stop me doing. I will never forget that he stood up to the heedie and said that he wouldn't stop me and that he thought that my friends and I were mature enough to handle this, and that he thought it was a good thing for us to do and showed a lot of initiative. I nearly fainted when I heard that, it was the first time I had really heard what he thought of me. I think he'd always just thought I was a pain, moody, distant, too interested in boys and a bit of a disappointment through my teenage years – and I probably was. So it was a great feeling to think that he actually thought I could do something. A lot of our parents backed us and a few turned up on the night too.

The biggest problem actually was what I was going to wear, well, isn't it always? But I found this fantastic brown suit in one of the boutiques in Motherwell (I think there were two) and I felt brilliant in it. I still have it to this day, though it was a small size 12, so I would probably get one leg into it now.

On the actual night, the whole thing was a blur. I was so uptight and nervous about the whole thing and making sure everyone else was fine and behaving that I don't think I danced at all. But it went brilliantly: no incidents, no fights and no drunkenness. It finished on time, we cleared up the hall and went home with a real sense of achievement and of having a great time. It's amazing because teenagers do things like this all the time and always have but we never hear about it. We certainly would have made the *Motherwell Times* if we'd wrecked the joint and started fighting, but success and raising money without incident never makes the front pages, does it?

So I prepared to leave Braidhurst High with a sense of self that I'd never had before. I'd done a good job that year, studying and enjoying school. I was growing up. I had a Saturday job in Curtess' Shoe Shop and I was very good at the multiple selling, as well as the gift of the gab (well, you had to be as the shoes weren't Louboutins, they were cheap and sometimes cheerful, but mainly cheap). I had the wonderful May as my manager who was warm, funny and a great boss and Margaret Love, one of the happiest and nicest women I have ever met – she openly adored her husband and her children and spoke of them in a way that I'd never really heard anyone speak of their own before, full of love, wonder and praise. She was quite religious, though never preachy, and she sang in church all the time (she had a great voice too – a bit of a Susan Boyle actually). I really enjoyed the workplace gossip and chat and the desperation for your tea break. So I had a bit of independence, I'd been going out with Jeff for about a year (we'd met on a holiday in Aviemore and started going out a couple of months later, though he lived in Glasgow, which was an hour-long trek on the bus to see each other).

During this period, Stella found that she had more time and, after a succession of office jobs, she decided that she wanted to return to college and finish her education. She went to night school over a couple of years and gained her Highers and then trained as a nursery nurse for the next two years at Motherwell Technical College. She loved it, even though it was hard financially. But the big change that education brought for her was a sense of independence and a feeling that she wanted more from life than just being a wife and mother. There was a lot of tension and fights around this time as Dad had to slowly adjust to the fact that she was out at college or working most of the time; it couldn't have been easy for him. The ideal family that they had built together wasn't turning out to be quite so ideal, and like many men of the time he found it difficult to adjust. Stella also learned to drive and managed to pass on her third attempt – much to the apprehension and fear of other drivers on the roads of Lanarkshire. Times were changing.

CHAPTER 14

DRAMA, DRAMA, DRAMA

In 1960s Lanarkshire, I didn't know there was such a thing as a drama school, I don't think many people did. I also didn't realise that being an actor was a real job. Maybe I was just especially thick, but apart from Hollywood films and realising that Doris Day did actually have a real life and that what she did on screen was acting as someone else in another story, I was clueless. My knowledge of theatre or that it even existed was from films and TV, so I knew what a stage was and knew that there were such things as theatres but I had never been in one (except for the Alexander Brothers show which I talked about earlier).

Because I had piano lessons I knew that there was such a place as the Royal Scottish Academy of Music, but I didn't ever really understand what the 'and Drama' bit meant. Musicians, and especially my piano teacher Mrs Hughes, pursed their lips and said the 'and Drama' sotto voce, indicating that it wasn't up to much and was obviously full of strange types. She'd never worked with some of the 'musos' I have who could drink and party for Scotland at the drop of a hat. Anyway, to her the only bit that mattered was the music college. She referred to it as 'The Academy' – a holy place in her view.

We did our piano exams there and it was a pretty scary. The RSAMD was in what is now Nelson Mandela Place, I am happy to say, but in the mid '70s it was St George's Place and right in the centre of Glasgow, next to the Ivanhoe Hotel and Buchanan Street underground. In fact, when you were in the theatre or certain classrooms the noise from the underground could be heard loud and clear and certain parts of the building shook. But it was a beautiful old building. So I had been in the hallowed building for music but ask me what they did in the 'and Drama' bit, and I couldn't have told you.

In my fourth and fifth year at high school a girl in my class changed my life. Bored out of my skull in maths, I was sitting gabbing to Christine Crichton and she happened to mention that she went to elocution lessons. After the initial guffaw from me and a 'Really?' she said that, yes, she did indeed go to elocution lessons though I was sworn to secrecy as this along with oboe or violin lessons could be a hanging offence in the eyes of some. Accordion, piano and flute were OK, and obviously the drums (preferably a really big one) but anything else and you were a weirdo. And elocution lessons – well, forget it.

I asked her what they were for and she said that it was to teach her how to speak properly. I was a bit confused as I thought that she spoke very well and could understand her no bother, as could everyone else, but then I realised that what she meant was that she was learning to talk 'posh' i.e. without a trace of the working-class roots. This was still in the days when it was believed that a heavy accent was a sign of poor education and class (wait a minute, what am I talking about, it's still the bloody same now). Anyway, she said that she was going to be trained as a teacher of speech and drama. I was intrigued especially when she explained that it was a real subject (we didn't have a drama teacher in our school) and that you went to the Academy in Glasgow, trained for three years, then did a year of teacher-training afterwards and you could then teach in a high school.

The skies opened, the sun came out and angels started to sing – well, not quite but you get the picture – a whole new world opened before me and I set about finding out more. I was desperate to be a teacher but I didn't know what I wanted to teach (well, children obviously) but the subject was another matter. The knowledge that you could teach something more practical and creative was just amazing and that conversation changed everything.

I went to my English teacher, Mr Lodge, and Mr King who was the head of department and they helped me get the details. I wrote off for an application form, sent it in and got my audition date in July at the end of term. I had my poem ready, *The Death of Marilyn*

Monroe by Edwin Morgan, a poem I had loved in class and I also had to read a piece from *Dr Zhivago*, which was another favourite. I didn't know what I had let myself in for.

An audition? I was 17 years of age, had never been in a theatre, had never had a dancing or singing lesson in my life, had done a small play and a couple of Gilbert and Sullivan productions for school and that was it. Audition? My parents were a bit confused about it too and didn't really know what I was talking about (in fact Dad referred to me being 'at the university' for a long time), and the notion of an audition was reduced to being like an interview. So I got my good navy-blue, three-piece suit bought from Bairds in Motherwell (height of fashion in 1975), with my huge platform shoes from Goldbergs and breezed into Glasgow on the train, and walked into the Royal Academy full of enthusiasm and excitement. The old Victorian building, or 'The Atheneum' to give its full name, made me very nervous straight away as it was very imposing.

It wasn't until I was shown into the waiting room that I started to suspect that I was out of my depth. There were all these girls in leotards and tights, with hair swept up tidily in a bun, limbering up. They all seemed to know each other and were chatting about classes and stuff. I had entered a whole other world. When I watched *Billy Elliot*, I cried at the audition scene because that feeling of being in another country was done so brilliantly and that was exactly how I felt. The language, the building, the whole environment were as foreign to me as an African desert.

I was called into the first audition, which was 'Improvisation'. What the hell was that? I walked into a large room with a table at one end where sat three people (whom I later found out were lecturers at the Academy, though the only one I remember was Pete Lincoln, the handsome movement teacher). They were very pleasant without being chummy and thankfully explained what I had to do in this part, i.e. improvise.

Basically, it meant that they would give me a situation like a fire or something and I had to get up and act out how I would behave and react if I were in that situation. 'Fair enough,' I thought. But then came the bombshell. 'Would you take off your shoes, please?'

'What?'

'Well, in order for you to move properly you have to take your shoes off.' They had obviously spied my incredibly high platforms.

My dilemma was not about being barefoot or even my tan tights under my trews. No, it was that I would be five inches shorter and my perfectly fitting blue trousers would be five inches too long and I would be flapping about the room looking ridiculous. Suddenly all those girls in the leotards and tights sitting in the waiting room started to make sense. They knew what they were in for and came prepared. But in true Lanarkshire style, I got stuck in and got on with it.

I was asked to climb an imaginary rope ladder, something I had never had cause to do in my entire life. Well, maybe when playing Swiss Family Robinson in the back garden, but not lately. I stood there, jacket off, sleeves of lovely white blouse with the fashionable puffy sleeves and row of buttons at the wrist pushed up, trews rolled up and barefoot, feeling ridiculous! I started doing an awful mime which lasted about five seconds of me climbing up a rope. I laughed of course and apologised for how rubbish it was and the panel smiled benignly.

Next I had to play a game of tennis. 'By myself?' I asked, and they said yes. So again I set about doing as they requested, except my literal interpretation of what they had asked was that I had obviously to be both players for the game to work! So instead of standing on one side of the imaginary net and serving, volleying, smashing and passing the imaginary ball, I hit the shot on one side of the net and then ran around to the other side to hit it back. I did this for a few minutes until I was red-faced and sweating from all the running (complete with trousers flapping around my ankles), looking knackered and becoming slightly confused at the looks of amusement on the faces of the panel. It was obviously a first.

Next was the dramatic fire scene. They asked me to imagine that I was in a building on fire and to show them how I would react. My mind went straight to shouting 'Fire!' out of the window but I didn't think that would work. So I opted for the last bastion of the rubbish actor, the running back and forth across the room a few times, with a panicked look on my face (I was already panting and sweating from the tennis match so that seemed to help). I ran to the window and shouted, 'Help!' and just as I was getting into it I decided to run to the door and pretend to try and get out. I unfortunately miscalculated and pulled the door the wrong way and it opened wide. End of fire scene, I got out.

Again, I got a mixture of amused and bemused reactions from the panel, who thanked me as I tried to get dressed. I have to tell you that I walked out of that room with head held high with as much dignity as a sweaty red face, a flat hairdo, flapping trousers and a 6 in. platform shoe would allow.

I then had to go and sing in another room and that was easy and the music woman (better known as Olive the singing teacher, who always arrived late, with dark glasses on, a fag hanging out of the side of her mouth and singing, 'Rhythm of Life', but more of that later). I did all right and she thought I had a 'fabulous singing voice, dahling', no one had ever called me 'dahling' before so it was a bit of a shock and I started to feel a wee bit better.

Next was the reading part and though I had learned the Edwin Morgan poem off by heart, I assumed they would have a copy of *Dr Zhivago* there, so didn't take my copy of the book with me. The shock of the improvisation audition, combined with the realisation of what I had let myself in for with this stupid drama stuff had started to sink in, and I just wanted to sit and cry. They took pity on me when they saw how upset I was and I compounded this with my usual self-berating habit of apologising, and telling them how stupid I was. I remember Russell Boyce (who later became head of the college) asking me if I was always like this and I said no, and this somehow made him laugh. I read the piece they gave me while he occasionally looked up from reading his newspaper and that was that. I can't even remember what they gave me to sight read because by that time I was having a nightmare day.

I left the building in shock. I was trembling and thinking 'That was terrible, and I don't want to bloody go there anyway with all those weirdos!' I got the train home and by the time I got there I was seeing the ridiculous side of what had just happened. By the time I reached our dinner table and told everyone what had gone on they were in fits of laughter and I eventually turned it into one of my funny anecdotes. It had my mum in stitches and naturally she made me retell it over and over to various aunties and so, of course, it just grew bigger and bigger the more I remembered and the more I played up the ridiculousness of it all. My ability to turn a scary or upsetting event into a funny tale has always been one of my saving graces and it works as a sort of therapy for me. If I talk about it and laugh at it, then it's always less scary and I can see it for what it is.

A week later I got a letter telling me I was in. I nearly passed out. I couldn't believe it. I was asked to let them know if I accepted and then to attend to register for the new term in September at the RSAMD first year annexe in Athole Gardens, in Glasgow's West End. We all rejoiced, even though I didn't have a clue what I was doing. All my family knew was that I had been accepted into this course that would eventually lead to my becoming a teacher – in my mother's eyes, I had arrived. All we had to do was wait on my exam results, see if I was eligible for a grant (remember grants, big in the '70s). If there was no grant, then there was no way that my parents could have afforded to let me go. I duly got my grant (not a big one, but I got my fees paid and a few hundred quid a term for books and other things) as well as travel expenses.

The results came through in August and I was devastated, I had failed my Higher English, the one thing I needed to get into college. I was totally confused as I had only just failed and got a complimentary O grade (which meant I had failed by a couple of points). It was the one I was sure of and my English teacher phoned me at home to see what had happened and to say that they were going to appeal. I had been third in the whole year in my prelim and thought that I'd done well. My bright future was dashed, but only fleetingly, as a couple of weeks later the appeal came through – I had got it, I could go to the ball.

So on 30 September 1975 I made it onto the tube and emerged onto Byres Road, which is a quite famous street in Glasgow, though at the time I hadn't a clue.

It's a bustling, busy street full of cafés and shops and lined with tenements, but they were grander houses than I had ever seen before and unlike most Lanarkshire tenements, some were on four floors. I walked across the road and up to Athole Gardens, into a beautiful Victorian square surrounding some private gardens. Yes, very posh, and I was way out of my depth (though I didn't know by how much) before I had even walked through the door of the college.

In my first year at drama school I just felt like a fish out of water – I was just so inexperienced and naïve on so many levels. Most of the students my age had been privately educated and therefore knew much more about poets, writers and the Classics in general. I had no idea.

We had a class on the history of drama, starting with the Greeks, and I genuinely hadn't a clue what our lecturer, the wonderful Peter D'Souza, was talking about. I didn't even know there was such a thing as Greek bloody drama, or *The Iliad* and *The Odyssey*. I didn't even know how to take lecture notes. I sat there at the ripe old age of seventeen and three weeks, trying to write down every single word he said, which meant that I was miles behind the rest, thus missing what he was saying completely.

The first meeting of the class let me know in no uncertain terms that I was in what I felt was an alien environment. We all sat around in a big room in the annexe with Russell Boyce, who had been at my audition. He was warm, welcoming and funny. So far so good. I looked around the room to see a disparate group of men and women of all ages from 18 upwards, in various types of dress – from the conservative rugby tops of some of the guys to the weird and wonderful hippy 'out there' stuff that would have made me and my pals in Motherwell point and laugh in the street. I felt sick.

We went around the group and told each other our names and a bit about ourselves. I realised as they started that I had nothing to say about myself – all these people talked about the jobs they'd had. One had been working for the United Nations in Paris as a translator; another a chief stewardess for British Airways; another a teacher for years who'd decided to come back and retrain as a drama teacher – all of them seemed really interesting compared to me and I didn't know what to say except that I was Elaine, from Motherwell, in an accent that now sounded so thick that I wanted to apologise immediately for it.

At the coffee break, I started chatting to some others like John Wood and Annette Staines (as in Middlesex, not as in Ajax, which she'd said as her funny introduction of herself. Why couldn't I have thought of something like that to say? It made everyone laugh and was clever too). They seemed quite nice and dressed like normal folk and were also closer to my age. I also spotted an amazing-looking girl called Gwen. She had huge eyes and had on a fab top, which I liked, and had the most wonderful accent from Northern Ireland (we became great friends be she'd end up my bridesmaid and is still a dear friend). But on that day we didn't speak as I was obviously far too young and straight to be interesting, even to me. I was out of my depth and inexperienced emotionally, intellectually and sexually.

I was no innocent and I had been going out with Jeff for about a year. He was a great guy, and he and his family were wonderful to me. I loved him a great deal but knew that the path that I was on was causing difficulties between us. He was a telephone engineer, bright and funny, though I think he found my going to drama school a bit weird and didn't quite understand what I was doing. I had a lot of growing up to do and I think deep down, he knew it. The gulf between my home life and the life I was leading at college became ever wider.

For the first few months, I was glad of the grounding and the ties with my real life at home. But the West End was beautiful in my eyes – the Georgian buildings, the bustle of Byres Road, the university and, of course, Laura Ashley. The first day I walked up to the top of Byres Road to see Laura Ashley I thought I was in Fairyland. The Botanic Gardens were beautiful, the BBC sign in the distance, and the Grosvenor Hotel and terrace looked like a scene from a movie to me. I loved all of it: the cafés, the Salon and Grosvenor Cinemas showing foreign movies I'd never even heard of.

I still stayed at home and travelled to Newarthill every day, or out to Jeff's family in Parkhead. I did feel that I was missing out a lot on college life, as most of the students had flats or digs but I was happy with the normality of it. But the pull of a different life was there, mainly because the life I had was constantly being derided. When I look back now it felt as though every aspect of my life was just not good enough. My working-class background, my accent, my education, my family and the area I came from – my general lack of 'proper' culture. But at 17, I am sad to say that all that I felt was a sense of shame about where I came from and constantly apologised for not being good enough, and that everyone else knew better.

Gradually, things started to drift, and I did need to get out and into a flat and live a more independent life, but there was resistance from family and boyfriend. I wanted to include Jeff in college life but going to college discos and dances were a bit of a shock to the system. Apart from the drink and the madness of girls in diaphanous gowns dancing round pillars (I think substances other than drink may have been consumed) there were folk with posh voices and neckerchiefs shouting 'dahling!' at the tops of their voices. We were used to Joanna's nightclub and dancing round our handbags.

This was also an environment where gay young men and women freely kissed each other and that was totally shocking for me as I hadn't even known gay people existed. But because I was with them every day, and knew and liked them all, I got used to it very quickly. In 1975 unfortunately, for a phone engineer from Parkhead, it was all a bit too much. My life became increasingly about theatre, college life, plays, writers, improvisation, voice and movement.

My first movement class was with the legend that was, and is, Grace Matchett. Grace had a tough reputation in that she didn't suffer fools gladly and I was really scared of her. She was, to my mind, very posh (well, most of the lecturers and students were non-Scots and quite middle or upper class. Anyway, anyone who didn't speak like me or my friends and family were deemed posh) and she was one of the first openly gay women I had ever met. Her first class had us there in black leotard and tights (boys as well) and had us moving to jiggling keys, sounds, bangs and clicks. I had thought that movement would be like dancing which I was quite good at, so this came as a bit of a shock to a wee lassie from Lanarkshire, well, actually, it was a bit of a nightmare.

We went to the main building in St George's Place every Friday and this was when we got to meet the other drama students in the years above us, and also the music students, in the canteen at lunchtime. It wasn't quite the kids from *Fame* but there were elements of it: musical instruments everywhere, drama students speaking too loudly in outrageous outfits and generally drawing far too much attention to themselves.

As first years we were pretty intimidated by it all but gradually we got more confidence in the whole place and started enjoying it. Our favourite prank was to go down to the 'janny's' office and put out announcements to the canteen. So of course we would hear the 'Would Hugh Jarse please come to the main reception?' and collapse with laughter, and it worked every time – very lowbrow, I know, but funny. Gradually, though, I started to get to know other students who confessed to being as bamboozled at times by the course and life in the college as I was, which helped me adjust.

The Christmas Ball was, for me, the most exciting thing ever, a real ball. And I had the ultimate in fashion statements, the white Laura Ashley frock, and I thought I was a goddess. But I'd got a job as a postie at Christmas, so I'd been up at 5 a.m. every morning for a week. I have to say I was rubbish at it. So by the time the ball came I was so knackered that I felt under the weather during it, and the next morning I couldn't move my head. I thought I was dying but actually had the worst case of sinusitis I'd ever had. I had to give up the job and spent most of my first Christmas holidays as a student in a dark room drugged out of my brain with painkillers.

When I got back to college, we were told about the College Cabaret. This was an annual event where the final year students and the lecturers were invited as the audience, the second years provided the food and drink, and the first years provided the entertainment. So auditions were held for acts who wanted to take part. I had sung a couple of times at events and so a couple of the other students said that I should audition. I had so little confidence then, particularly in an environment where everyone else seemed so confident and talented. I went in to audition for the student committee and I felt sick. The theme was 'The '60s' so I sat down at the piano and sang a Crosby, Stills, Nash and Young song, 'Our House', which I loved. They hardly looked up and then said, 'Well, we're not sure where to put you in the show but we could use you to cover while the others are changing for the big number?' I said OK. So I was in the show, but it was far from enthusiastic.

The big day came, and I'd seen little of the others as they were always off rehearsing and I was an act on my own so I was basically just told to turn up in '60s gear and that there would be a piano there. I watched the other acts at the rehearsal and they all seemed so knowing and worldly – all song or dance routines about wanting to be a star, or Stephen Sondheim pieces which I'd never heard but thought were great. I thought I would be on, cover the change and off, and that would be it.

On the night I put on the kaftan, put flowers in my hair, slunk on quietly in the dark as I was introduced and sang the song. I stopped the room. I of course thought they were quiet because I was rubbish but when I finished, the room erupted and the whole audience stood up. I almost fainted with shock. They kept shouting more and eventually I said, 'I don't know anything else,' and they shouted for me to just do the same one again. All I could play was one of my own songs, which I did and it was fine, but things changed that night – I realised that I did have talent.

Of course I was back to being a wee first year in my jeans and Miss Selfridge top and no one really noticed me in the main building, though I realised I had become a bit of a threat to the other students whose noses were out of joint because they hadn't got a similar reaction in the show. I was just this wee mousy lassie from Motherwell, not a proper actor like them.

Months later I was now going out with an actor, as Jeff and I had broken up in the spring, which was very sad but somehow inevitable, given our ages and the ways our lives were going (I loved him very much and it was even sadder because we still cared about each other a great deal when we parted). Anyway this actor was in second year, a really nice guy called David Mills (who died suddenly, after graduating). He was friendly with another guy, David Ghan, and his girlfriend was a girl from Paisley called Phyllis Logan. She was a stunning actress and the one that everyone in the place loved because not only was she really talented, but she was very down to earth and kind to everyone, including me. We ended up going out for a meal one night and I said something about singing and she suddenly went, 'You're her . . . you're the girl from the cabaret. I have been looking for you for months . . . you were like Cinderella, no one knew who you were and you look so different . . . you were brilliant.' I was so chuffed I floated home that night.

By this time I was living in a flat off Great Western Road with some of the other girls in my year, Susan and Pam, so life outside the college was much more exciting. I'd had a summer job as a waitress in a hotel on Loch Lomond, which was a great experience, though terrifying having to deal with mental chefs, bullying waiters, crazy coach-trippers and hellish living conditions. But I survived, though having gained a stone by eating my way through the holiday, trying to deal with life without Jeff and confusion about what I was doing. When I got back I needed something else to do. The flat was great, and the West End was student heaven, pubs, drugs, bands, men and for the first time able to make my own rules – which is always a bit scary. But creatively I was bored.

The course wasn't stimulating, and what had been new and exciting in the first year was now dull in the second. Also as a teaching student you didn't get to perform as much, probably twice a year, and they had to be big plays with large casts and I wasn't the type of actor that would ever get a big role. All the plays were from the English or American stage – we did practically no Scottish work at all. A production of *Ane Satyre of the Thrie Estaities* every five years is just not good enough is it? We were basically taught that there were no good Scottish playwrights and no work worthy of drama students to study from Scots.

Yet in the theatres all over Scotland, it was Scots stars and shows that were packing them in. Jimmy Logan, Rikki Fulton, Jack Milroy, Una McLean, Mary Lee, Johnny Beattie, Dorothy Paul and many, many more were filling theatres across the country with everything from Sam Cree plays and pantomimes to variety and summer shows. But we never heard their names and were not encouraged to go and see them either. Good theatre was basically English or American, and variety and vaudeville, the theatre that Scots loved and did brilliantly, were derided. They were frowned upon and looked down upon by the college and middle-class society in general. Sad to say that it is still the same, but more of that later. But out in the real theatre world a bit of a revolution was happening.

At around 15 years of age, I was babysitting for my parents, who were out at another dinner dance, and I stumbled across a play on TV. I had always liked dramas on television and *Play for Today* was pretty popular with Mum. But I had never really seen any Scottish dramas and certainly not contemporary stuff. The fare was generally historical stuff with kilts and lochs and Jacobites – with an occasional *View from Daniel Pike* starring Roddy McMillan thrown in – so the chances for our writers to be produced and developed were pretty thin on the ground.

But this particular night they were showing a contemporary play called *The Cheviot, the Stag and the Black, Black Oil*. It was written by John McGrath and had been performed by a fantastic team of young actors in the 7:84 Theatre Company. They were a political company (the name highlighted the 7 per cent of the population who owned 84 per cent of all the wealth. Tragically it is worse now, it's about 4 per cent that own 90 per cent of it) and they felt this scandal should be made more public.

The play took the form of a ceilidh (something I as a 'Lowlander' had never been to or even seen in my lifetime). It was vibrant, political, funny with great songs and music and it told me things about my own country that I had had no idea existed. Brilliant actors like the wonderful Alex Norton and Billy Peterson were in it too. It changed my life, it changed my view of drama and of what was possible and I have never forgotten that feeling while sitting there on a Saturday night in my jammies in front of the box. Little did I know that one day I would be working with 7:84.

Around the same time this company was touring Scotland though, the Traverse Theatre was commissioning new playwrights like Tom McGrath, John Byrne and Hector MacMillan. On one of my first ever visits to a real theatre I was blown away. All too often when young people go to the theatre they get turned off and bored but I was lucky. This was the Young Lyceum Theatre Company performing *A Midsummer Night's Dream*. I had never seen Shakespeare – in fact I had only ever been bored out of my brain reading *Hamlet* at school so I wasn't too keen on going but it was magical. Young actors, combined with a superb set, and supported with brilliant, innovative lighting and a stunning range of contemporary costumes (hot-pants and glitter were the order of the day). It was brilliant, but still I thought it was something that I would never be able to do or even dream of – acting and theatre were for others, not me.

Billy Connolly had written a couple of plays *An Me Wi' A Bad Leg Tae* and *The Red Runner* and the punters were packing in to see the plays in Edinburgh and Glasgow. When I saw them at the Pavilion Theatre in Glasgow, it was such a relief to hear my own accent and humour on the stage, in direct contrast to what I was being taught at college. *The Slab Boys* by John Byrne was wowing the critics and audiences too, and was full of amazing, young, talented actors. Again, it showed me that there was another style of theatre and art that was as valid as anything I was being taught at drama school.

On the noticeboard one day, I spotted an advert for a singer in a band. So I decided to bite the bullet and go along for the audition. I hadn't really done anything since the cabaret and my dreams of becoming the next Joni Mitchell weren't being realised. A great piano player (and very nice man to boot) called Iain Findlay turned up and asked me to sing. The big hit at the time was Julie Covington's 'Don't Cry for Me Argentina', so he persuaded me to sing that, and fortunately I knew it and my range was very similar. I sounded quite like her too. I know I did a really good audition, and he was impressed by what I did and how different I was from most of the club singers who were around (I was a bit more contemporary). I didn't have the range of a good club singer – but I had something. So I played a bit on the piano and sang, and he offered me a trial with the band on the spot.

I was really excited and went along to the miners' club in the village of Larkhall to meet the band and do a bit of rehearsing too. The drummer, Ronnie Leckie, wasn't too keen on me. I think he saw how inexperienced I was; I was only 18. I would be the first to say that I don't have a great range as a singer; the pyrotechnics and leaps that some excellent cabaret performers can do are not skills that I possess. So doing a big Shirley Bassey number wasn't for me. Despite this, they let me stay and I did work hard and I learned more about dealing with an audience in the clubs than in any class at drama school. God, they were tough gigs.

I realised that as a woman, to succeed in the clubs I had to get the other women to like me first. So the low-cut number appealing to the guys wasn't the way forward; in fact, it went against you. I stuck to the velvet jumpsuits (very big at the time) and I got away with a lot because I was young, or 'the wee lassie with the band'. But if you appeared too full of yourself, or over-confident, then that could be met with a silence, frosty stares or worse – them not listening to you at all. I learned to introduce numbers and started to talk to the audience, but I found it hard. I wished I could have the gags and jokes of some of the comics, like Andy Cameron, Mr Abie, Clem Dane and some of the other guys whom we supported.

Andy was my favourite, as he had great warmth and a great sense of where he came from and who the audience were. He had a fantastic take on sectarianism and was quite groundbreaking at the time. He has never been given credit for it. You have to remember that even in the 1970s the religious divide was still very much present. Private clubs freely operated a 'No Catholics' rule and certain clubs were no-go areas for punters of a different religious persuasion, colour, creed or sex. I often thought they should just have a sign out front saying, 'JUST US . . . NOBODY ELSE ALLOWED IN.'

Dave Anderson of Wildcat wrote a great song about clubland, which I have sung in shows many times, called 'Wan Singer, Wan Song', which was the cry of many a compère of the bad wig, bad suit and quasi-American accent persuasion:

> Youse all know me, I'm Harry McDade,
> Through the week I'm a plumber to trade,
> But come the weekend,
> Ah've got it made,
> I'm a singer [cue huge echo . . .].
>
> Youse are here for the crack and the booze,
> We don't have any darkies or Jews,
> And youse'll get barred if any of youse goes yer dinger.
>
> Wan singer, wan song,
> No politics, no religion,
> No Catholics, no homos,
> Just wan singer, wan song.

This was at a time when in one club they opened the show with 'Brothers, sisters and Protestant friends'. Two of our band were Catholics, so when we played there they didn't let on and changed their second names to more Protestant-sounding ones. I was asked in one club to remove the plain silver cross that I was wearing. I asked why, because it was just jewellery and I wasn't Catholic or religious at all. The compère replied, 'Oh, it's no' me, hen, it's just that one of they eejits oot there might think there's a wee man on it and they'll haul you aff the stage with it.' I removed the cross. My mum and dad came to that club in Bellshill but she was recognised as being from a Catholic family and spent the whole night feeling really uncomfortable.

Andy Cameron got an act out of all that madness. He used to come out in a Scotland football shirt, but one sleeve was Celtic and the other was Rangers. He played all the clubs, whether they were all Catholic or all Orange or mixed. Gags about the insidious religious divide could be dangerous, especially in drink-fuelled situations, but he managed to do it really well. His opening line was, 'Don't worry, missus, I'm wan of youse. My wife, she's wan of them, but I'm wan of youse!' So he was immediately playing to the underlying allegiances of the audience while poking fun at them at the same time.

There is a story that is told about Andy (which he denies) that supposedly happened at a Catholic Knights of St Columba club. Many priests and deeply Catholic folk went to these clubs and it was obvious when you went in, as there was a giant crucifix at the back of the stage just behind the drums. Apparently, there had been a robbery in the club the night before the gig, and the TV and some money had been stolen. The comic – whoever he was – leapt on the stage after his introduction, looked at the crucifix and back to the audience and said, 'I see you got the guy that stole your colour TV!' He never got another line out, as a riot ensued.

The punters loved Andy. So did I. He was kind, warm, encouraging and I realised watching him that I would rather be a comic than the 'wee lassie in the band'. But that just wasn't an option. I never saw a woman comic in all the time I did the clubs.

I knew my place and I was fortunate in that I was quite pretty, had a reasonable voice and got by onstage. I got better at dealing with audiences and speaking to them and could even occasionally tell a joke or two, or be funny spontaneously. I got to do songs that suited my range more – dramatic songs like Roberta Flack's 'Killing Me Softly' – and I tended to live for those moments, rather than another chorus of 'Under the Moon of Love'. I did it for about nine months and gained so much experience and material for the future.

But it all ended for me one night in the Rolls-Royce Club in East Kilbride. I had been talking about leaving the band; the pressure of college and everything else was proving too much for me, and I was also bored. But this night put the tin lid on the clubs for me. I am the first to admit that I was pretty terrible that night, due to the fact that I had accidentally knocked over a pint of orange and lemonade into Iain's £1,000 piano just before the gig. I felt awful, a total idiot, and though Iain kept assuring me that it was all right, I knew how furious he was. I was in tears for about an hour before the gig but got myself together before the show. The atmosphere was terrible. Iain had to play the old club Leslie organ (which was hellish and had none of the synth effects that we needed and that he loved). I just couldn't pull myself together and sing properly because I was so upset and I couldn't even do the chat to the punters either. I just wasn't enough of a professional to put my troubles behind me and get on with the show. Anyway, we got through it, but at the end of the night a woman (drunk as a lord and held up by two other equally drunk lords) approached the stage and said, 'See you, hen, you're the worst fuckin' singer I've ever heard in my fuckin' life!' and walked off. Everyone's a critic, eh? I was a young lassie of 18, inexperienced and not at my best, I admit, but I have never really understood what pleasure she got out of that. But that was the end for me and I handed in my resignation that night.

I had already had a talk one night with Ronnie, our drummer, who was a great guy even if he was tough on me because he felt that the band should have somebody better and more experienced fronting it. He taught me a lot, though, and I did get better and better ('Don't Cry for Me Argentina' once even got me a standing ovation in the officers' club at Barlinnie Prison, and no, they weren't locked in either).

I had arrived early at a gig one night a few weeks before and was sitting singing and playing piano on my own when Ronnie came out of the shadows and said, 'Elaine, I have to tell you something.' I got a total fright and said, 'What?' I thought he was going to sack me. 'That was really good, Elaine,' he said. 'You have really got something special and I am telling you that you've got to go and do what you can now before it's too late. Don't waste your life here. I didn't take the chances when I could have and I have regretted it. Now, I'll be a club drummer for the rest of my life unless Elton John happens to pass by the club one night. Go and try, and if you don't make it, then at least you tried. But you'll never forgive yourself if you don't.' I knew that what he was saying was absolutely true and over the next few weeks I set about thinking about leaving the clubs and trying to do a bit of rock and soul singing. I needed a change.

Living in the West End, I had got to see a lot of the bands that were doing the rounds and got to know a lot of the musicians too, some of whom crashed in our flat from time to time. Zeke Manyika, who later worked with Edwyn Collins in Orange Juice, was a flatmate for a while, as he dated one of the girls who lived there. He knew loads of the jazz-funk guys in Glasgow and we were all fans of bands like Cado Belle. So I was seeing all these rock and soul bands in pubs like the Amphora, His Nibs, the Maggie, the Curlers and the Burns Hough and I wanted to do more of that kind of music.

I answered a couple of ads and did a stint with a group of lovely guys who'd been in a cult band called Findo Gask. We covered a lot of Linda Ronstadt songs and I liked it, but it all sort of fizzled out. I then came across a great band and a bunch of fantastic guys who'd had a lot of gigs and success as a band with a female singer called Uncle Sam. She had left and they wanted a replacement, so I went along to audition for them. Gary Culpan was the main man because he owned the PA and the van (he's always been a great businessman and went on to run a big property business and did up old houses for the likes of myself and Kirsty Wark, but at this point he was a drummer with a van). The bass player was another great guy who is still a good friend, the wonderful Jamie Travers. I actually bought my first flat, in Earl Street in Scotstoun, from him and his wife, Carol, and I'm godmother to their eldest daughter, Louise.

Well, you can take it from that that I got the job and I loved it. I met the funniest and best people: singers like the legend that was Johnnie Burns and Big George, bands like Ryan's Express (who actually sounded more like Steely Dan than Steely Dan) and Sirocco – all of us out gigging out the back of a Transit van throughout the west of Scotland, from the Victorian Carriage in Greenock to the naval bases on the Clyde. This was rock 'n' roll at last. And we did songs by bands I loved, such as Fleetwood Mac (my show-stopping number was 'Songbird' with the wonderful Davie on piano). We caused a wee bit of a stir for a few months, and we all harboured dreams of the A&R guy spotting us and whisking us off to pop stardom – and some did actually come to see us. Basically, though, we were good, but we weren't good enough.

My sister Louise had decided that all the organ playing was too much for her and she had given up the concert parties. She was growing up and actually finding the pressure to perform too much – unlike me, she didn't really like being the centre of attention. My mum wanted her to stop too because she thought it was all having a detrimental effect on her, so, much to Dad's sadness, he relented (it was the end of his career as a stand-up and compère). He kept her organ for a few months but eventually sold it and because I was doing so well with the band he bought me a mike, an amp and some fold-back speakers. Unfortunately, he saw this as a reason to turn up at the gigs. So I would look out at a smoke-filled rock gig and see Dad sitting there, although I think we were always a bit too loud for him.

My mum had also started to take control of her own life and was back at college herself. She took to coming into Glasgow with some of her friends and on a couple of occasions she'd even turned up at our flat when she knew that we were having a party – which was a bit embarrassing to say the least. I mean, on the one hand, it was great to have a mum and dad that were a wee bit hip, but it didn't leave much room for me to grow and develop. My mum was only 42 and obviously, for the first time in her life, felt she had a great deal of freedom, but it was still very confusing for me. It was also an indication that their marriage was in difficulties. It had been rocky at times before and I do know that she had threatened to leave at least once (I later found out that she was going to leave us too). But in the end she hadn't been able to do it. Dad had pleaded with her to stay, apparently, but had left for work that day fully expecting her to be gone when he got home. She wasn't, she stayed and they went on to have my young sister Diane, but I think a deep crack in their relationship had developed.

So, as my mother started to find herself a career and a new, liberated life, the cracks appeared more regularly. It was always difficult for me, because she had always leaned on me emotionally. When I was 14, her secrets and worries were actually too much for me to carry. She would sit and talk about her marriage and what was wrong, forgetting that this was my dad and a man I loved. It was really confusing for me, though I coped. However, many years later we were able to talk about that and she explained that she had had no one else to confide in and I had always seemed so mature. But she did admit that she had been wrong and apologised, which is something I really admired her for doing. It takes courage to face up to past mistakes. I was never really angry at her, because I understood that she was very lost and confused herself.

The whole rock band thing lasted about six to nine months and I had a ball. Great times, but as ever it all ended the way most bands do, with everyone getting on each other's tits and getting into some sort of a fight over the vast sums of cash we weren't paid (we were getting thirty quid a gig between six of us, and that was to cover petrol and the van too). It was the classic *Spinal Tap* scenario: girlfriends arguing, roadies stoned out their boxes, and egos. So we wound up the band, but I stayed friends with many of them for years.

My college work had really suffered, though, because I was gigging all the time and basically not turning up for what were to me really boring lectures. I was still passing exams and pulling the finger out when I needed to, but I was far from a dedicated student. The course felt increasingly irrelevant to me and my life as a pop star, and I only really lit up when I got to do a piece in one of the plays. I and a few others got pulled up by the staff for our work and given warnings about attendance. But it made little difference to me. I was learning more about the business outside the college than in and willingly neglected my studies. I realised around then that I had a bit of something onstage as an actor, even though I still felt that it wasn't something for me.

I played Eurydice in Sophocles' Greek tragedy *Antigone* for one show. It was a good part, but small (she comes on, gives a powerful speech and then dies, which is great, as you can then get to the dressing room for a cup of tea). For some reason, I got a lot of praise for it. I decided to do my hair and make-up à la Liz Taylor (I was very dark-haired anyway, so it was big eyebrows and eyes too) and that with the Greek toga-style costume gave me quite a striking look.

But I felt I was unimportant, so I just did it and retreated offstage. Afterwards, an actor on the course, Don Crerar, came up to me and told me that I had wonderful stage presence and I should remember that because most actors would sell their soul for it. I hadn't a clue what stage presence was but he explained that it was 'watchability'. When you are onstage, the audience can't stop watching you; you hold the stage and their attention. I was chuffed to bits to get praise from an actor – in fact, I was just chuffed an actor had spoken to me and taken me seriously.

Then, in my final year, I did a play by Noël Coward called *Waiting in the Wings,* about a group of elderly actors in a retirement home, which sounded to me like my idea of hell. I played Cora and did it as well as any 19 year old can play a retired actress of 75, but my pal Gwen stole the show, as Mum told me quite forcefully and rather a lot at the time. (Now here's the weird thing: as I write this book, I am playing a character named Cora for the first time since then and I am appearing in the Noël Coward Theatre – cue *Twilight Zone* music.)

Near the end of my second year, a pal, the lovely actor Joe Sheridan, told me that he was going to the Citizens Theatre to see 7:84, the politically orientated theatre troupe I had seen on TV as a 15-year-old girl. I had heard of them and their other shows like *Little Red Hen* but hadn't ever seen them, and it didn't ring a bell until he mentioned that they had also done the *Cheviot* play that I'd seen that night on television. That night at the Citz changed my life. I saw what I wanted to do for the rest of it by watching *Out of Our Heads* by John McGrath.

There was a band, they all played and sang and acted, they spoke in Scottish accents and were talking about things that I understood: politics, alcohol and its effect on people's lives – especially those of women. (In fact, the speech that Liz MacLennan did about not being normal was a speech I later did in a voice exam, though I attempted a more naturalistic accent. It was a great speech.) They performed the show in a funny and moving way, and I loved it, floating out of the theatre knowing that that was it, the job I wanted to do, to be on that stage with those people. I had a dream, and one based not in Hollywood but in my very own backyard.

In my third year, I had to do a dissertation for Glasgow University (they ran the academic side of the teaching course) and decided that I would do it on 7:84. By this time, the company had split into two and the musical side had become Wildcat. We'd had some lectures about them and I loved their work. It was also a chance to get to meet them, to interview them, as there was little research material. I wrote to them and found out that they were appearing at the Dolphin Arts Centre in Bridgeton with a show called *His Master's Voice* – all about the record industry and punk music. I turned up to interview the artistic director, Dave MacLennan, and as I sat there in the dark watching the rehearsals I was terrified. I had all my questions prepared but was so star-struck I couldn't speak. Dave Anderson, director, writer and actor, walked past me and barked, 'Are you press?' to which I replied no, and he walked on without saying another word.

Dave MacLennan was lovely to me, although he was freezing and sitting in a woolly hat and a big coat. I then got to meet my heroine, singer and actress Terry Neason. She very kindly encouraged my ambitions when she found out I was a singer in clubs and we recounted tales to each other. Our beautiful friendship didn't last long, however, as when I took her up on an invitation to visit her flat and collect some records, she seemed preoccupied; I think she was entertaining a young man. Overall, my thesis was far from an academic triumph, but I passed, which was the main objective, and I had met some of my heroes along the way.

Around this time, I got involved in student politics. I had been on the SRC (Students' Representative Council) as a rep for a couple of years and helped organise dances and stuff, but 1976 and '77 were big years in student power. Many colleges, led by Moray House in Edinburgh, had staged sit-ins and revolts against the education cuts being proposed by the James Callaghan-led Labour government. Many of the Scottish political figures that you see in government now got their political awakening during those days of direct action and many were involved in the NUS (National Union of Students).

We found out that our teacher-training places for our postgraduate course were to be savagely cut back. We had supported the action of other universities and colleges by fund-raising and going on demonstrations; we'd even staged a mock funeral outside the education offices in Edinburgh in protest at the 'Death of Education Through 1,000 Cuts'.

We were all in funeral gear with a mock coffin (typical drama school stuff, but we made the news). But this time the cuts were at our own door. So we arranged our own sit-in at the college. It was carefully planned and we brought supplies for an overnight stay. We marched in an orderly fashion into the office of Ted Argent, the head of drama (who was far from pleased), and asked him to leave, as we were occupying the college in protest at the cuts. I and a few others slept on the floor of his office that night after a picnic of sorts and a few beers. I didn't like it much: uncomfortable, boring and not a heated roller in sight for the morning. A few weeks later, we did the same at Jordanhill College – marching all the way in with our banners and occupying the principal's office overnight. We got a lot of flak from the RSAMD for that – we were seen as trouble – but it was a great political awakening for me.

In the middle of all this, I had also had a really bruising love affair with a musician and I was devastated when it broke up. I became one of those weeping girls that you see at parties, the ones who have a couple of drinks and collapse in a heap at the mention of his name. My band had split, I was heartbroken and I was barely getting by with my college work, so politics filled a void. My friend Gwen was a real help and I will never forget her patience during all my tears and madness. I just couldn't see a way out. I went out with other guys but I was still too much in love with the one I'd broken up with, and it was made worse because we had loads of friends in common.

I got called into Ted Argent's office and told that they were really concerned about my work and my commitment to the course and actually said they felt that I should leave. They knew I was doing extracurricular work outside the college, which you weren't supposed to do, and I gathered there was a degree of jealousy from other students in my year, with one classmate declaring, 'Why are you wasting your time here when what you really want to be is a singer?' And to be fair, I wasn't pulling my weight in classes, and if you can't be depended on to turn up, then you can't ever hope for a professional life. I always turned up for the things I liked, but for others I didn't, and that was becoming too frequent. So I found myself pleading to be kept on and asking Ted Argent if he thought I wasn't talented. He said, 'On the contrary, you are very talented, but if you can't be trusted to turn up, then you aren't a team player and that is not tolerated.'

I walked out of his office devastated. I didn't know what to do. I was so close to graduating and I knew I was far from the worst case; I was just stupid enough to get caught. There were others who had failed exams or had had to repeat a year, or who just played the game better (always had an illness or a nervous disorder up their sleeve and were much friendlier with the lecturers than I was). They were much cleverer in their approach to the course or they simply turned up at the right times and looked as if they cared. My head was in the clouds − or up my own arse − at the time, but I was brought down to earth with a bang. How was I going to tell my parents I was in trouble? How was I going to tell my mother? They thought it was all going fine. I was back to being 11 again and my mum being told I was an awful student. I felt like I was a failure, like I was 15 again when I didn't pass all the exams I had hoped because I didn't work for them. Now I was being thrown off my college course.

I went to my friends in the SRC in floods of tears saying that I was going to be thrown out and they asked if I had actually failed anything, to which I said no. It was decided that they'd support me in fighting for an appeal and in the meantime they told me I had to turn up for everything and ask for a meeting with David Lumsden, who ran the Academy. I also went in to the wonderful Val Parker (who ran the drama school from her wee office) and asked her if she would keep a register of all the times I was in and on time between now and the end of term. She did and was really encouraging with me, for which I will be eternally grateful. I turned up early for everything, got all my work done on time and was a good student (at times I'd be sitting in classes on my own as the other students skived off, but I was there). I went to members of staff and asked them if they would speak for me if it came to a vote, and Pete Lincoln, Grace Matchett and Bill Murray did just that. I finally got a meeting with the principal too, sitting shaking outside his office, and discovered with relief that he was kind and understanding. I explained about my broken love affair, how I hadn't wanted to go on, my lack of concentration and focus, and how I'd stopped all the gigging. I then produced my timekeeping sheets and my list of the lecturers who supported me, as well as pointing out the fact that I had never failed an exam. I promised to do my utmost for the remainder of the course and not let them or myself down again, and I meant it. I basically pleaded for my life.

I had to wait outside until they came to a decision. They called me back in after an agonising time and I was told that they had been impressed by what I'd said and were prepared to give me another chance. I wept openly between cries of 'Thanks!' and 'I won't let you down!', and I almost fainted on the way out as Val Parker gave me a big hug. Saved! I was saved!

So I did knuckle down for the remaining four or five months, and on the day I graduated in June 1978, the principal shook my hand as he handed me my scroll and said, 'Well done, Elaine. I knew you could do it.' I felt fantastic and so relieved, and I vowed never to get myself in that position again in my life. My mother was finally happy that she had a college graduate she could boast about. True to form, she asked me why I couldn't have had a hood with a white ribbon around it, because she felt the pink clashed with the wine and the white would have looked better in the photographs. I did explain that I would have had to do a degree in music to get that, but it didn't seem to make a lot of difference. We went for a big meal with my friends – Gwen and her wonderful parents Walter and Nessie from Northern Ireland and John Wood with his parents from Edinburgh.

The photos were hellish. I looked like I'd had a foot pump taken to me, even with the Farrah Fawcett flicks. I was so tired and puffy due to the stress and relief of just getting through the course and graduating that I'd obviously been comfort eating for Scotland. My parents knew nothing about all this stuff, of course; I think it was an unwritten rule between us that when things went wrong I wasn't to tell them and upset them.

I think the pattern of yo-yo dieting and weight gain began then. I had gained a lot of weight working in a hotel over the summer going into my final year (even bursting my cream trousers one night at a disco in the college, much to my humiliation – and they were a size 14). So I dieted and shed the weight, but it was the start of my battle. The big sign of stress and angst for me is always when I gain weight. I think that I try and eat my way out of trouble or just try to keep the fear way deep down in there with a lot of food. Given the stress of just graduating, it was no surprise, really, that I'd put on weight.

We then set off for my cousin John's wedding to Diane in Middlesbrough, and I remember it being a great journey. It was just me and my parents for the first time in years. We stopped off en route for a meal. I saw Dad have a glass of wine for the first time and he was really happy and jolly – well, it's not every day that your daughter becomes a college graduate. As my mum and I discussed my ambition to go on to teacher-training college, Dad turned and said, 'You do what you want, doll, you've done enough for us.' The emotion released with those words was wonderful and exciting. I felt that I had permission at last to live my own life, just for me, though in practice, for Mum, that would never be true – the ties were too binding. But distance would help, and even though Edinburgh was only 40 miles away, it was the other side of the country, and in 1978 that felt a long way away.

CHAPTER 15

EDINBURGH

As a 'Westcoaster' – as I was often referred to in Edinburgh – I'm not supposed to like Edinburgh. Even though I would never call myself a Glaswegian either, I was still seen as one because of my Lanarkshire accent. Actually, the accents of Glasgow and Motherwell are very different; we didn't 'parliamo Glasgow' (i.e. have all the phrases and rhyming slang of the Glasgow vernacular). Yes, we did have the vowels and the glottal stops, but we had more of a country 'Auld Scots' way of speaking, whereas Glaswegians were different. We laughed at the way they spoke too: 'sters' for stairs; 'mo'a' for motor; 'bu'a' for butter; 'ma' for mum; 'weans' for children. This wasn't the way we spoke at all, but in Edinburgh it didn't matter – you were a 'weegie' if you were from west of Bathgate. Old rivalries between two cities that are only forty miles apart run deep.

Much as I loved Glasgow, I couldn't wait to get away by the time I graduated, as I felt I couldn't breathe any more. I was desperate to leave behind the flat, the friends, the broken romances and the bands. I'd had enough and wanted to be a teacher, reinvent myself and leave show business and singing behind me. That's when I came across Moray House College of Education on the Royal Mile. I didn't know Edinburgh at all so had no idea where to live. John Wood was an Edinburgh boy and suggested I stay in the university's halls of residence until I got somewhere permanent to stay. So I did, and I got accommodation at a place just off Liberton Road, which meant I could walk to Moray House if I wanted to.

I had never been in halls of residence before and there I was in what felt like a public school for girls. It was an old Victorian building. My little cell with its single bed looked out onto gardens. There were rules about no males allowed in rooms and visitors having to be out by 10.30 p.m., and a bell rang for meals, etc. – pretty weird, really, compared to the wilder life I had just left behind me. Most of the girls there were starting the Primary School Teaching Course, so were only 17 years old and very 'girly' in their outlook on life, whilst I, of course, was a mature woman (aged 20).

I had a laugh there, sneaking in late, or sneaking men out (not lots, you understand, I wasn't running a brothel), and I got friendly with a mature student called Roxanne Quaranta – a beautiful Italian-American woman who was doing a one-year course specialising in teaching the deaf. I don't think she knew what had hit her when she arrived from the heat of Tucson, Arizona, in Edinburgh – the poor thing was cold for a year, as this was well before central heating. But she hooked up with a lot of the US students who were in Edinburgh, and therefore so did I, and it was great.

We partied and laughed and most of the time I felt as foreign as they did. For the first year in Edinburgh I met hardly anyone who actually came from the city; it was either Americans, Aberdonians or Westcoasters. We met when she heard me playing a Joni Mitchell song on the piano in the main living area. There was a beautiful grand piano, which I played whenever I could, but I usually had to wait until the room was empty. She had stood there quietly listening to me sing and play and then spoke up afterwards, giving me the fright of my life. We found we had lots in common, being hardcore Joni fans, and both finding the set-up in the halls a scream – it was as if we were back at school. So, discovering we were obviously two rebels together in a strange city, our friendship was sealed.

I stayed for a term until I got my bearings, and then I got a small room (once I got a three-quarter bed in the bedroom, there wasn't room for much else) with a skylight in a flat looking onto Blackford Hill. I had never really been that far away from my family and those ties that hold you down, and Edinburgh was just far enough away to let me feel free and in charge of my own life for the first time. I was still an eejit but I felt I had learned a great deal in Glasgow – mainly through my mistakes. One thing I now knew was how to work hard to achieve my goals. I didn't want to do the band thing any more, I felt really discouraged and drained by it and had decided that it wasn't for me. I wasn't good enough and didn't really fit.

At Moray House I was disappointed to find that the drama department was so small that they didn't do any shows or plays; I wanted to keep being creative. But along with John Wood, I met some great women and especially my friend Evelyn Handleigh. We didn't like each other, though, at the start. Well, truth was she didn't like me. She was quite a serious person and after we became friend told me that she'd thought I was only another airhead who talked all the time, just like too many of the girls she'd been at Queen Margaret with. But after one incident she changed her mind.

We all had to do a mini-lecture on a chosen subject to the group. I can't remember what mine was about, but I remember it was a Friday and most of us were heading off for the weekend and Evelyn was heading back to her home in Kilmarnock. She had a beautiful white long-haired cat with piercing blue eyes. She was taking it home to the vet and she asked if it would be all right to bring it into the class in its basket. I said no problem and proceeded to get on with my lecture. Well, after five minutes this cat started squealing and yelping and I just found it funny, but Evelyn was mortified, and even when it was put outside in the corridor the yelps got louder. She apologised profusely afterwards but I said that it was fine and didn't matter, and I genuinely meant it. She said that she couldn't believe that someone would be so good about it, as she would have been complaining to the lecturer and making a fuss. We became firm friends, and I ended up renting a room in her flat in Henderson Gardens, down in Leith, for a year. I was eventually to become her bridesmaid when she married a few years later, and we kept in contact until she died unexpectedly in 2008.

I still harboured a dream of getting some experience as an actor and knew that I wanted to keep performing. The real dream was of being in 7:84, or Wildcat, but I didn't know the best way to go about it. I think I still thought that I would just be spotted and given a job. I asked one of my lecturers, Gareth Wardell, if there were any drama societies and he advised me to head up to Edinburgh

University Theatre Company (EUTC), as they had a really strong group at Bedlam Theatre and Hill Place. Gareth was a lecturer I liked a lot and on a project with him he invited us back to his house in Corstorphine, where I met the wonderful Pam Wardell, his wife – an inspirational woman who became a mentor to me. Around our second meeting, Gareth told me that he thought I would do well as a teacher but that I really should be acting, as he felt I was a natural for a company like 7:84 – my dream job! I admitted that to me it seemed like a pipe dream; I felt it would never happen and anyway I was enjoying my teaching.

I was far from an A-plus (though funnily enough in psychology and sociology I was) but my grades were good, my teaching practices above average and I was falling in love with education again. But I need to be creative, I really need that outlet and, to tell the truth, if you weren't into the pub culture in Edinburgh, it was a difficult city to get to know. I loved living there and loved the buildings, the history, the freedom I had and the new friends I was making. But I never felt that I was getting to know the locals and how they lived. It is a very middle-class city in that it is very business-orientated with lots of private schools. You found that people would tend to stick together within their own social groups in their own sections of the city: Barnton, Corstorphine, Colinton, Trinity, the Grange and the New Town, to name a few. All the working people tended to live on the outskirts, in areas such as Pilton, and in Leith.

I was used to the west coast, which has a lot of wealth too, but there is a feeling that, regardless of your background, school or how much cash you have, everyone is the same – we're 'aw Jock Tamson's bairns' and all that. It's maybe an urban myth, but in Glasgow they wear, drive and spend their cash, whilst in Edinburgh they like to save it and hide it.

Edinburgh buses have their numbers on the back as well as the front, which an uncle of mine said summed up the Edinburgh mentality – in Glasgow, you don't want to know the number of the bus you've missed. I couldn't understand that in the flats I lived in when it was your turn to wash the stairs, a sign was hung on your door to tell you; in Glasgow, you would just be told in no uncertain terms that it was your turn and woe betide you if you didn't do it.

But actually for the first couple of years I loved the reserve of Edinburgh. I loved the fact that it wasn't as in your face as Glasgow – at times that can be too much. Everyone knows everything about you and will tell you what they think about everything to your face. That can be wonderful and friendly, but the ego of the Glaswegian knows no bounds and at times it is just overwhelming. So Edinburgh was great but still took a bit of getting used to and even after a few years I still yearned for a friendlier place (like Partick Cross) where people spoke to you at bus stops.

I went up to EUTC and auditioned for various directors who were putting on different plays, and one of them was a wonderful Glaswegian called Alan Brodie. He was a law student with a vast interest in and knowledge of theatre. He was putting on a play by David Mamet called *Sexual Perversity in Chicago*. It was a really hip play and this was one of the first productions of it in Scotland. Mamet was a huge playwright in the USA at the time (and still is). I can do a decent American accent – and was surrounded, as I said, by Americans at the time – and there were two other Americans in the play. Jennifer MacDowall from New York played Jen, the gentle 'other woman' up against my man-eating Joan, and she was terrific in the role. But Joan was a fabulous part to play too, as she was so tough and unlikeable. The production was a hit and was packed out every night, and although we all did it in our spare time and weren't paid, I still loved it.

We ended up at the National Student Drama Festival in Southampton, where I was paid the ultimate compliment by Americans in the audience who told me they'd thought that I was the only American in the play. I hadn't understood why Alan didn't want me to speak at any of the events until our play was on, but he later confided in me that he wanted people to be shocked when they heard my real accent, which they were when I piped up at the after-show talk. A guy from Chicago said he almost fainted when he heard my strong Glaswegian accent. Jennifer won the best female acting prize, which was tough for me, because I had the flashier role and had gained more notice, but she was a good friend and I can honestly say that I was really pleased in my heart for her. That sort of jealousy never gets you anywhere anyway – if you wish for someone else to fail, it only makes you miserable.

In my last year at college, I got a chance to do a teaching practice at Firrhill High School in Edinburgh. I walked into the school to see a show before I started and I have never felt so at home in my life. That has happened to me a few times in my life: I walk in somewhere and know that this is where I am meant to be. That's how I felt that night. I did a teaching practice there for a term and I adored it. I also got to work with one of the finest teachers I have ever seen in Pam Wardell. It was a real privilege to watch her caring, compassionate and funny nature in action close-up, and she displayed a real desire to make a difference to the lives of the kids and the school. I did well there, got good marks and Pam asked for me when a new job was created as her assistant. I did three days in the high school and two days in the surrounding primary schools, which let the primary school children have an experience of drama before they arrived in the high school.

So in August 1979, I had my first real job, with a salary and a flat, in a city I loved, and life was good. I remember getting my first monthly payslip and thinking, 'How am I going to spend all this?' I was actually on a bigger wage than Dad and he was 55 and had worked all his life. Naturally, I found a way to spend it all, and very quickly, too. This was also the new era of Margaret Thatcher and many people had become involved in politics due to what was happening in education and the rest of society in general. I joined the teachers' union, the EIS, and became a committed and active member.

I really enjoyed politics – and still do, as you'll discover later in this story – as it was actually very exciting at that time. It was full of young people who still believed that change could be brought about by joining together, and to a certain extent we succeeded. I was on the picket line in the teachers' strikes, on marches every other week and got heavily involved with groups such as Women's Fightback. We were still far from a society where women were equal and things were not helped by the first-ever female prime minister – who seemed to have picked up all the worst aspects of men in power.

On one particularly cold February night, I went along to an EIS meeting at Moray House to speak about the plight of drama teachers. I was a member of the Drama Teachers' Association; we were having a lot of difficulty within schools and in education generally, as we were still regarded as a fringe subject. Facilities were poor and we had problems attracting academic kids because we had no exams in the subject, so we were asking the union for some help and support.

I was sitting with a friend and preparing what I was going to say when a couple of guys and a woman walked up the aisle to sit behind us. I couldn't stop looking at one of the guys; he was very handsome and dark, not too tall (a bit like Al Pacino – I had just seen *The Godfather*). I just felt as if I knew him. My skin sort of went all prickly and I leant across and asked one of the other women who he was. 'Oh, that's Bob Morton,' she said. I couldn't stop looking at him, and I honestly felt like I'd been hit by lightning. Of course, he hadn't even noticed me as I sat there before the meeting started, thinking thoughts like would he be married, have two kids, a mortgage and a nice safe teaching job? I tried to focus on the meeting and dismiss what I was feeling. The feeling sort of freaked me out because I was in a relationship with a lovely guy, Graham, from Ipswich, who was in the army. We'd been going out for a few months after meeting at a friend's wedding. I really cared about him and we were even talking about his coming to live in Edinburgh, but I knew that if I could feel this way about someone I'd just seen, then something was wrong. I was in trouble.

I spoke at the meeting and was quite funny about drama and the preconceived notions of the teachers just making kids act like teapots for half an hour. It went well but I have to say that my performance had been mainly to attract the attention of the handsome guy behind me. We all retired to the Blue Blanket pub on the Royal Mile and I ended up with the man in question sitting right next to me. I then proceeded to make a fool of myself by trying too hard to be funny. I was feeling good, had of course been on another diet and was about nine stone for the first time in years, and I was wearing my favourite white shirt and blue velvet-cord dungarees.

Now, what you have to remember is that I was sitting with a group of folks who were all avid left-wing trade unionists, people who were not known for their sense of humour unless it was about Marx, Stalin or the evils of capitalism. But I was undeterred and launched into a gag about an Irishman, which, though funny, was actually a racist joke. My political understanding hadn't really reached jokes about the Irish or other nationalities really being racist. Jokes about black people or Asians, absolutely; but I had been brought up with 'Paddy' jokes (as told by my Irish grandfather), so I had no idea I was out of order. However, in this company I was. When I did the punchline, no one really laughed and I didn't understand, so of course I launched into my backup gag, which was much the same. The politicos were kind (I was a young, well-intentioned working-class woman), so, smiling, they said, 'Right, come on. None of that racist stuff here!' Eh? Racist? I just didn't get it and realised something terrible had gone wrong with my plan, watching in embarrassment as the conversation drifted back to politics.

But actually I had got the attention of Bob Morton, who thought the whole episode was in fact much funnier than any of my gags. He loved watching the trendy lefties (largely from middle-class families and very earnest and worthy) trying to cope with a genuine working-class woman. He and I chatted about Glasgow and the bands I had been in, and it turned out that he shared a flat with some guys (Dick and Wullie, no less) from a great Edinburgh band called The Dominators. He said that he would put me in touch with them if I was looking for some more singing work.

So the lefties and I retired to the wonderful Bennet's Bar – next to the King's Theatre in Tollcross – and I met up with some people I knew, so we sort of split up. At the end of the night, I shouted goodbye to my friends and asked if anyone was going up to Blackford Hill so I could cadge a lift. It was then that the beautiful Bob stepped in and said, 'I'll give you a lift.' I couldn't believe it, and of course Calum and Ann (two of my pals I'd confessed to that I totally fancied the Al Pacino lookalike) were in fits, with Calum commenting on how impressed he was by my quick work. They couldn't have been further from the truth.

We got outside the pub and I asked him where he lived, and he said down on Leith Walk but he didn't mind giving me a lift. I was really pleased, as I thought, 'Well, he must fancy me! He's sought me out and offered me a lift to the other side of town.' We got to his car (not the lovely sports thing that I'd imagined but an old banger of a Volkswagen that took about five minutes to start), and as we drove off, he started a very businesslike conversation, asking about my work and the plays I had performed in, so it was a bit odd. Of course, because I was so nervous, I chatted incessantly, about anything. We got to the flat and I asked him if he wanted to come in for a coffee and he said yes. 'Oh right,' I thought, 'he does fancy me!' We went into the flat, had a coffee and talked about politics for almost two hours, and then he got up to leave, saying how nice it was to meet me and thanks for the coffee, shook my hand at the door and left. I was totally bamboozled, but also totally smitten.

I had the rehearsals for a show (Jonson's *Bartholomew Fair*) to do, my teaching job and a bloody boyfriend, but I couldn't stop thinking about Bob. I knew I couldn't lie to Graham – and nothing had actually happened – but I also knew that if I felt this way about another man, then I was not in love with him. I broke the news as gently as I could and was able to truthfully tell him that there was no one else, because there wasn't. Nothing had happened between Bob and me, and in fact we hadn't even spoken again. But a few days after our meeting he'd met a friend of mine at a party and had asked about me, saying he thought I was quite a woman (I don't think that was a compliment), and he gave her his number for me to call so that I could get in touch with his pals in the band.

I did the play and actually got a good review from a very young Joyce McMillan, who wrote that 'Elaine Smith as Ursula the pig woman would not be out of place at any Glasgow fish market'. How right she bloody was.

I ended up meeting Bob for a drink, though when I plucked up the courage to phone him I was so nervous that I asked to speak to Bob Morrison. He replied, quick as a flash, 'Well, I'm Bob Morton, will I do?'

'Oh yes, you're him,' I blurted back. He then asked if I could call back as he was watching *Blake's 7* (note to self: never get in the way of Bob's favourite TV show). We met up with his lovely, funny and talented 'Fifer' musician friends after the show one night and then once more he offered me a lift. 'Aha,' I thought, 'he does fancy me after all.' He came in for a coffee and guess what? We talked about politics, then once again he shook my hand and left. I was totally confused. I had never invited a guy back for a coffee who hadn't at least tried to kiss me or make an advance unless he was gay or an old friend. I didn't know what was going on and after another couple of similar meetings I just had to admit that he liked me as a pal and wasn't interested in me in that way.

But I was head over heels by this time. If he touched me, it was like an electric shock; the sound of his voice made my knees buckle. It was bloody wonderful and awful all at the same time. Worse, my ex-boyfriend had jumped on a train to try and persuade me to stay and to tell me he loved me. But by this time I knew that my affections lay elsewhere, even though, as yet, we hadn't even kissed each other. I felt terrible about hurting him but I knew it was over. He left broken-hearted saying, 'I hope he treats you well, Elaine.' Truth was, for a couple of years he did anything but.

I don't want to go into the gory details of all the fights and the splits, but suffice to say eventually we became more than friends and 29 years later we are still happily married with two beautiful, wonderful, daughters. I'd like to tell you that it has all been a wonderful romantic journey from the beginning, but it hasn't and isn't. But when I think about what I felt that first time I saw him . . . I just knew we'd be together. I felt I knew him instantly, we connected, and I love him even more now than I did then. He still makes my heart leap. Right, that's enough of that.

I had started working with the Scottish Youth Theatre, for Gareth Wardell, who was their artistic director at the time. He asked me to be a tutor/warden with a woman who was to become a great friend, and still is to this day, Chris Henderson. In fact, when she and Brigid, her partner, tied the knot a couple of years ago I was her 'best burd' at the ceremony. We got on brilliantly from day one, made each other laugh, and we both love football, politics and tennis. Chris was a primary teacher from Castlemilk (or 'Chateaulait', as it's called) in Glasgow who had gone back to Moray House to train in community work, and she knew Gareth and Pam from her teaching days. Also there running things was a fellow drama teacher from Airdrie Academy, an American firebrand and brilliant woman called Lynn Bains, who went on to become head of drama at Queen Margaret College in Edinburgh.

I enjoyed the summer school and the kids were fantastic, but in the middle of it I had an awful experience. I was attacked and assaulted (fortunately not raped) by a guy who broke into the halls where the kids were staying. They were all at rehearsals and I was there on my own. It was like a Hitchcock movie. I walked into the bathroom and was combing my hair and looking in the mirror when he came out from behind the door. By the time I had turned around he had me by the throat and was pushing me into the bath. It all happened in seconds and I don't know where I got the strength from, but I pushed him off and found my voice. I screamed as loud as I could and ran and ran. Eventually I reached the kitchen where the cooks were and they phoned the police. It was terrifying and yet I was really calm and just grateful that I'd got away from him. Even now, I can see the guy's face. I have no doubt that he was watching the halls and would have gone on to attack other women. He's probably in prison now – I hope so, anyway.

Being interviewed by the police was actually worse. This was 1981 and sex crimes were still sort of regarded as a woman's fault. I was asked first if he was my boyfriend, to which I said no, and then when I told them what had happened they took notes but were very dismissive until they found out I was a teacher and then they sort of bucked up a bit. They never found the attacker and we were much more protective of the students and ourselves after that.

I was then attacked in Princes Street one night about two months later. I was standing outside Woolworths, just along from the Café Royal. I was with Evelyn and we couldn't decide whether to go dancing or go home, as it was about 10.30 p.m. I had a black silk dress on, so it was fine material, and three guys ran up fast towards me and one of them grabbed my dress and literally ripped it off from the waist down. Then one shoved his hand up between my legs. So there I was standing in Princes Street in my knickers, with Evelyn throwing her jacket around me to cover my dignity. I was in total shock as it had all happened in about ten seconds and then they ran off down the street laughing. I was humiliated and shocked, and I couldn't understand what they thought they would get out of it. On reflection, I think that they were just drunk pranksters who were doing the old schoolboy thing of pulling women's underslips down and didn't realise that I wasn't bloody wearing one.

There was a lovely tag to the story, which helped restore my faith in men, and that was that as I was standing there holding my frock together, four young Sid Vicious lookalikes ran up to see if they could help. They then took off some of the badges from their jackets to help me pin my dress together. They had seen the whole thing from the bus they were travelling on and had got off and chased the guys down Leith Walk, but they'd lost them and decided to come back and see if they could help. We went straight up to a police box to report it and the police were fine but dismissive. One of them joked that if they caught any of the guys who did it they would let me pull his trousers down. I said I didn't think that would help the fact that I felt completely shocked, violated and upset. Again, their attitude changed when they found out I was a teacher and two detectives did turn up at the school later in the week.

These incidents certainly gave me an insight into what it feels like to be attacked and the reaction of the police, which only increased my determination to help women in these situations, as I really was one of the lucky ones. My involvement with the women's movement (which had been pretty rigorous up to that point, with organisations like Women's Aid, Rape Crisis and Zero Tolerance) increased after this and I am still committed to it to this day.

I still loved teaching and was becoming much more confident in the job I was doing. I had also moved staffrooms and ended up in the new building, where I met a group of guys who were the funniest men to work with. It got to the stage that I used to look forward to tea break because of the banter and laughs that we had with the one and only, the great A.J. Savage, Eddie Cooper, Allan Hunter, Dave Peat and Dave Clark. I think they would tell you I gave as good as I got, although when they ganged up (as groups of even intelligent men tend to do), I found it hard to cope – but those incidents were rare. I was still young (22), enjoyed a good laugh and was full of enthusiasm about education, and teaching in particular. I think they saw it as their job to set me straight, perhaps, and toughen me up. I enjoyed their company a lot and still see Eddie and Allan, with their wives, when I'm in Edinburgh. They have always been great supporters of my work and I really appreciate that.

By this time, I'd got more and more involved in politics. I started reading the books that would change my life, like *The Women's Room*, *The Ragged Trousered Philanthropists*, *The Female Eunuch* – which radically overhauled my belief system. I joined Women's Fightback and met some fantastic people there. We fund-raised, went on demos, discussed books and theories and had some good parties as well – women only, of course! I was often to be found of a Saturday morning selling the paper at the top of Leith Walk, complete with the uniform of Palestinian shawl and loads of earrings and badges. I'd had all my hair cut off as a sign of my commitment to women and my anger at the patriarchal society (though I have to admit that my shoes and bag still matched and I always wore lipstick – I mean, give me a break!) I sold a lot of papers because I was nice to the punters and made them smile a bit, not easy in Edinburgh on a cold Saturday morning. My life at that time was politics; my friends were all political and I was always on demonstrations – from raging against unemployment or US involvement in El Salvador and Nicaragua to supporting CND every other week. It was an exciting time to be in politics, and there were many battles to fight within the Labour movement itself too.

But the Left, or actually the Far Left, was a very funny and strange place to be at times. They took themselves so seriously and were so earnest, and I have no doubt that they believed it all at the time. The infighting between the small groups was also hilarious, with the People's Front of Judea scene in *Monty Python's Life of Brian* being the most accurate picture I could think of. The fights were ridiculous, between the IMG, the RCP, the SWP, Militant, the CP. They would all meet in Mathers Bar at the top of Broughton Street, just round the corner from the Trades Council at the top of Leith Walk. They all drank in separate bits of the bar, of course, because they hated each other more than they hated the capitalist swine they were supposed to be fighting against. There were only about 50 of us in total but they saw themselves as the vanguard of the revolution. I would often reflect, while sitting there watching it all unfold in front of me, that if the revolution happened in Corstorphine, we would probably still be in the pub putting motions together and arguing about what bus to get to it to join in.

Overall, the main thing lacking in it all was a sense of humour, as it was so serious and dour. It was no wonder to me that they all had to drink, or steal each other's girlfriends and husbands, as their lives were so bloody serious. It wasn't actually much fun saving the world.

An absence of a sense of humour always indicated to me a lack of intelligence, and it seemed that there were many people on the left of the political spectrum who seemed to be using politics, and the desire for revolution, as a route for dealing with their own emotional dysfunction and their own anger at their world and their lives. That's not to say that their fervour and passion weren't genuine, but I did discover a lot of posturing and many folks who came from privileged backgrounds seemed to be at the front of the queue when lecturing the rest of us about why we should all be living in a council house.

There was a lot of animosity between the women's movement and some of the macho left-wing groups too. At one big fund-raiser I was involved with, a rammy broke out because the guy who was doing the good socialist stand-up starting attacking the women's groups. Naturally, the women in the audience started going crazy at him and rushed the stage. A fight broke out between all the politicos, with chairs flying and lots of pushing and shoving, but it was the Left, so there were no real punches. It was horrible and an awful atmosphere, as eventually the comic had to leave and the whole thing stopped. It was all resolved within about ten minutes, though, when the disco started up with 'I Will Survive'; the dance floor was immediately filled with victorious women dancing round their duffle bags, with the men still raging on the sidelines. No doubt they all danced, got pished and made up in each other's beds later in the night. I am not saying I was any better, as I was an arse too at times. I was no different from the rest. Politics gave me a sense of purpose, a feeling that I was doing something to change the world, and I have to say I am proud of all the campaigns I was involved in. They educated me, shaped my political views and opened my eyes to the problems of the world.

Personally, I was pretty unhappy and confused in my relationship with Bob and what was going on, and I have to say he was pretty confused too. This was the 1980s after all, and women were making many more demands of relationships and about what they wanted.

I arrived in a relationship with Bob with a head full of love, romance, white weddings and happy ever after, and I ended up a left-wing feminist who wanted to destroy the patriarchy, keep my own name, never get married and live my own life (which caused a few arguments with Dad, to say the least). I was more aware and informed and better read about the world I was living in, but I ended up hurt, rejected, exhausted and very confused about who I was and what I wanted in life. So I made a promise to myself that I was going to change my life.

I wanted to buy a flat and have somewhere of my own (I was still renting rooms and needed my own space). I also wanted to go to the USA, as my friends there kept telling me I would love it, and I was seriously mulling over the idea of trying to make it as an actor full time. With all the plays I was performing in, as well as a lot of directing productions at school, I had plenty of people telling me I could make it professionally. I still didn't know how to do it but I knew that I had to try and sort my life out fully.

First, I bought a flat back in Glasgow. My old bass player Jamie and his partner Carol were selling their place in Scotstoun. It was a flat I loved and had spent many a great night in, so it felt like home already. They were finding it difficult to sell and I set about trying to buy it. I worked out that I could afford to have the flat and live in it at the weekends and rent my friend Evelyn's box room back in Leith. They were selling it for a princely £9,000 – a lot of money to me in those days. I set about getting a mortgage from the district council and then raising the deposit of 10 per cent of the asking price, which was hard. Jamie and Carol kindly reduced the price and even helped me with the deposit, which allowed them to move to their new house and avoid paying a bridging loan. I loved the flat and was soon travelling back to Glasgow as much as I could.

I decided that I needed to get away for the summer so I planned an adventure to see my old pal from the halls of residence Roxanne, who lived in Tucson, Arizona. The plan was that I would fly to Los Angeles, she would meet me and we would have a couple of days there before driving to Arizona. I was then going on to meet Jennifer (my other American pal from our days performing in *Sexual Perversity in Chicago*) in Atlanta and drive through the Blue Ridge Mountains and on up to New Jersey and New York where she lived. I bought my Freddie Laker ticket (remember him?) from Gatwick to Los Angeles and was all set to leave Bob and all the mess behind for a few weeks. I had told all my pupils about my trip and they were as excited as I was.

Two weeks before I left I got a call from Roxanne to tell me that her father had been diagnosed with terminal cancer and she had to be in New York with the family and couldn't meet me in LA. I had a non-refundable ticket and didn't know what to do. My dream trip was in ruins, as I couldn't just arrive in a city like LA on my own. My third year drama class were a bit mental, but great kids. A lot of the kids that I recommended for drama were the ones that no one else seemed to want, but I just loved their spark and humour and got loads of great work out of them because they felt that they were wanted, even if it was just drama. They were always asking about my trip and I had to tell them that it looked like I couldn't go because I didn't know Los Angeles very well.

Jackie Wilson, who was a great girl and pretty tough, piped up, 'Eh, Miss, I know someone in LA.'

I said, 'Yes, I'm sure you do, is it family?'

'Naw, Miss, I met him in the Wimpy Bar in Princes Street and he's my pen-pal.'

'Oh, that's great,' I said.

'Hey, Miss, I could write to him and ask him where you could stay – that would be good and then you could go on and meet your pal if you'd like?' Initially I dismissed it but when I thought about it I decided maybe if I could just get advice about where I could stay overnight, then I could just make my way to Tucson and see Roxanne. So I asked if I could put a note in with her letter to explain and she agreed.

About a week later, I got a phone call from Matt Stevens' answering service to ask me to call regarding my trip. I did and he was terrific. He said that he would pick me up from the airport and explained how he had ended up in a Wimpy Bar in Edinburgh. He had actually won a trip to Europe on an American TV game show. He and his friend were in Edinburgh, saw the sights and ended up in a Wimpy Bar being asked for a fag by our very own Jackie Wilson. They got talking and she asked if she could be his pen-pal, and he gave her his business card and that was it. All true!

So he got my flight details, I phoned Roxanne to say I was coming (though I didn't tell my parents about the change in plan) and I set off at the ripe old age of 22, on my own, to a country I'd never been to. If my own daughters told me that, I would be going daft but I was full of hope and optimism and it never occurred to me till later what I was doing. I headed for Gatwick very nervous and excited. I sat next to a great girl called Randy (I sympathised with the reaction that name would get in the UK, and she laughed). We got talking and I told her my tale and she was so kind to me. She told me that she lived in Westwood in Los Angeles and if this guy that I was meeting turned out to be a weirdo, then I was to call her and go and stay with her. So I had a backup plan.

We got to LAX and I headed for the 'Aliens' door and said goodbye to Randy. I was knackered, sweating (well, I was wearing my then favourite cream wool suit and blouse in an effort to look smart) and humping a giant suitcase as I entered the arrivals hall. I was met by an enormous cheer, and a tall, tanned guy in shorts and a T-shirt with a moustache jumped over the barrier and hugged me! I didn't know what was going on but it turned out that Matt had turned up at the gate with a sign saying 'Elaine Smith' (something that wasn't done in the USA at that time). It had sparked a bit of interest from the others who were waiting and they asked, 'Hey, don'tcha know who you're waitin' on?' To which Matt explained that he was waiting for a school teacher from Scotland (he thought I would be like Miss Jean Brodie) and that we'd never met. So people hung around out of interest to see if I would arrive. Randy got through before me and saw the sign so went up and told him that I was coming and what I was wearing – hence the cheer as I came through the door. It was amazing.

He whisked me down to his car (a sports soft-top) and as I looked at him I sighed with relief – because he was as gay as a goose and camp too! I felt so safe and loved him instantly. We drove along Sunset Boulevard, through Boystown, the gay district, along Rodeo Drive and past Griffith Park, and as I looked at the Hollywood sign I thought I had died and gone to heaven. He had an apartment in Silver Lake that looked onto the sign and he gave me his bed (he was staying with a boyfriend to let me have my own space). I was surrounded by his gay pals from around the area who were all intrigued by the exotic story of the schoolteacher from Scotland. This was the early '80s, pre-mobile phones, and I was so fascinated by the lifestyle, as well as cable TV. And there was still something unusual and exotic about foreigners.

I had the most amazing time with all these great guys, going to clubs, the gay bars, and even visiting Disneyland in Anaheim, as well as Universal Studios. I headed down to San Diego with Matt and then got a Greyhound bus to Tucson. It actually said 'Tombstone' on the front – I felt like I was going to visit John Wayne. I did the ten-hour journey across the desert to meet up with Roxanne on my own. I felt so grown up; I felt wonderful.

It was an amazing trip, with people constantly telling me how much they loved my accent (the guys and gals in one LA club cracked up every time I swore as they thought it was the most hilarious thing ever and didn't sound like swearing). I told them that I loved their accent too, but the Americans – due to their place in the world and lack of travel – looked puzzled and asked, 'What accent?' Go figure, as they say.

I flew on to Atlanta to meet Jen and her family and we had a magical three-day drive in a huge station wagon across Kentucky and Maryland, through the Blue Ridge Mountains to Philadelphia and New Jersey. They lived the American dream: the beautiful house, the executive salary, the two cars and the good-looking, bright kids in school. Of course, the truth was very different, as I knew from Jen, but for me, looking in, it just seemed perfect. And then I got to New York City – 'the Big Apple' – and I just adored it. Nowhere on the planet do you feel more alive. I dreamed of living there. It was as if I got all my hopes and dreams back on that trip and I came back to Scotland feeling more sure of who I was, and finally over Bob. I hadn't been in touch for months and I at last felt in charge of what was going on.

I arrived back home feeling fabulous, and jet-lagged, and as I got on the bus to school, a very pleased Bob Morton got on it too and sat next to me. My heart lurched as he told me that he'd just got a job in the modern studies department at Firrhill. I had suggested him when a job came up with Eddie Cooper before the summer, not really thinking that he'd get it, but he did. So there he was, the object of my desire, right in front of me, and in the same bloody staffroom – every day. What chance did I have?

But I still had my dream of getting into the business and he and I did love going to see shows by Wildcat or Borderline. One night when we were out for a drink after a show he took me to task. No doubt he was sick of me going on about wanting to join 7:84 and the like and he tore into me, saying that it was time I got my finger out and did something about it and that he didn't want to know me in ten years when I was saying that I 'could've' or 'should've'. I was so angry that I stomped off, but he'd told me a truth I didn't want to face.

The next day I bought a copy of *The Stage* and there was an advert for a political theatre company in London called the Broadside Mobile Workers' Theatre. I phoned them and arranged an audition and got a day off from school. The acting bit went fine but they were a very earnest political company so I was grilled on my politics for about two hours – all that was missing was a light shining in my face and someone saying, 'Ve haf vays of making you talk.' It was a total grilling and I felt real pressure to come up with the right political line on what I felt about the world – difficult with the Far Left because the 'correct' view can differ from group to group and on a daily basis. What was more, I didn't quite know who this group were aligned with.

I think I did OK, and they offered me the job, but I wasn't an Equity member so couldn't take it. I had come back home with mixed feelings: I wanted to get away and start a life as an actor, but the company were so earnest and humourless that it might have put me off for life. In hindsight, it was lucky for me – God knows where I would have ended up. But getting the job gave me confidence to keep trying, so I wrote to Dave MacLennan at Wildcat asking for an audition. Dave called and we arranged to meet in the Café Royal in Edinburgh (a magic pub that I'd worked in for a few months to earn some extra money). I was really nervous but he was so kind and remembered me from the interview for my thesis years before. We had a drink and a great chat and he explained that they didn't have any jobs then, but he promised to keep me in mind and said he thought it would be good for me to come down and meet the band when they were rehearsing.

We arranged this and I turned up at an old building in Canonmills where they were all set up. When I look back, I can see how the band would have reacted when MacLennan went in to say this girl was coming to an audition because he'd never seen me act or heard me sing (and he actually can't sing a note). The welcome I received was a bit lukewarm to say the least. I remember that I had put my good shirt and my velvet knickerbockers on, though Dave Anderson remembers me as the most macho person he'd ever met, with no sign of nerves. I was actually cacking my pants!

I sat down at the piano and sang Joni Mitchell's 'Woman of Heart and Mind' and the atmosphere changed. They listened and even applauded at the end. I sort of stopped the room and Dave was up asking me to sing things and then I played my standard, 'Leaving on a Jet Plane', and the drummer Mike Travis and the rest of the band joined in. It was superb and I loved every second. I left on cloud nine, with no job but a promise that they would be in touch. I knew my life was about to change. Nothing happened for a few weeks but then I got a call from MacLennan saying that he had passed my name on to John McGrath, who was casting a season of plays called 'Clydebuilt' and thought I would be perfect for it. He also explained that they had seen a few other good young performers and had plans to expand the company and that I was in those plans.

The next day, I was teaching my O level drama class about John McGrath and his company when Christine from the office came in to say that there was a phone call for me from a Mr John McGrath, and I actually burst out laughing and went to take the call. John was charm itself and said that Dave had told him about me and that I'd make a perfect Lady Macbeth. 'Yes, Elsie Macbeth,' I said (always trying to be funny, of course). He asked if I would come to his office and read for a part and we arranged a date. I went in, met my hero and read for the part of Kate in *Gold in His Boots* and got it. I was ecstatic. I was to start in two weeks' time.

As I was celebrating, I got a phone call from their administrator Christine Hamilton to get my details, Equity number, etc., there was a silence when I said that I wasn't a member. This was in the days when you couldn't work as an actor unless you were in the union; it was a closed shop, meaning that only so many new members were allowed in per year. She said it was a problem and I thought that my hopes were dashed. But John phoned me later to tell me that he'd had a word with Equity and they were allowing him to use their last provisional membership for me.

I handed in my notice to the school, went out with the guys to celebrate and couldn't get drunk because I was so high. I knew that this was what I had been waiting for. A new career, and I could finally get away from my relationship with Bob, which I felt was just getting worse and worse – though he was incredibly supportive of my move and new job. I think secretly he'd stopped himself from falling for me (well, apart from the distraction of other women) because I was younger than him, and perhaps he felt that I would eventually leave and go into show business, where there would be little place for him. But I was so excited about my new opportunity. I moved back to Glasgow and was able to live full time in my flat. Then I headed off for my first day as a professional actor.

CHAPTER 16

SHOWBIDNESS

So there I was, back in my wee flat in Glasgow, I'd been on a trip to the States and was now a working actress – a whole new life. It took a long time for me to be able to call myself an actor. First, because it was just too embarrassing, and second, I still didn't believe it myself. I sort of giggled and said, 'I'm an actor,' as a sort of a mumble behind my hands when anyone asked what I did for a living (and that lasted for about ten bloody years).

It was a shock to my parents that I was giving up the teaching job. They were naturally worried about how I would pay for my flat, as I had a mortgage and I only had a seven-week contract to bank on money coming. I convinced them (and myself) that it was the right thing to do and that I would manage somehow, as I had a vague promise of work in the forthcoming summer from Dave MacLennan and Wildcat, although it was no guarantee. But in my heart and soul I knew I was doing the right thing.

I was so excited, as well as crippled with nerves, when we started the read-through that morning. All the other actors seemed to know each other and the cast was a 'who's who' of actors spanning the previous two decades who were working all the time in Scotland: Jake D'Arcy, Finlay Welsh, Charlie Kearney, Billy Riddoch, Tam Dean Burn and the wonderful actress Jan Wilson. Jonathan Watson was part of the ensemble too, and he is someone who has ended up sharing a screen and stage with me for the last 30 years. I'd been at drama school with Johnnie and I liked him a great deal. He was the year below me but had hung around with my friends, mainly having a laugh and drinking in the Ivanhoe pub. Thankfully we had remained friends, as I was to play his girlfriend, Kate, in the play. Johnnie had been working as a professional actor for a couple of years so I don't really know how he felt about being paired up with me as a professional novice – probably a bit pissed off that he had this new girl to deal with.

As it was, it turned out it was the older actors who took me under their wing and it was wonderful to hear their stories and tales of colleagues, their disasters and triumphs, all retold in the pub, I hasten to add. That was something that shocked me at the time, how much they all drank, especially in rehearsals. Before the show was a definite no-no, but afterwards, well, unbelievable – except for those that were already alcoholics! Much as I grew to love them all, with the kindness they displayed towards me, I vowed that that was not the way I was going to go in my career – acting and drink were not to be mixed. I did have a drink at lunchtime that first day (half a lager or something) but I was too nervous to even notice. Anyway, I got the first day over with (the read-through is always the worst bit for me, as everyone sitting around a table always makes me feel that every word I say is rubbish).

It was the big freeze in January 1983 and most of the city's buses were off the road because their diesel fuel had frozen in the tanks. I'd got a lift in the morning but had to try and get a bus back to Scotstoun from Argyle Street. To avoid the cold, I took a short cut through Central Station. I felt such relief at getting through the day that I didn't look where I was going and my foot caught in a bit of wrapping. As I tried to release it, I fell over and broke my bloody arm. I got up, with the help of some other folk in the station (who'd obviously watched me do my comedy routine of trying to stay upright while falling arse over tit – very Eric Sykes). I thanked them and walked to the bus stop, pretending everything was fine. I waited over an hour for a bus while the pain got worse and worse. I fluctuated between panic and calm, terrified that I had done something serious and that I would lose my new job and all hope of being an actress. I got back to the flat, where my pal Nick was (he was staying over for a few days) and he took one look at me and I burst into tears.

I explained what had happened and half an hour later I was in casualty at the Western Infirmary begging the doctor not to put a plaster on my arm, which he told me had a hairline fracture. I did the best acting performance of my career thus far as I moved and swung my arm around saying, 'I'm fine, it's not sore, honest,' when in reality it was agony. All I could think of was that I had given up everything and with my arm in plaster after only one day of rehearsal they could easily recast my part, and my career would be over before it began. The doctor relented and made me promise to come back to see him in a few days, put my arm in a sling, gave me painkillers and sent me home. I went into rehearsals next day and in a weird way it broke the ice, because everyone was so concerned about me when I told them what had happened that they treated me with kid gloves. John McGrath, who was directing, looked very concerned but I assured him that it would all be fine before the show opened. It was and I didn't end up with a plaster on it, although I have an arm that still clicks and occasionally aches to this day – but, hey, I've got a career.

I loved the whole experience of rehearsing: the laughs, the intensity, the fear and being part of a team. As we got nearer to the dreaded opening night in front of the audience, the fear increased. We opened in Cumbernauld Theatre, and it went well; I remembered my lines and didn't bump into the furniture. I didn't set the heather alight, but I was good enough and learning all the time. Everything was new yet familiar, all at once. I got used to the whole idea of the discipline and the show really quickly. We toured around small theatres in Scotland and then came in to the Mitchell Theatre in Glasgow (which was my equivalent of Broadway at the time – I loved it). I think coming to a packed Glasgow theatre was when my parents realised what I was doing was legitimate, especially as they recognised some of the actors from TV (which always seems to help) and 7:84 were at the height of their popularity. At the end of the run, I didn't know what I was going to do but I'd got myself an agent, Pat Lovett in Edinburgh, who was hopefully trying to get me some more work.

I had some time off after the tour (actually, it's called unemployment, but I'm an actor so I was resting). I loved having the time off, as I felt like it gave me time to adjust to my new life. I had money because I'd cashed in my superannuation from teaching and I knew that I had the promise of a job in the summer with Wildcat. So I decorated my flat, went to see my friend Gwen, who was now training as a probation officer in Manchester, and generally had fun, which I felt I hadn't been doing for so long. Life had been very serious – teaching, politics, my relationship with Bob, as well as with 7:84 – so I decided to simply enjoy myself.

A dear friend who had always encouraged me in every way and helped me have a lot of fun was Anne Lamond, and we spent a lot of time together during my 'resting' period. Anne taught drama in a school in Livingston and was quite frankly the finest drama teacher I have ever seen. She had been the year below me at the Academy and then came to Firrhill High as a student of mine. Through dark times, she was always a great friend. At the ripe old age of 23, she and I hit Byres Road on a regular basis and had a great time. We were both into mystical stuff and loved going to see fortune-tellers – of which there seemed to be lots at that time. Many were complete charlatans, probably out-of-work actors trying to pay the rent with a bit of dressing up and fortune telling. We loved it, though, as it was all part of our search for who we were, as well as a desperation to find out where our lives would take us. Would we find the man of our dreams? And when? Would we have the careers we wanted?

One day we saw a woman in a back lane that housed the very hippy De Courcy's Arcade. Her name was Lenor (somehow I don't think that was her real name). When I went in, she didn't seem that promising; she read cards and was a middle-aged woman with a big hairdo, glasses and a sensible jumper. Not a turban or a crystal ball in sight – how could she be any good? She asked me to shuffle and pick a few cards and I did. I wanted her to tell me that Bob was the man of my dreams and that it would all work out fine, but she didn't. She took her time and then she started. Her first line was, 'Oh, my dear, you should have been an actress.' I looked at her and said, 'Well, I am,' and she countered, 'No, no, I see you with children . . . like a teacher, but there are no desks . . . but you should be an actress!' I explained that I had been a teacher until a few weeks before and had just come into the business. She was so relieved that she spluttered, 'My dear, you are on the right path.' She carried on looking at the cards and then launched into this remarkable reading that described the next job I was about to do. She described Dave Anderson of Wildcat, telling me that this man was surrounded by music, had grey hair and a moustache and he was going to help change my career over the next couple of years. She then went quiet and said, 'In about 18 months from now, you are going to meet a man much older looking than his years, he too has grey hair and a beard, and this man will change your life.' I couldn't really work out what was going on and asked whether she meant romantically and she replied, 'No, but he will change your life.' I can't recall the rest of it but it was short and sweet – not exactly what I wanted to hear, but fine. We left, and later, over a few drinks, told one another what she'd said.

I forgot all about it, but a few weeks later I took Mum to see Billy Connolly at the King's Theatre. He was doing a benefit concert for the Prince and Princess of Wales Hospice and I could only get tickets at the back of the gods. My mum hated heights and though she loved Connolly she heard most of the show rather than actually watched it, as she was gripping the back of the seat all the way through. As ever, Connolly was brilliant. But as we got up to leave I noticed a familiar face a few rows in front of me; it was Lenor. I felt a bit awkward as she said hello, as I didn't want to tell Mum why I knew her. I smiled and greeted her and she just stopped in front of me, looked down at the stage and then back at me and said, 'You'll do that.' I laughed and said, 'I wish,' but dismissed it as fortune-teller bunkum. In any case, I was going to be a serious political actress, not do stand-up – and 'nice girls' didn't ever do that anyway. I forgot all about it. Sixteen years later, I was standing in the wings of the King's Theatre, about to do the recording of my stand-up show for BBC Scotland, and I looked up into the gods where my mum and I had sat, and at the full house, and I remembered Lenor's words. (Cue *Twilight Zone* music again.)

Luckily, Wildcat did come through with their offer of work. They started The Brand New Wildcats and put on a production of *His Master's Voice* – the production I had seen and loved at the Dolphin Arts Centre when I was doing my thesis. I was playing the role of the mother, which my idol Terry Neason had created, so it was a pretty daunting task. In July, we all started rehearsing in Glasgow, preparing to open at the Pleasance (a famous Edinburgh Fringe venue) at the Festival the following month, and then tour. My dream had actually come true. I was in the company I wanted to act with, in the theatre I had watched them in so many times, and appearing at the Edinburgh Festival, where only a year before I had taken my pupils to see shows

– now they were coming to see me. I ended up playing theatres across Scotland for the first time. I'd never even been to Dundee or Aberdeen and it was wonderful getting to know these cities. There I was back in a Transit minibus, with a group of relatively young actors, having a ball – as well as many a fight or drunken argument and sing-song too.

I graduated into the main Wildcat company and got to work with my heroine, Terry Neason. We were doing a show called *Welcome to Paradise*, which was about the links between Scotland and America, beginning with the journey of a Highland family from a couple of hundred years ago heading off to the New World to build a new, exciting life. It was a funny yet sad piece that had some great music. I got to play lots of different parts, from an American journalist to a Highland girl and a Glasgow mother à la Lotte Lenya. The Lotte Lenya song led into a classic variety routine – though I had never seen a classic routine, and it was only later that I found that out. For me, it was just a funny scene, but it was called the 'maw [me], paw [Dave Hicks] and wean [Myra McFadyen]' sketch. In layman's terms, it goes, 'formidable mother and gormless father with child desperate for a pee while attempting to tell their landlord about their damp house'. Damp was a huge problem in working-class tenements in Glasgow. The sketch showed the ignorance and disdain that ordinary people were treated with when they tried to do something about the mushrooms that were growing out of their walls. The classic response from the council at the time was that the residents were breathing too much, or having too many baths. I loved doing that sketch and it frequently brought the house down because it was really funny, yet it also made cogent political points and observations – and all in a song.

Dave Hicks was from Lanarkshire too and I knew him from some bands and the stage crew at the Academy, and Myra had been the year above me at drama school. Both were witness to a very funny but nightmarish night for me in Dunfermline – at the Carnegie Hall, no less. Until this point, I had a space between my two front teeth. I had my teeth extracted in the '60s (in the days when dentists were allowed to do that) because they had grown in a bizarre way, so at the age of eleven I'd lost my two front teeth and had a plate with 'falsers' attached. For some reason, the dentist thought that I would have had a natural space in my teeth and in subsequent years it had stayed the same until Bob said that I should get it fixed, as it 'looked a bit strange' (thanks, darling). So I went back to the dentist and instructed him to get rid of the space; unfortunately, it was scheduled for the day we were going to Dunfermline, but I didn't think there would be a problem and there wasn't, except for the fact that I had a new lump of plastic in my mouth. (Don't worry, I later had excellent bridgework done and got rid of the plate – I didn't have the cash in those days.)

So we did the sound check and everything felt fine and I got ready to go on and do my big dramatic Lotte Lenya number. So there I was in a spotlight, got a chord on the piano and started: 'The family came to Glasgow, it was 1849, and the men worked in the shipyards and the mines.' Unfortunately, with reverberation from the speakers, the volume and my new teeth, the lines came out with a slight lisp, as I was having difficulty saying my 's's! I was mortified when I heard, 'The family came to Glashgo, it wash 1849 . . .' I couldn't believe it. The band were all pissing themselves laughing as they realised what was going on and, worst of all, I knew I had really difficult words coming up. How the hell was I going to say 'shipyards'? But in true showbiz style I ploughed on and sang, 'And the men worked in the shshshipyardsh and the mineshsh.' I was in a complete sweat and panic but kept going, not helped by the band, who were wetting themselves by this point, with Myra and the rest in a heap on the floor laughing in the wings. I eventually got used to the teeth.

I stayed with Wildcat on and off for three years and loved it. It was everything I wanted it to be. I loved the songs, the company – give or take a few egos and eejits – and I still loved the politics of it all.

Fortunately, Wildcat were very different from Broadside in that the political consensus was assumed and not shouted about or drummed into people. There were also different political views (some further to the right than I could believe). But the ethos of the company always remained intact: our shows were written by the 'Two Daves' and we were out there as a company entertaining, educating and highlighting the terrible way our country was being run. The job was not to take one political line or tell people how to vote; it was to point out what was being done in our names by the Thatcher government of the time.

This was against a backdrop of massive cuts in healthcare, education and traditional industries like steel-making, mining and manufacturing across the country. The work fitted perfectly with my own views at the time and I loved being on demonstrations and picket lines with Wildcat as well as being the entertainment for many a fund-raiser, for everyone from the STUC and the Communist Party to nurses and firemen. This was at a time when trade unions were still strong and able to represent their workers well, when wrongs were questioned and campaigned against and occasionally righted, when unity was strength and power. It was still a time when ordinary people felt that they could do something – maybe not change the world, but we felt our voices mattered. Not the same nowadays, I have to say. My personal belief was that I was fighting for the people I was raised and brought up with and I wanted to help in the only way I knew how: to walk with them, entertain them and raise as much money as possible. So there I was with hundreds of others on the picket line at Ravenscraig, or marching in Ayrshire with the miners (to hear the wonderful speeches of Mick McGahey and Arthur Scargill), or speaking at rallies for the workers at Caterpillar or for devolution in Scotland – and occasionally giving them a song into the bargain.

I was so proud to be part of Wildcat, as well as being an actor and a political activist. In between my contracts with Wildcat I went off and did other jobs like pantomimes (of which I'll talk in detail later) and landed a job on a BBC Scotland radio show called *Naked Radio* that would lead to many bigger things. But I always returned to Wildcat, and that mixture of music, acting and politics was perfect for me. We did shows about the Health Service crisis, which took us to the Shaw Theatre in London, and I got to meet Tony Benn MP and a few other of my political heroes. A show we did called *Dead Liberty*, about the Miners' Strike, was a huge hit and packed out across Scotland. Some of the shows were like nothing I'd ever experienced, a wonderful coming together of people for one just cause.

The Crack was a favourite show of mine. It was a play about the divide between rich and poor in society, centring on a Glasgow working-class family and an upper-class family of the 'dressing for dinner' variety. We all took on the different parts in each family and it was great fun, and for me it was a chance to play a type of role that I'd grown to love: that of the heart-of-gold, ordinary woman struggling against the odds. It was also in this show that I started to work with an actress whom I had long admired, although our paths had never crossed. Elaine Collins had become a bit of a star in John Byrne's wonderful play *The Slab Boys* and Elaine was cast in the original as Lucille. Funnily enough, we had been brought up just a few miles from each other and our mothers used to push their prams along Brandon Street in Motherwell in 1959, with their two daughters called Elaine sitting in them and nodding to each other and smiling as they passed. I had seen some local press stories about Elaine in the *Motherwell Times* and was of course a bit envious of this young actress and her fame.

We met when I went to see Phyllis Logan in another John Byrne show, *The Loveliest Night of the Year* (eventually renamed *Cuttin' a Rug*), but it was only briefly, and again I was a bit intimidated by the whole 'dressing room' thing in the Traverse Theatre, not quite sure if I was intruding and envious that they were doing such a great job. So when the Two Daves said that Elaine was coming to work with us I was delighted. The cast was a great one – Dave Anderson, Elaine Collins, Myra McFadyen, Dave Hicks, Rab Handleigh – and fortunately Elaine and I became great friends and remained so for almost 20 years, working together on *City Lights* for TV and living together when she was our lodger in the flat (with occasional visits from her eventual husband, actor and writer Peter Capaldi).

Wildcat always did original songs and one of the minor criticisms that my dad had was that we didn't do any songs that ordinary folk knew. I tried to explain that we were a political company and that the songs were such a part of the story and the Daves were such good songwriters that we didn't need to use pop songs; we used the styles of the popular songs (rock, reggae, soul and country) but they were original. *The Crack* was the one and only time that changed. My character was the wife of Dave Hicks' character, who was a bit of a drunk and a lost soul (at this time, Dave had been quite ill and had been out of the game for a while with cancer, but he was back in remission and doing well in the show). There was one scene that always went down brilliantly with audiences. I got to sing a song that suited Dad no end. In the play, a working-class daughter brings a posh boyfriend home to meet the parents. Much drink is taken and, in true working-class tradition, a sing-song ensues. I'd told Dave Anderson about Dad's comments, which he found really funny, and we came up with a way of weaving covers and originals together as a dramatic device.

I started the sing-song with the Julie London classic 'Cry Me a River' (a song to be heard at many a Glasgow party), which then wove into an original song by Dave, in which Martha revealed her own life and troubles, ending with 'Cry Me a River' again – though this time sung in true Glasgow-drunk style with a very big rallentando finish. I loved doing that number, as it was like all of my life rolled into one: the parties with my family, the clubs I'd sung that song in, the politics of a woman's life – and all of it done in a funny and poignant way. Artistically and dramatically it was a great device.

The work that the company was doing then was really filling a gap in the market and the audiences were increasing all the time. The mixture of politics, comedy and songs just fitted the bill and was exactly what a vast section of the audience wasn't getting elsewhere. Variety was still popular, but it was seen as a bit old hat and out of touch (too many accordion players and old gags), and though people like Rikki Fulton and Jack Milroy were still wonderful, their audiences were becoming older. The programmes in place in the actual rep theatres were looking increasingly staid and conservative, apart from the avant-garde work being done at the Citz under Giles Havergal and the attempts by the Traverse Theatre to get new productions out to a wider audience. The big, popular audience, though, were desperate for something for them and we seemed to service that need, though occasionally what we were trying to do and what the audience wanted were a bit too far apart.

The success of *The Crack* led the admin team and Dave MacLennan to take the next show to the heart of working-class variety in Glasgow: the Pavilion Theatre. Unfortunately, however, we went with the wrong show. The Pavilion is a great old palace of entertainment in the centre of Glasgow and had a loyal core audience, particularly in the 1970 and '80s, who tended to go to see whatever was on in the theatre that week. It's safe to say that they were used to a diet of comics, variety and light-entertainment shows. So *Business in the Backyard*, about the situation in Nicaragua and El Salvador, although it had great music and stuff, was a bit of a difference.

On the opening night, Bob, who was by this time working for Wildcat, sensed there might be a bit of a problem when he was trying to get the audience in from the bar and into the auditorium. As he tried to get them in, one of the punters said, 'It's awright, son, there's no rush, it'll just be the dancers on the now,' obviously assuming that the play was some sort of variety show, where the 'turns' don't come on until later in the bill. God knows what they thought when they saw all of us up a mountain in camouflage gear pretending to be Nicaraguans. On another night, when I came out of the stage door these lovely wee women came up to me and said, 'Oh, hen, yer group were good, what are yeez, the Wildcats? Aye, it was good, different fae the usual . . . we got the dates wrong . . . we thought we were coming to see Hector Nicoll [a very funny Scots comic at the time, though somewhat blue and politically far from correct] but we still enjoyed it, hen, yeez are a good group.' I don't know whether they started giving cash to the Sandinistas afterwards but they seemed to have had a good night out.

There was a wonderfully serious side to all this, of course. I was quite passionate about what was going on in Central America; the horror of the death squads and what the US-funded dictatorships were up to was getting through to the mainstream news and it was horrifying to watch. So it was great to feel that we were at least doing something to help and letting people know what was going on in the name of US freedom. We had the Nicaraguan ambassador in the audience on the first night, who got a standing ovation from the Glasgow audience (even if they did think he was Hector Nicoll). I got more involved in the fund-raising with Scottish Medical Aid for Nicaragua and the wonderful Des Tierney (whom I knew from my political days in Edinburgh). He eventually persuaded me to do a trip with them to Nicaragua, after we did some benefits and set up Artists for Nicaragua, which raised money for artists, dancers, writers and musicians who were struggling to get even basic things like guitar strings or ballet shoes due to the US embargo of the country. But more of that later.

It was my last show with Wildcat as a permanent company member. I told the Two Daves that I was ready to go off and do some other things and they were really understanding about it. I knew that I had made friends for life and that the time we'd all spent together was very special. It had been wonderful and rewarding, but it was time to move on. I'd done a couple of Christmas shows with Borderline Theatre Company when Wildcat were on a break and had had a great time. At that time, it was run by the wonderful Morag Fullarton, and the legend that is Eddie Jackson (who is still there today) was their administrator. They had built a great reputation as a touring theatre company in Scotland and Morag always had a tremendous eye for talent and putting on a good show. It was a combination of good productions, new writing and good actors. Early shows had cast lists including Robbie Coltrane, Freddie Boardley, Phyllis Logan, Gregor Fisher, Brian Pettifer, Pat Doyle, Elaine Collins, Katy Murphy, Tony Roper, Alan Cumming and many, many more. They commissioned works from John Byrne, Tom McGrath, Alex Norton and Liz Lochhead, as well as doing small productions of classics like *Guys and Dolls* and work by Dario Fo.

It was one of Fo's shows, *Trumpets and Raspberries*, that Morag offered me, and that was the first time that I got to play the wife of one of the funniest men I have ever met – the one, the only Andy Gray. We'd first met in the bar of the Mayfest Club (which Bob was running at the time) at the Mitchell Theatre in Glasgow. He was in *The Slab Boys Trilogy* directed by David Hayman at the Citz at the time – before it transferred to the Royal Court in London – and was drinking with Johnnie Watson. I went over to speak to Johnnie and within minutes of being introduced I was in fits of laughter, drinking Alabama slammers and fending off Andy's advances. (I learned not to take his interest as a compliment. I was a woman and I laughed at his gags so that was enough for Andy to advance, particularly after a couple of drinks.) He was, and is, fun personified, but I was exhausted after ten minutes. We went on to work on a pantomime together and a few episodes of *Naked Radio*, but doing the Dario Fo show together was just a great opportunity.

We rehearsed in Glasgow in the old RSAMD annexe, which was like starting acting all over again for me. After the read-through, when I was feeling rubbish about my performance, especially next to Andy's, I got a real boost when Morag told me that the designer (who was up from London) had immediately asked who I was and said that he thought I was brilliant. That calmed the nerves a bit.

It was a great cast: Brian Pettifer, Hilary Lyon (who became a good friend and survived the tour and sharing a dressing room with me, God bless her) and her future husband Alan Cumming (yes, this was pre-gay Cumming). I struggled in the first week of rehearsals, though, as I watched Andy being incredibly funny and brilliant in the lead part. I tried to keep up with him but it just didn't work and I could feel it. As I struggled, I realised the key to playing Rosa in the show was to not try and be funny – a lesson that has stood me in good stead ever since. The comedy in the show derived from the fact that Rosa believed everything that was happening, even to the point of believing that placing a mincing machine on her husband's head was actually helping him. If she ever hinted that she was in on the gag, then the whole thing just didn't work, and once I hit on that it all fell into place. It was a fabulous show.

We took it to the Fringe in Edinburgh. The venue was my old college, Moray House, and our local was the Blue Blanket, where I had met Bob for the first time. That pub saw many a sight as we convened for refreshments with the likes of Billy Connolly and Jimmy Nail, and my biggest thrill was getting to meet a long-time idol, the writer Peter McDougall. The show got great reviews and packed houses, and Andy got the Best Actor on the Fringe award, which he richly deserved.

I was also doing a cabaret show at Hill Place under the name Nippy Sweeties with Liz Lochhead and Angie Rew. For those not of the weegie persuasion, a 'nippy sweetie' is slang for a wee whisky chaser. 'A pint of heavy and a nippy sweetie when you've a minute, barman,' was a cry often heard in a Glasgow hostelry. It's also used when referring to women of the hard-nosed variety: 'See her, she's a right nippy sweetie, isn't she?' Meaning she is a woman not to be taken lightly. It seemed a perfect name for us three! The show was called *The Complete Alternative History of the World Part One* and was, as Liz said, 'A feminist show from the "don't kick them too hard in the balls" brigade.' I'd finished my first performance on TV in one of Liz's plays, she'd written a cracking part for me in *Same Difference* for Wildcat and we'd co-written a couple of songs together for the Nippy Sweeties show. It was a funny, moving show with three women: a writer, actor and musician coming together and entertaining a Scots audience. It was a huge hit too – although we were, as ever, largely ignored by the press and the teams up from England, who seemed to come to the Fringe to review acts from their backyard and make stars of them – not many Scots were of interest to them. But, doing more than I should as usual, I would be seen by many tourists running up the Royal Mile from one performance that had ended at 10 p.m. to get to the other theatre for a 10.30 p.m. kick-off. The things you do when you are young and just so bloody chuffed to be asked.

Generally, I was having a ball, and finally feeling like a proper actress. *Trumpets and Raspberries* was such a hit that we were asked to come back to the Fringe the following year. By this time, *Naked Radio* had also become more popular, so Colin Gilbert and the Comedy Unit decided to put a live show on at the Assembly Rooms in Edinburgh. So there I was again, doing a show in one theatre and rushing (though this time with Andy too) to the Assembly Rooms to start a different one. Again, it was a hit and sold out but was largely ignored by the southern press and the companies that decamp to Edinburgh for the summer.

It was standing at the back of the Assembly Rooms watching *Naked Radio Live* that made Colin Gilbert and his team decide to develop it in another way, as unbeknownst to us they had a commission from BBC2 for a new sketch show and they were in Edinburgh searching for new actors, comics and talent to put it together. Watching us do the show, he apparently had a lightbulb moment and thought, 'Why don't we use this team and add to it?' They already had the writers, the set-ups, the actors, and so that's exactly what they did. They had been to see Helen Lederer and John Sparkes do their stand-up on the Fringe and thought that putting us all together would be a good idea – building on what was already popular and bringing in others from the south to satisfy the network. *Naked Video* was born.

CHAPTER 17

TELLY

During my time at Wildcat, I was asked to go up to BBC Scotland in Queen Margaret Drive to meet the head of the Comedy Unit, Colin Gilbert. At that time, he had been producing and directing *A Kick up the '80s* with some great talent such as Tracey Ullman, Miriam Margolyes, Roger Sloman, Ron Bain and the up-and-coming Robbie Coltrane. I'd first seen Robbie in Edinburgh in *The Slab Boys* and thought he was incredible. He was a rising star and there was talk of a TV series of his own, but at this time I thought I was going for an interview for a radio comedy show.

I met this grey-haired, bearded guy, whom I later discovered was only in his 30s, and found him warm and funny. He chatted about what I was doing and said that he'd seen me in the Wildcat show and enjoyed it and they needed a woman for this show who could do different voices, etc. Apparently, when he asked a fellow drama graduate, Ian Aldred (who was a BBC announcer and anchored the show), if he thought that I would be good at doing different accents, he replied, 'Yes, she would be – at different Glasgow accents.' I've never quite forgiven him for that. Actually, although I have a strong Glasgow accent, I do have a good ear for others, especially regional ones.

So we got to the end of the interview and he said, 'Well, everyone is out there and the photographer is outside; I think they're going into the Botanic Gardens to do the pictures.' I just smiled and nodded and was ushered out to meet the other players: Gregor Fisher and Ron Bain (whom I'd never met before), Tony Roper (whom I'd met through the Scottish Youth Theatre at the Traverse) and my old mate

Johnnie Watson. That was it, I was in. I'd got the job and I didn't realise it until I was standing getting my photograph taken. That job started my association with the Comedy Unit and changed my career for ever.

We were to meet the following week for a day's rehearsal and then the show would be recorded live at the Tron Theatre on a Friday lunchtime. The writing was funny, by some great writers like Phil Differ, Bob Black, Niall Clark and Ian Pattison (very few, or no, women of course), and I loved it all. I was the only female performer so was generally the wife, the mother, or the nurse and the men generally got the better characters. Most of the people we parodied from the news and political world were men too, so it was logical that the men got the most parts. But gradually the writers got to know me and started writing more female characters and some specifically for me, which was great. Though occasionally I came a cropper trying to do a decent Mrs Thatcher and also Zola Budd (the famous South African-born long-distance runner), which was a nightmare.

The siting of the Comedy Unit in Glasgow was a great idea and Colin Gilbert saw no reason why, if BBC Bristol was the centre for animal and nature programming, Glasgow couldn't be a centre for comedy. Colin asked me to do a little part in a new sketch show called *Laugh??? I Nearly Paid My Licence Fee* with Robbie Coltrane, though I would only be doing a couple of days' filming for it. At the same time, Tom Kinninmont was producing a series of six new plays called *The End of the Line* and I was asked to audition for a part in one of the plays, called *Sweet Nothings*, by the wonderful writer Liz Lochhead. It was a play about a sit-in in a bra factory (loosely based on the Lee Jeans dispute of the late 1970s when the women occupied the factory for months, and I, as a young politico, did many fund-raisers for them). The lead actress was one of the finest and best-loved actresses in Scotland, the terrific Eileen McCallum. She was supported by a stellar cast of great women: Annie Kristen, Dorothy Paul, Siobhan Redmond (who played her troubled daughter). Jimmy Kennedy played her husband. I got the part of one of the young women in the factory and wife of Freddie Boardley. It was my first play for television and I was completely in awe of the cast and crew. All the actresses knew each other well and I felt very much out of the loop, so I tended to sit on my own. After a couple of days, I ended up in the production bus with the others, waiting to be called for my scene. We started talking about holidays and I told them about my trip to the USA and my arrival at the airport with Matt. They laughed out loud as I told it and at the end Dorothy Paul turned to me and said, 'Come on, you can come up here and sit with the big girls.' I was made up – I had arrived! – and I remained in awe and adoring of Dorothy and those other women for many years.

We started on the filming of the TV series of *Naked Radio* and there were a lot of nerves about this being a network series made in Scotland. We as actors did our best to do every other accent that we could so that we wouldn't be condemned as 'that Jock show'. Actually, all the audience research after the first series showed that the Scots element of the show was its strength: audiences across the UK liked it and it also made it stand out from the others.

I felt at ease in the TV environment, though it was a new style of acting and performance. It was about hitting your mark and getting the shot right (as well as your lines, hopefully). Theatre is much more an actor's medium, whilst TV and film are much more about the technical apparatus and the technique – the technique being that things are smaller and more realistically played generally, even in comedy. No need for the 'projection of the voice' or elaborate gestures, because the screen is so small and there are microphones too, so a lot of the drama school training went out the window. I like both film and TV for different reasons, mainly that in television you get the chance to do it again if it's rubbish, though these days the lack of rehearsal and the speed of filming and budget restrictions don't allow even that. Take 25 is a rare thing and reserved only for the biggest stars and the biggest projects – now it's turn up, lines learnt, no rehearsal and on with filming, which is terrifying. At least in the 1980s there was time to rehearse.

Our routine was very like *Naked Radio* except that we worked five or six days at a time. We would meet and read through all the sketches and scripts – of which there were many – and we would see whether we thought they were funny or not. We had about thirty writers at times including guys (yes, generally guys; I think we had about two women writing in the whole ten years of the show's life) like Harry Enfield, Paul Whitehouse and Nigel Planer, and Scots like Ian Pattison and Bob Black. What was funny was determined by the producer, script editor and ourselves. Now there were three women in the room generally (if the lovely Gillian Ewing was there from the office). What was deemed funny was what the majority decided, and they were all men. Both Helen and I confided to one another that we would only ever send scripts in under another name because the humiliation of the rejection from the powers around that script table would kill us. I only started to write when I left the Comedy Unit, realising that what men and women find funny in the world and what they want to write about and the style they want to write in are quite different. A Victoria Wood sketch, or something from *French and Saunders,* wouldn't have fitted well into the *Naked Video* punchy style, but I learnt a lot and very quickly.

It was far from a glamorous life on location, as the hours were long when filming. I can honestly say that I have never got the gig on the Greek beach being fanned by assistants and getting paid enormous sums. Location for me means a pick-up at 5.30 a.m., a bacon roll and a tea in a paper cup, an hour in make-up and a performance of a sketch in a bad wig, in a field in Ayrshire, waiting for the pishing rain to stop – all for a BBC wage. And if it's bad for the actors, then think of the poor crews who have to be there hours before everyone else to set up sound and light systems, and then have to stay late to 'de-rig' the whole thing too.

Although we did lots of location filming around Glasgow, we also had a live studio element in the shows, and that was strange because you had all the buzz of the theatre and a live audience but had also to pretend in a way that they weren't there – the folks at home on their couches aren't interested in the live audience and they are who really count. Many times, a sketch that went well in the studio wouldn't make it to the screen because it just didn't transfer well. We were also in and out of make-up changing wigs and stuff, as we were doing sketches and had to look different in each one. Luckily, I have one of those faces that changes with different wigs and make-up so sketches were relatively easy to fit into.

But that young BBC team were just great; these were the days when make-up artists were trained in everything from making bald caps to creating spots and bruises. We were lucky in having people like Julie Dorrat (who went on to create the whole *Rab C. Nesbitt* look), Jacqui Mallett and the wonderful Robert McCann. He was so beautiful in all ways, as a man and as a professional. All the girls wanted Robert to do their make-up for a big night out, as he made you look the best you ever could. He was a real artist and it's no surprise that he ended up as Nicole Kidman's personal make-up designer, as well as doing many other Hollywood icons, like Jodie Foster and Tom Cruise.

Initially, though, the sketches were the usual fare for me as an actress. Helen wrote a lot of her own material and she did her character monologues in the wine bar, as well as a few other sketches, so the bulk of the other women's parts – the wife, the mother, the nurse, the girlfriend, the fat bird ('It's not my fault, it's glandular, I've got this gland that makes me a greedy bastard') – fell to me. It meant that I got a lot to do but didn't make me that identifiable. I became 'that woman from *Naked Video*', well until the magic of Ian Pattison came about in the form of two women characters he wrote called 'The Divorced Woman' and 'Woman at Ironing Board or 'Wife of Guy with Bandage'.

Ian has a dark, incisive and at times outrageous take on the world (on several occasions there were lines that had to be cut, which, though funny, were simply not allowed to go out on TV, especially at 9 p.m. in 1985). But his angst and darkness are our gifts, as is his desire to poke and prod at the underbelly of Scotland and beyond. It was just perfect fare for the young and for those tired of the 'up a close in our tenement' type of fare that had been prevalent for too long. He, like Billy Connolly, used it, used the rich language and descriptive cynicism, took it on and moved it forward. Some of my favourite ever lines were written by Ian Pattison:

It's not chocolate that's a substitute for sex. It's sex that's a substitute for chocolate. Have you ever met a man that could measure up to a Curly Wurly?

A fanny bag? A fanny bag? Well, I have had my arse in a sling many a time but I have yet to see the day when I would be carrying my arse around in a special bag!

I've been up that Govan Library, Rab, reading about life, and you see, Rab, what yer great philosophers, yer Nietzsches and yer Schopenhauers are saying is, 'We're all mad bastards.' I've simplified it for you, Rab, but that's the gist of what they say.

Naked Video eventually ran for eight series on BBC2 and we got great viewing figures and a fabulous response, even though we were outside the loop as far as the BBC in London were concerned (mainly because we weren't hanging around the Groucho Club, I think). In ten years, no awards, no nominations even, but I think if we had been made in London we would have been much more visible and had much more of a push from the Beeb itself. Though within 'the business' it has had an effect; it's amazing the amount of young comedy performers who want to talk to me about *Naked Video* and tell me about sketches I barely remember. It was a thrill to go and do an episode of *Little Britain* and have Matt Lucas tell me about running home as a teenager in time to watch it. I'd already worked on another show with David Walliams who told me the same thing; of course, I felt like their mother – well, I was playing Matt's mother in the sketch!

The Comedy Unit then decided that they wanted to do a sitcom and one of our writers on *Naked Video* – the wonderful Bob Black – came up with *City Lights*. This also ran for eight series in Scotland and was a huge hit there but never quite made the transfer to the south. Like other great Scottish comedy programmes and performers, from Rikki Fulton and Jack Milroy to Ford Keirnan and Greg Hemphill today, it seems that the bigger they are in shows in Scotland the more difficult it is to break into the southern market. In my eyes, it doesn't diminish the talent; it's just that what makes them so massive in Scotland is the thing that makes them more inaccessible to a wider British audience, which is a shame for them, but wonderful for us. On the flipside, both *Naked Video* and *Rab C. Nesbitt* managed to grab a wider audience but probably had less of a massive appeal in Scotland alone.

Anyway, Colin Gilbert asked me to read for a small part in *City Lights*. The lead actor was a young man called Gerard Kelly, whom I had never met, but I had admired him from afar when I saw him in the award-winning film *Donal and Sally* – about a love affair between two teenagers with profound special needs. It was brilliant. There had also been a pilot of *City Lights*, which he was great in. It was the beginning of what has become a 20-year relationship of performing together, but it didn't start off that well.

Kelly had been told by some people in the business that I was to be watched and a bit of a nightmare, and I had been told the same about him, so I think we were always a bit wary of each other. Although we got on and had a laugh together, we never really got to know each other that well at the time. The fact that I was only in a few episodes each series didn't help and he was also manically busy for all those years, with lots to learn every week for the recordings. It was a huge job for him and he became a household name in Scotland virtually overnight. *City Lights* was a massive hit. It came right at the best time for Scottish audiences and regularly pulled in over a million viewers. It wasn't cutting-edge TV, or even groundbreaking comedy, but it was groundbreaking culturally in Scotland, because we rarely got to see Scottish contemporary life on our screens. We hadn't had a sitcom for about 20 years, since the glory days of *Para Handy*.

For Scots audiences just to see their country, their surroundings, and hear their own accents was rare, so *City Lights* provided all of that. I am amazed when I watch *Taggart* or any Scottish-produced show that the people I'm with are often fascinated more by trying to find out where they were filming than what's actually going on. 'Is that the People's Palace there?' Or, 'Is that Kelvingrove?' For those reading this who don't live in Scotland, I should explain that much as you might think that in Scotland we have our own channels and therefore can make lots of our own programmes, the reality is totally different. Money is controlled by London and BBC Scotland gets an allocation of funds every year to make some 'opt-out' programmes, meaning that we opt out of the schedule coming from London. But that has to cover regional news, sport, culture, comedy and drama, and there isn't enough cash to do any of that on a big budget, so quality does tend to suffer at times. The money is just spread too thin. Also, we have to take all our national news from London, as it's cheaper to do that, but that then means that Scottish news is treated as regional news and we only get to cover 'Scottish' stories. As a result, we end up with a very narrow view, with stories about 'the last kestrel to be seen in Sauchiehall Street', and nothing about the Black Watch in Iraq (from a Scottish perspective) because we aren't allowed to cover those stories or even send journalists there. Both *Nesbitt* and *Naked Video* were made with money from London, as BBC Scotland could never have afforded to make them; they would have eaten up their whole budget for the year.

Anyway, none of us was prepared for how big *City Lights* became. It was a show that actors and 'the biz' didn't like (though people were always more than happy to take a part in it), but the TV punters adored it. Kelly played Willie Melvin, who was a sort of Billy Liar – a dreamer who lived with his mum, had good-for-nothing pals (in the form of Andy Gray's aptly named Chancer) and a girlfriend, played by Elaine Collins. Willie was forced to go back to night school in an attempt to better himself and that's where he met me. I played Irene, a great funny character – a new-age, desperate kind of girl with poor dress sense and a slightly pathetic need to please who had a mad crush on Willie. She also had a catchphrase that haunts me to this day: 'pure dead brilliant'. This had actually emerged as a phrase in *Naked Radio* in a sketch that Bob Black had written. The use of the word 'pure' is so Glaswegian, and kids at the time were always saying things like, 'I was pure on the bus,' or, 'I was pure walking down the road, right?'

I had been doing a show with Wildcat in St Margaret Mary's High School in Castlemilk and a few wee lassies who had been in and out the hall during the show to have a fly fag came up to say hello at the end of the production. One said, 'Haw, yer show was pure brilliant, so it was,' which made me laugh, and on the way home that night in the van we were all doing, 'Look at that pure lovely car, that's pure great!' When Bob Black wrote a phrase in a sketch, 'That's dead brilliant,' I asked if I could put 'pure' in front of it. They agreed and I did and it got a huge laugh. So Bob decided to put it into my character in *City Lights*. Little did we know that it would end up on the side of buses in Glasgow – brilliant at first but a nightmare when every arse on the planet thought it would be great fun to shout it at me in any situation. A natural response, of course, as folk just thought they were being funny, but after the 50th time having 'Pure dead brilliant!' shouted at you on any given day out shopping, or just eating out, it tends to wear a bit thin.

I did get a great laugh in B&Q one day when I was in with my daughter Katie and was loaded down with shopping, and the inevitable wee guy in a tartan bunnet spots me. He must have thought, 'Oh, there's that wumman from the telly, Ah'll just wander up nonchalantly (cos I don't want her to think that I'm impressed by all that actor pish). Ah'll let her know that I can be as funny as her.' So he duly sidled up, didn't introduce himself, just poked me in the side and did a wee dance-shuffle thing and said, 'Aye, dead pure magic, eh?' I couldn't be arsed putting him right and telling him that if he was going to do my catchphrase he could at least get it right. I just looked at him, smiled and walked away – leaving him thinking I was an uppity cow, which is what people seem to think if you respond with anything less than a laugh, a joke, and 'thanks for noticing me'.

It became a bit of a goldfish bowl in Glasgow at that time, and much as I was enjoying the fame thing and getting noticed, it was very weird too. How Gerard Kelly coped I have no idea . . . he couldn't walk down Argyle Street without being mobbed. And that's the thing about fame. It can bring many positive things and as an actor it's nice to have people come up and be nice to you. The other side is that you walk out your front door and you have to be 'on' in a way. And in Glasgow there are always those kind individuals who cross the street to tell you how shite they think you are too. You can never get above yourself in this town. But you can't blame the public for noticing you when you are on their screens at least three months of the year – I was doing *Naked Video* and *City Lights* by this time and they were both very popular. I loved going to London to get a bit of anonymity and see pals, but actually I was walking along Oxford Street one day when a guy shouted at the top of his voice as I passed, 'Haw! Pure dead brilliant, ya bastard!'

I think he was from Surrey.

CHAPTER 18

REAL LIFE

B ob and I, at the beginning of my showbiz career, had initially been having a kind of long-distance relationship. Bob was very disillusioned by both teaching and politics in Edinburgh and wanted to do something more creative. In many ways, I hoped that my moving away and having a different career would help me end the relationship with him, because I was tired of the lack of commitment and all the confusion, and I wanted to get on with my own life and maybe even meet someone else. But much as I tried I couldn't – there were other lovely men (and some not so lovely) who showed an interest, but Bob had a habit of coming back into my life just when I was about to forget about the whole bloody thing.

The truth is that I had loved him from that first night I met him and was in love with him from then on; he was always 'the one' for me, nauseating as it sounds. He was and is my grand passion, though that doesn't stop me wanting to chuck him out the window sometimes, and occasionally I have tried to do that. However, it didn't mean that I was prepared to put up with the way things had been. After many months of travelling between cities (he was still in Edinburgh) and many break-ups, we decided to give it another go. He asked if I wanted to get married and, though flattered, I thought better of it. I just thought he was trying to play the ace up his sleeve before he really meant it – it just didn't feel right. But we decided to try living together and he moved into my wee flat in Scotstoun.

After a few months, we decided that maybe we should buy somewhere bigger together and Bob had a hankering to go back to the East End of Glasgow, where he had been brought up. It was an area that still had many ghosts for him. Both Bob's parents had died very early in his life (his dad, Tommy Morton, when he was 12 and his mum, Annie, when he was 18). They themselves were only in their early 50s and the family of seven kids was divided up among the relatives (well, the younger ones were). It was a tragedy played out too many times amongst too many poor families across the west of Scotland.

At the age of 19, he was alone and living in a flat, with his parents dead and his family split up. When I think of what he and his brothers and sisters achieved from such a background, filled with poverty and hardship, I am overcome with complete admiration and respect for the great job his mother did rearing seven kids virtually on her own. It shows what a single parent can do, though the cost to her own health was massive. She would be so proud of what her family has become, and the tragedy of her never knowing stays with us all. Her oldest son Frank (whom she lived to see married) did a degree in languages at Glasgow University; Michael is a journalist and TV producer; Paul is a priest; Gerry (who did a spell in Barlinnie Prison when he was young) eventually helped bring up the younger kids and went off to start a successful life in Canada; Bob did a degree in economics; and his sisters Bernie and Ann went on to successful careers as a nurse and a chef respectively, as well as becoming wives and mothers. Between us we have produced 13 grandchildren – none of whom Annie lived to see, sadly. Bob left Glasgow as quickly as he could after her death, getting a place at Edinburgh University, needing, I think, to forget the sadness and the life he'd left behind in Glasgow. He stayed in Edinburgh for 11 years and only really started to come back when I was living there. I didn't meet any of his family for two years.

So Bob's desire to be back in Glasgow and to be back in the East End was a sign that he was ready to start facing his past and maybe to build a new life. I started to understand that his unwillingness to commit and settle down (and not just with me but with any of the other women throughout his active love life) was actually about those formative years and the trauma of what he and his family had been through. The decision to buy a flat and put down roots was momentous for him.

The East End was an area I knew because of my old boyfriend Jeff, and it was much easier for me to get out to Lanarkshire to my parents and sisters, so I was quite happy to go there too. Dennistoun was an area I had always liked. It was a mixture of lovely Victorian and Georgian tenements with some really bad housing too on the south of Duke Street, and thus had a great deal of poverty. It still retained a real sense of its working-class roots and I loved that Dennistoun had a great sense of itself. Unlike the area now, which is quite trendy and rebuilt, it didn't have an organic café within 20 miles. Coia's Café, serving egg and chips, was as exotic as it got – though Coia's thrives to this day, all trendy with great food, and the newer locals love it. Back then, it was still easy to buy a good-sized flat there, and at an affordable price. The West End and even the South Side of Glasgow were too expensive for us, as an actor and a supply teacher didn't earn a lot.

We found our flat in Golfhill Drive. It was a four-bedroom, high ceilinged, top-floor flat that had been used as bedsits, so was in a bit of a state. It was cold, with no central heating or double glazing, so there was a fight every morning to see whose turn it was to get up and switch the fire on before we would dare get out of bed. But the house had loads of space and brilliant cupboards, incredible walk-in wardrobes, a huge kitchen and a bathroom with an old Victorian bath too. So we set about painting, decorating and putting a new kitchen in (thank God for MFI) with the help of my dad's building skills, or actually his foreman skills, as he was definitely the boss. Uncle Fred (Dad's youngest brother) was christened by my brother-in-law Jimmy and forever known to us as 'The Legend' for his ability to be the quietest person you've ever met and then at the slightest touch of drink turn into a singing, fighting man with a tendency to go AWOL for days at a time. But he was a fantastic worker and they helped us buy the kitchen and hump it up four flights of stairs. Bob was allowed to be the general labourer and I was allowed to be the caterer – and food (fried egg and bacon sandwiches) had to be ready on request. 'And none of your fancy tea either' would come the cry from my dad. (I'd made the mistake of giving them Earl Grey one day and you'd have thought I'd given them poison.) On another day, I made the mistake of buying a selection of bread rolls from the local baker's and they had poppy seeds and bits of oats and cereal on them. They tended to just wash their hands and sit where they were working. Fred had been sawing all morning, so there was sawdust and wood shavings all over the floor. I duly gave them their 'real' tea (Typhoo) and their egg and bacon rolls. After a few seconds, I saw Fred trying to wipe all the seeds off the top of the rolls. I said, 'Do you not like seeds and grains, Uncle Fred? They're good for you, you know.' He looked a bit bewildered and then looked closely at the roll he was holding and said, 'Aw, I thought they were bits of the sawdust off the floor!' I got a look from Dad that just said, 'Our Elaine and her fancy ideas.' They never got anything but plain white rolls after that.

There was slight disapproval from certain sections of the family about us cohabiting (it was only 1985), but Dad just never mentioned that his daughter was living in sin, and my mum was so into getting on with her own life and hacked off with marriage that there was no real pressure there. She felt that it was right to see if a couple got on with each other before making the lifetime commitment.

Bob and I still had a lot of growing up to do and we had many a fight and a walkout (mainly by yours truly) and a subsequent reunion. I was still working hard and taking any job that came along and found myself doing the Christmas show *Merlin* at the Lyceum in Edinburgh. Unlike the pantos I'd done in other theatres, this was a Christmas story, i.e. no laughs or slapstick allowed. The reasoning behind this seemed to be that middle-class children are too sophisticated to laugh and have fun, unless it's fun we adults approve of. Actually, I am all for Christmas shows that combine styles of theatre to entertain kids. One of the problems with the big commercial pantos doing the rounds at the time was that they didn't tell enough of the story and the kids got bored and lost the plot during the routines that the showbiz comics did for 20 minutes. The Christmas shows were an attempt to do more for kids, and rightly so, but their lack of humour drove me mad.

I was incredibly bored, even in rehearsals, and when the King (played by the lovely Bob Carr) had a line, 'Who are you?' I did the old Scottish panto response, 'Fine, thanks, hoo's yersel?' (This won't mean much to non-Scots but all the Jocks reading this will be rolling in the aisles, I promise.) I was told by Ian Wooldridge the director (even though he'd laughed out loud) that it wasn't appropriate, to which

I replied, 'Why? Do people not laugh in Edinburgh?' Having lived there for years, I knew that they did indeed love a laugh, but sadly we weren't allowed to do the gag. The whole thing felt very po-faced and up itself in my opinion but I'm sure the kids of Merchiston and Barnton loved it (kids from Pilton and Craigmillar would have been bored out their skulls, as they know very quickly when they're being patronised). I was playing Mrs Eeery Cheery ('Oh yes I was,' – we weren't allowed to do that either) and a couple of other parts. I was a bit concerned that all the women in the show were bad or harridans (the Witch, the Queen, and even my nice lady turned out to be evil) except the virginal Gwen (played by Gerda Stevenson). All the men were good, funny or heroes, of course. I didn't enjoy it.

I was travelling by train back to Glasgow every night to a house that was still a building site (we'd discovered dry rot and could actually see through to the flat below for about a week while the floor was lifted) and I was doing two and three shows a day at times. I was knackered and of course got the flu like the rest of the cast, but we soldiered on. We had one day off for Christmas Day but we had to be back for three shows on Boxing Day. I had started to feel ill about three days before Christmas and noticed that I only felt OK when I was lying in the bath. I had a sort of dragging pain in my pelvis and then discovered a lump in my 'nether regions' while in the bath. I thought it would just go away but the more I worked and the more tired I became the bigger it got. I told some of the girls and they of course said that I should go and see about it. But when? It was Christmas Eve and I was in agony and only laughed once, when my fellow 'thesp' and pal in the show, Billy McElhaney, asked if I 'still had that boil on my arse'. To which I replied, yes I f****** did!

It was going to be Bob's and my first Christmas on our own, due to the fact that I was knackered and had three shows on Boxing Day and had to get through to Edinburgh. I woke on Christmas morning in a bit of pain, had a bath and felt a bit better. We did all the present stuff and watched a bit of TV but it just got worse and worse. I had another bath and we sat down for dinner and the brave face I'd been putting on it (though I think Bob would beg to differ with that and tell you that I was a moaning git) collapsed into floods of tears. I couldn't eat and told him I was in agony and he took charge (he's great in a crisis) and said, 'Right, we'll never get a doctor so we'll go to the Royal Infirmary A&E.' He had a few more mouthfuls of turkey as we tried to call a cab (we didn't have a car at that time) but it was useless so we decided to try and walk and get one in Alexandra Parade en route to the hospital.

I was having difficulty staying upright, as I was only getting relief from the pain when I was bent over, but we made it down the four flights of stairs and out into the streets, which were deserted. It was 6 p.m. on Christmas Day, dark, misty and there was not a cab in sight. We walked to the hospital – which was about a mile away – and all the way I was in absolute agony. We were seen after about an hour and I was told that I had Bartholin's syndrome, which is an infection (quite common, though I'd never heard of it) of the glands at the mouth of the vagina. Lovely. 'Can I have the antibiotics now?' It was not to be, as even worse news came. They told me that it was too advanced and that I would have to have an operation the following morning to remove it. 'But I'm an actor,' I cried. 'I have three shows to do tomorrow.'

'I doubt that,' said the doctor, and I dissolved into tears. They sent us home. I was to return the next morning at 8.30 a.m. and eat nothing. Merry bloody Christmas, eh? After a succession of calls to others when we got home to find out the director's home number, I called Ian to tell him the news (writing this, I realise that all this was the pre-mobile era and how different it all was trying to get in touch with people then). He later told me that he'd never sobered up so quickly in his life. He got in touch with the understudy (believe it or not, it was the first time I'd ever had an understudy in four years) and I headed off to bed. I was in such pain I didn't give a toss any more.

I got to hospital the next morning, was put in a 'gynie' ward and had to wait till the end of surgery because my syndrome was highly infectious and once they had operated on me they had to scrub the walls of the theatre and it couldn't be used for at least 12 hours. The staff were fantastic and quite fascinated that I was an actress (I don't think they'd encountered many in the East End), but I was more an object of curiosity than anything else – this was before any fame, so they weren't star-struck by any means. I was given my pre-med, which was fabulous; suddenly I felt no pain, had no worries and felt totally safe and secure as I was wheeled down a corridor by a porter who told me, 'Don't worry if your teeth are oot, hen, Ah've seen it all before and a lot worse tae!' I still had the plate at the time and had been mortified to find out that I had to remove it before the operation.

I came around later that day to the sound of a woman shouting into the payphone at her bed, 'Aye, Magrit, that's it done noo, they've taken the hale lot away and left me wi' nuthin.' I later discovered that she was describing her hysterectomy – or 'hysterical rectum', as she referred to it! I ended up sharing a day room with this woman and a few others, and they were the basis for every Glasgow woman character I have ever done. They were funny, cheeky, lippy, bolshie: 'Ah just tellt that doactor, yer no' putting that up there and if you try it, you'll be getting it first! Ah did.' The operation stories were wonderful, full of exaggeration – 'They gie'd me 16 pints of blood, Magrit . . . oh aye, they hid tae or Ah was a goner' – and we all sat there rapt. The black humour, so common in dark situations, was amazing and actually gave us all a sort of a strength. Fear seems to be dissipated by a good laugh, and illness is also a great leveller – no point in any airs or graces when you all have something wrong with you that needs fixing. These women were great and I have to say that the nurses especially were angels.

One awful night, the husband of the woman in the bed opposite me came in pissed and started shouting. All the nurses had been particularly kind and attentive to this wee woman and I figured that she was very ill. Her children had visited and I knew that things were serious. Her man was obviously distraught and in classic west of Scotland style could only show what he was feeling when he was drunk and angry. He stood at the bottom of her bed shouting, 'You don't gettit . . . yer no' gettin' home . . . ye've got fuckin' cancer . . . d'ye hear me? Yer fuckin' dyin', right?' It was horrific to witness and I've never forgotten it. The poor woman was left crying as the nurses and porters had to eventually remove him. She died a few days later.

I was there for five days and got back onstage to do three shows on New Year's Eve. I had never, and have never (touch wood), been off sick in any run of a play before or since, and have always felt that the only reason for not going on would be if I were hospitalised or sat in a traffic jam for six hours and it was physically impossible to get there. A sore throat isn't an excuse. The show has to go on, dahlings! But meeting those women and those workers had a huge effect on me. I just loved their take on life and their strength in facing everything thrown their way. They were funny and dignified, and that was when the seeds of Mary Nesbitt were sown.

I used lots of their energy in the next show I did with Wildcat, about the Health Service, *Bedpan Alley*; as I told my tales in rehearsals the Two Daves set about coming up with a 'lippy wumman' patient who knew every medical procedure on the planet intimately, or so she made out. It worked brilliantly within the show, because most of the audience knew, or were related to, a woman very much like her. I certainly could think of a few.

Our flat became a sort of actors' boarding house for friends up from London who were willing to venture out of the West End. When my friend Elaine Collins came up from London to do *City Lights*, she came to us and stayed for six months, on and off, which was great. Her then new partner, Peter Capaldi, was a regular guest and it was the start of a friendship and bond that lasted for many years.

People were always dropping by and staying with us, and we rented rooms out to students we had both known when they first arrived in Glasgow. I had always wanted to have a house like that – to be open and friendly – and in the main we enjoyed it.

Bob had given up teaching and was working with Wildcat as a development officer (which gave him a great grounding in and knowledge of small-scale touring in the theatre, which would prove invaluable when we later established our company together). He set up and ran the Mayfest Club, and did many other freelance jobs, but he was still a bit lost about where he was going and what he wanted in life. I dare say it was hard for him, as he was living with someone (namely me) who had no doubt that what she was doing was absolutely right for her and was becoming more successful at it. Financially, I'd started to earn a lot more too and that was difficult for him to accept at times.

Mum had finished her Highers, learnt to drive, trained as a nursery nurse at Motherwell College and was enjoying being an independent woman. After some years in nurseries around Lanarkshire, she was working in a school in charge of a few children with spina bifida, a

Betty (Gran), Aunt Magda and Aunt Margaret in Girvan, 1951.

Stella's class, *c.*1945. This was sent to me by one of her ex-classmates after she died and I treasure it. She is third from the right, second row.

Uncle Andy, Dad, Aunt Frances and Mum in 1954.

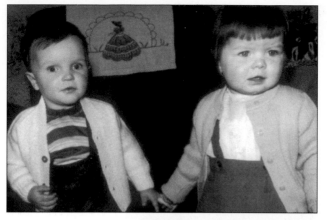

'C'mere, son, I'll show you.' Cousin John and me in 1960.

'Can I eat this?' On the beach at Bridlington with Aunt Frances, John and a very glam Mum, *c*.1960.

Does she really have to stay? Louise and me, *c*.1961.

Hey, check the Farrah Fawcett flicks! What was I thinking? Graduation, June 1978. Nessie (Gwen's mum), me, Gwen and Mum (Stella). Our mothers' daughters.

Wedded bliss! Dave Anderson, Bob, me, Mum and Dave MacLennan, 1 July 1988.

The beautiful Kate, and me trying to look like a mum.

Mother and daughter, 1992.

Jimmy Smith and his 'dolls': Louise, me and Diane in 1998.

My man, Bob, where he is happiest. His only comment about this photo was: 'I've caught better fish than that.' Once a fisherman . . .

Naked Radio rehearsal shot in 1984, with Dave McNiven (musical director), Ron Bain, me, Andy Gray and Tony Roper.

The *City Lights* cast in 1987: Iain McColl, Andy Gray, Gerard Kelly, Dave Anderson, Jonathan Watson (aka Graeme Souness!), Jan Wilson, Elaine Collins and me. How young were we? (© BBC *Scotland*)

The burds! Honest, I was only 28! First-ever publicity shot for *The Steamie* in 1987. The cast was Katy Murphy, Ida Schuster, me and tenement goddess Dorothy Paul.

How earnest was I? Politics is a serious business.

Performing *Shirley* changed my life.

The Uglies: with the wonderful Babs Rafferty in 1996.

Showbiz *c.*1996.
Don'tcha' just love it?

Will you marry me? I'm sure that's
what he was asking me at the time.
Ewan McGregor and me at a charity
showing of one of his films, 1998.

He's an arse! Andy
Gray and me at the
photo shoot for
Little Voice in 2008.

Merry bloody Christmas!
For better or for worse . . .
together again! October 2008.
(© The Comedy Unit)

Here come the girls: Pat,
Siân, me, Julia, Lynda and
Gaynor . . . and no, it
wasn't an extra big copy of
The People's Friend, thank
you! (© John Swannell)

We've been together now for
40 years . . . well, 30, actually!
No' bad for two old duffers.
(© Upfront Photography)

job she loved, although it was very hard (both physically and mentally) on her and left her exhausted. She decided that she wanted a change and went into house sales. She started with Broseley Homes and they soon discovered that Stella's gift of the gab (or the fact that she had 'been vaccinated with a gramophone needle', as her father was often heard to remark) proved a winner in a sales team. She was dedicated, hard-working and enthusiastic, and it gave her a new lease of life. She was subsequently poached by Miller Homes and she sold most of the flats in the old Hamilton College site, which led to her making many friends (among them Helen Smith) there and also getting to be on first-name terms with half of Lanarkshire.

Finally, the cracks in my parents' marriage became bigger and bigger, and my mother decided she had to leave. She had nowhere to go and Bob said quite calmly that she should stay with us for a bit, as our flat was big enough. It was, and is, typical of him to go immediately to try to help, and I know that not many men would have offered to have their mother-in-law to stay for months. Maybe because his own mother had died when he was so young, he had more of an idea of the importance of a mother and realised that in many ways we were lucky to still have parents to care about.

However, this wasn't exactly what I had imagined when I'd wanted the 'open house' feel for our home and the thought of my mum coming to live with us was not an easy one for me. I was back into the role of caring for her and her living just a bit too close again. I think I went a bit loopy with it all and felt a bit lost, but the good girl in me who dearly loved her mother could not turn her away. I was desperately trying to come to terms with everything going on in my life and to work out who I was myself and not doing too great. The fame stuff, the relationship stuff, the break-up of my parents' marriage, it was all pushing me under, and I decided to seek counselling. It was a great help for me and I would recommend it to anyone wanting to learn and grow.

I went in feeling confused, weird and a failure on many levels. I started with that time-honoured phrase, 'I don't really know why I'm here, I'm not mad or anything,' and proceeded to bubble for the next hour in a clear demonstration of not coping. Counselling proved a great tool for me and has done so over many years. I have had years without it, but when I have struggled in bad and awful times, I have had no hesitation in trying to sort it out by finding a caring place for me to talk through what is wrong. It provides a place for me that is safe, where I don't burden or bore to death my friends and family with my angst. I like the fact that I can go in, hand over the cash and say, 'Right, listen to this for an hour.' No guilt.

In a late-night conversation with Gregor Fisher over a few drinks, I admitted to him (shamefully, of course) that I had sought counselling. He was a good listener, and wise too, but made me laugh when he come out with, 'Aw, it's a lot of pish. Life's hard. We've all got to climb up the mountain of life and get on with the good and the bad . . . there are no free rides to the top of the mountain . . . no easy route.' I replied, 'Well, that's a fair point, but anyone who thinks that counselling means that someone else does the work for you is an idiot. You still have to climb the mountain, but if you don't know what equipment to take with you, how to get to first base, put up your tent or even put the crampons on, then you've had it . . . counselling helps provide you with those tools.' More than anything I simply wanted Stella to be safe and happy.

So, in 1987, she duly came to live with us and it was actually fine, though it had a terrible effect on my relationship with Dad. At times I felt it pushed me into taking sides, which I didn't want to do, but I couldn't see my mother on the street either. Dad was in shock for the first few months – almost in a bit of a denial – probably relieved that all the fighting was over and then having to deal with the realisation of what had happened. It was not an amicable split and I don't think they ever had a civil conversation again. They exchanged hellos and said 'Merry Christmas', but that was about it, and that wasn't easy to be in the middle of for any of us.

The split had a profound effect on all of the daughters. Louise and Diane will have their own feelings about it and it would be wrong for me to try and speak for them. I can only speak for myself, but I felt confirmed in the knowledge that marriage was pointless and that relationships would never work out, which left me with a lot of baggage to deal with, and poor Bob on the receiving end of my confusion too. My sister Louise had been through her own traumas in relationships and wasn't living at home, so was a bit more understanding and removed, while Di was still at home and I think felt very sorry for Dad and his situation. It wasn't an easy time for any one of us.

In the middle of all this, plus TV and climbing up the fame ladder, came a very special play: *The Steamie*, written by Tony Roper. Tony handed me the script to read one morning in rehearsals. He'd talked about it to me over a cup of tea one day and asked me to read it. This is always tricky for anyone, but when a pal asks you to do it you have to. It is very difficult, to be honest, so you tend to avoid it to save the friendship, in case you hate it. So I took it home and put off reading it for a few days, and then I decided that I had to bite the bullet. I went to bed with the script and a cup of tea and read it in one sitting – and I loved it.

Now, don't get me wrong, I didn't think it was the hit of the century, or even the hit it would become, but I did think it was both funny and poignant and had great roles for women (unusual at the best of times). I thought it would be a great show for Wildcat and that with songs it would work really well. I had a really good gut feeling about it. That feeling has been something I have relied on for these past 30 years, and I am rarely wrong. I get it when I think something won't work, as well – pure instinct, obviously, but I rely on it. There were things that I thought needed help in the play; I felt that it veered a bit too much towards the sentimental. I thought that songs by Dave Anderson would let the play comment on itself and give another dimension to it.

I was relieved to be able to tell Tony that I liked it and asked if I could take it to Wildcat. He agreed about the songs too and said that he was just happy for any theatre company to see what they thought of it, because every other theatre in Scotland had turned it down, even Borderline, who had commissioned it in the first place. It was felt that nothing much happened in it; to a certain extent they were right, but that was its beauty. Here was a simple play about four women doing their washing in a public wash house (or 'steamie') on New Year's Eve (Hogmanay). Throughout the play, the women talk about their lives in a really moving and funny way. The casting and the performances were of course key to getting this to work, as well as the right director.

For some reason, Tony wanted me to play Dolly, a 60-year-old wee round 'bauchle' of a wumman, with tackity boots, broken veins and a stickie-oot arse. I didn't think I should play her, believing that I should have played Magrit, the tenement goddess with a hard life, a caustic wit and a broken heart. But I eventually went along with his view, as I just wanted to be part of it.

We were lucky in getting Alex Norton to come on board as the director, and after a lot of auditions we got the wonderful Dorothy Paul to play Magrit, Katy Murphy to play Doreen, Scottish theatre stalwart Ida Schuster as Mrs Culfeathers, myself as Dolly, and comedian and actor Ray Jeffries as Andy. Rehearsals were the usual mix of terror, laughs, worry, fear and frantic learning of lines. But I still had a good feeling about it. We opened at the Jordanhill Theatre and the response was phenomenal. We had a total hit on our hands and this was just the start. I had never been involved in a show that had such immediate impact. None of us had known that the show was going to have this reaction and it felt terrific to be part of something that touched the lives of its audience so much.

The trade union NALGO (National Association of Local Government Officers) had sponsored our three-week run during the Mayfest Glasgow festival, which meant that tickets were really cheap, and it also meant that we got to play all the poorest areas around the city. I had done a lot of these areas with Wildcat before but never in a show where the audience were actually queuing before we arrived. We got standing ovations in Barlanark and Easterhouse, had kids sitting eating chips in the front row in Castlemilk, standing room only in Drumchapel, and reviews and reactions to die for. Everywhere we toured sold out and the response was the same. The tour was extended and a commercial tour was seen as a must for the following year. Tony asked Bob to set up the tour, as he knew that Bob had some experience with our small-scale touring company RPM, and he set about doing that. Unfortunately for Bob, he had to do it while Katie was in a wee rocking chair in the office, because we'd gone and got ourselves married and had a baby between the first and second tours. It was a great experience and one that I am very proud to have been a part of, bringing this play to life and performing it on the stages of Scotland.

Bob and I had made it through many of our own traumas. After a particularly bad split in 1987, when I went off to work in Amsterdam with Wildcat and then with Tony Roper in *Betty and Boaby's Macbeth* at Dundee Rep, we thought it was all finally over. I have to thank Tony for his patience with me then. I don't think he'd bargained for a tour with a heartbroken co-star, but he was so kind and patient with me and gave me lots of great advice too. Bob and I were both really upset, as you can imagine, and as usual with men (or maybe it's just Bob) he realised what he was about to lose just at the last minute. He turned up one night in Dundee and, as ever, my heart lifted and that was it – just in the nick of time.

We got back together and six weeks later I discovered I was pregnant. We were thrilled, shocked, stunned and at the same time decided we wanted to get married, so we arranged our wedding at Glasgow University for 1 July 1988. Dave Anderson played the piano for me and I came down the aisle to 'Ain't Nobody's Business If I Do'. Liz Lochhead wrote us an epithalamium (which was apparently what the Poet Laureate used to be commanded to write on the marriage of royalty), and Dave Anderson and Tony Roper read for us. We were married by the Reverend Hugh Ormiston – a very handsome minister who had all the women of a certain age swooning. We met him during the Miners' Strike when he was the chaplain to the NUM (National Union of Mineworkers): a truly Marxist minister – our kind of guy.

Our big regret was that Bob's parents weren't alive to be there and that his brother Paul, who was a priest by then, wouldn't come to the service because it wasn't Catholic. We weren't religious at all and felt it would be hypocritical to have a huge religious service, and Hugh was wonderful in what he did. Paul did come to the meal and because I love him dearly he was forgiven, but it was another sad episode in the ongoing religious divide. It was also Dad's 60th birthday and all my aunts and uncles were there, along with members of Bob's family that I'd only ever heard about. My friend Gwen was my bridesmaid and Peter Capaldi was our best man.

In all, we had about 500 folk attend, from all the *Naked Video* team, like Andy Gray, Johnnie Watson, Helen Lederer and co., to Kirsty Wark, Andy Cameron, John McGrath, Peter Mullan, Phyllis Logan,

Katy Murphy, Dorothy Paul, Charlie Sim, Paul Young, and a roomful of our old teaching comrades. Then there were my politico friends, musicians from the bands I'd been in and my greatest friends, like Anne Lamond, Pam Wardell and Chris Henderson, as well as people that we'd met while pished in the Tron Bar and invited to come along. We actually have some photos from our wedding where I have no idea who is in them – I'm sure some folk just wandered in off the street. It was a real event, a great day and a great night. Looking out from the top table as the bride, 11 weeks pregnant and making my bridal speech (well, you knew I would have something to say, didn't you?), I was so moved at all the faces from different parts of our lives that had made the effort to turn up. It was wonderful.

So there we were, in the space of a year, married, with our own flat, expecting a baby, with my mum living with us too. How did that happen? Our lives were about to change again, though, with the arrival of the firstborn: the wonder that was, and is, Katie. We didn't know what had bloody hit us.

CHAPTER 19

A WORKING MOTHER

I worked all the way through my pregnancy. I was writing a weekly column for the *Evening Times* in Glasgow as well as filming, and fortunately my role in *City Lights* could accommodate my pregnancy. She was a hippy type who wore floaty outfits, and far from a glamourpuss – those glamour roles never came my way. I was filming *Naked Video* when I fell pregnant and much as there was lots of joy and happiness from the cast and crew, most were men with wives at home who looked after the kids, so after the initial congrats I was just expected to carry on. I expected myself to as well.

Most of my peers were men and the women who were pals had no kids either, so I was the first in my group to go on and have a baby. This was also in the days when women thought that we could do everything and have it all – high-flying career, kids, home – and that we could do it without any cost to ourselves, our kids or our relationship. Our grannies shook their heads, watching women swap one job as a housewife for three jobs and wondering why we would want our lives to be that way. So I carried on, believing all the press about women having kids no bother and being back at work in a couple of weeks, with a flat tummy and plenty of sleep. The reality was pretty different. I was sick as a dog, throwing up before having to rush back in the studio and do a monologue.

The character in *Naked Video* of Rab C. Nesbitt (yes, he had a name by this time, his grandfather having been Rab A. Nesbitt and his father Rab B. Nesbitt) had become more and more popular. Gregor and I had actually done a couple of sketches together as husband and wife (she'd become Mary as opposed to 'Woman at Ironing Board'), one in a furniture shop and the other in a psychiatrist's office. A favourite line in that sketch was Nesbitt's response to the diagnosis that he was a psychopath. Both he and Mary start cheering and dancing in celebration, explaining that being told that news is a bad thing for some but, 'Up our street, it's like a knighthood, pal!'

There were rumours that a full-length pilot episode of *Rab* was being commissioned and we all loved the idea but generally weren't sure if it would sustain a whole episode. The plan was to film it in early November as a New Year's special if it all worked out. We were also going to do a Christmas special for *City Lights* so when I found out I was pregnant and had got past the first three months I went in and had a chat with the producers about my dates and to see whether I would be fit enough to do the shows. My official date was 26 December but with a first baby, the doctors told me, it could be four weeks either way. That was fine for the *Nesbitt* dates in November. The *City Lights* date weren't set yet, but it was decided to get my scenes done as early as possible during the filming part and to avoid the studio recordings, which would be in December.

All went according to plan (though I was still sick as a dog). Bob and I had a beautiful honeymoon in the States, visiting my old friends from Edinburgh days: Jennifer and Mark in Brooklyn, New York, and Roxanne, who was by now living in North Carolina, in Charlotte and Lake Norman (though being 14 weeks pregnant, in the middle of a lake, in a steel boat, in a lightning storm is not something I would want to repeat). We had a wonderful time there. But this was Ronald Reagan's '80s in the good ole South, so I don't think we met a black person (apart from those sweeping and cleaning in public places) in an area with a huge black population. There were a lot of 'good ole boys' too, mainly of Scots origin, I hasten to add.

We headed back up to see Lynn Bains and her wonderful mum Sydney in Westchester, New York State. Overall, it was a great trip. In New York, I had my first visit to Joe Allen's restaurant (driven there in Lynn's father Ed's stretch limo) and then went to see *Steel Magnolias* off Broadway.

We got back to Glasgow and set about getting the house ready for the new arrival. Around four months into the pregnancy, I had to have the blood test to determine whether anything was wrong with the baby (I was too young for amniocentesis). I understand why people want these tests and why the medical profession uses them, but they set parents a terrible dilemma and decisions are allowed to be made that generations before had no say in. It's a terrible position to be in. My mother recounted being in labour in Bellshill Maternity Ward with my sister Diane. In the next cubicle to her a woman was crying, having just given her Down's syndrome baby away for adoption. She heard her say, 'Why me?' As my mother lay there feeling so sad for this woman, her thought was, 'Well, why not me?' That's always stuck with me. It is, I suppose, a natural human trait to want bad things to happen to others and not ourselves, but in reality it's just a selfish thought and a misunderstanding of the random nature of life.

There is no rhyme or reason for certain tragedies befalling us or others – much as I have a certain belief in karma and people getting what they deserve at times. Bad things happen to us all and there is no way to control it, but it does seem that the more we try to make things fit and to control life, the worse life is. When tragedy and death turn up at your door, there is no use bolting it shut, as it'll just come in the window when you aren't looking. But all of that set us into a more serious mood about what was ahead. What if something was wrong? I remember, as I waited for the results, going into the office in the flat and saying to Bob, 'If something is wrong with this baby, I can't get rid of it. This is our baby and if something isn't right, it'll still be our baby.' Fortunately, the test came back with minimal risk and there was no need for any more.

We finally got central heating and double glazing in our freezing flat. My mum was living with us by this time and had bought us our new carpets for the hall. And we got the baby room together too. It was all very exciting playing at houses and expecting this perfect little sleeping baby to arrive and complete the calm, warm life I imagined! One big disappointment was that due to my youth (I was only 29) and my pregnancy, I had to turn down the role of Dolly in the TV version of *The Steamie*. Its success had guaranteed that STV would film it and put it out at New Year, a perfect time for it.

Hal Duncan, the veteran TV director, was going to direct it and was insistent that I should do it, but I said I thought that I would look too young for the screen. He said we could do great make-up, so I asked for a test. The experienced make-up artist Anne Hamilton was called in and we duly did the screen test. She did a great job and I looked convincing, until I was under the lights and saying the lines – where I just looked like a young actress with lots of make-up on. We were all disappointed but I realised that when it was to be shot I was going to be seven months pregnant and for sixty-year-old Dolly that might be a bit of a stretch.

I said that the only person who should play it was Eileen McCallum, and she duly did and gave a great performance. It was a huge hit and has become a permanent fixture in Scottish TV history. It won a Scottish BAFTA for Tony Roper and for Eileen as best actress (well deserved, for that and many of her other roles), and worse, it got the Roses for the week's best telly (as opposed to the Rasps for the worst) in the *Sunday Mail*. It was hard for me to take as the actress who had created the role, but if I was to lose out, it couldn't have been to anyone better than Eileen. As ever, she was gracious in her victory and mentioned me in her acceptance speech, so I forgave her!

Also, if I had done *The Steamie*, I'd have missed out on the first episode of filming *Rab C. Nesbitt* and I have always tried to play the long game with my career. No overnight success for me – I wanted a long, fruitful and fulfilling career. Good job, really, as overnight success has taken about 30 years to come my way! I filmed 'Rab C. Nesbitt's Seasonal Greet' at around seven and a half months pregnant. My imminent delivery was actually written into the script and Mary was obviously with child. The weird thing is that no one has ever written to ask us what happened to the baby Mary was carrying!

In the middle of this, Kirsty Anderson, daughter of our good friends Dave and Tina, died suddenly. She had returned from the wonderful wedding of Dave MacLennan and Juliet Cadzow on the Isle of Luing. (Their relationship had started at our wedding in July and everyone was delighted to hear that they had totally fallen for each other and were getting married.) Kirsty had been a flower girl. Kirsty had been around my life since I first joined Wildcat and was a beautiful, shining light of a girl. She had many health problems, which she faced up to amazingly and triumphed over. She was a bit of a wee miracle. She was now at high school and doing well. There would always be a worry because of her disabilities, but she was thriving. The worst of ironies is that what killed her had nothing to do with her own problems but seemed to be a virus that could have killed any of us if it had got into the system. The shock was appalling and the grief and turmoil that Dave, Tina and young Davey experienced was something that human beings should never have to suffer. I was eight months pregnant at the funeral, feeling awful that I was about to give birth when Kirsty had been taken away so cruelly. It was one of the worst days I have ever spent.

Nesbitt was shot and in the can and all that was left was the *City Lights Christmas Special*. I had given them my dates and they had said they would get all my material done in the filming in November. The story was a sort of *It's a Wonderful Life*, with Willie Melvin ready to end his life for various reasons. As he is about to jump off the bridge into the River Clyde, an angel appears to make him reconsider. The Comedy Unit was cock-a-hoop when they learned that Billy Connolly had agreed to come and play the angel, and rightly so, I may add! The schedule was redone to work around his dates and somewhere in there I think they forgot I was pregnant (easily done, when you have a huge star to accommodate). I got the filming dates through and realised that I was in only a couple of location scenes and that all my big scenes were in the studio on 14 December, in front of the live audience. It slightly panicked me because I knew that my date for delivery was really close to that, and I said so. I was assured that it would be fine but I got very jumpy about it.

There is a tendency for things to be heightened and become very stressful in theatre and television, and realising that what we are all doing is trying to entertain people and make them laugh gets forgotten at times. Nobody dies, generally (we are not performing intricate brain surgery), but for some individuals there is a need to make themselves believe that it is life-or-death stuff. I gave a good performance and contributed well to the show but never felt a valued part of it.

One awful day, I turned up on location having learnt the wrong scene (I read the wrong day on the schedule) and was mortified when I realised that I had three very funny scenes to learn in ten minutes! I was shaking, with the looks of disapproval very obvious, as if I were confirming the suspicion that I was an unprofessional amateur. As

I started the scene (and of course fluffed my lines due to nerves), I looked up to see the writer Bob Black behind the camera. Well, that was even worse. I wanted to die then and there as I fluffed my lines again, and again and again – six times in all! Eventually I got it right, left the set and promptly threw up. It was awful, but I have never read a schedule wrong again!

Now, I am not blameless in all this. Though I want to do things right, I can also be opinionated, emotional, wear my heart on my sleeve (and I don't suffer fools gladly), but I am a woman in basically a man's world. As a result, I have always thought I didn't fit, especially when I was a younger woman in my 20s and 30s. But I don't want this to become a 'poor me' version of my life – we are all victims of circumstance and cruelty at times, but I have had many more choices than so many other people. I am far from being the permanent victim in life. We all have to grow up, get over wrongs and slights, and get on with it – life is too precious to waste.

For many men (and women) I have worked with, or been friendly with, that struggle in me proved too much and I have lost or damaged many relationships, which I regret. I was young and naive to a certain extent. I think that possibly my saving grace is an ability to reflect on and apologise for selfish, thoughtless behaviour. I am no heroine, but my first move is generally to try to be better and to care, even if I get it wrong. If it's rejected, then there is nothing I can do. I am forgiving of other people getting things wrong and I am certainly someone who gives others a lot of rope, but I have to say that when I turn away, I turn away and there is rarely a way back. I'm with Bette Midler on this: I hold a grudge!

I am older now and, at 50, I know I am not as quick to judge, though I still sort out whether someone is an arse or not very quickly and I am sadly rarely wrong! But I will always go the extra mile to try and see another's point of view and understand all their fears and insecurities. I have found over the years that all bad behaviour comes from fear. It doesn't excuse the bad behaviour or the terrible way that people can behave, but it does explain a lot. My worst fault, as friends, family (and enemies) will tell you, is that I am late, pathologically late, as Dave MacLennan once described me. I am generally not as much as an hour late, or even half an hour, but if you say meet at 2 p.m., I will be there at 2.10 p.m. I always seem to find something else to do just before I have to leave, even when I know I could do it later. I also leave myself the minimum time to get somewhere, as the hopeless optimist in me always thinks that I will make it, even if it's across London. Other friends give two hours for a journey that should take an hour; I give fifty minutes. My sisters tell me my hair appointments are fifteen minutes before their real time in an effort to get me there.

Over the years, I have pissed off production folk in the Comedy Unit by coming in five or ten minutes late on too many occasions. I am never intentionally late, though. Alex Norton told me that being consistently late generally means that deep down you don't want to be there, and maybe that's true. I certainly wasn't enjoying my time at work at this point and wanted to be elsewhere, thinking about baby clothes! Generally, however, even when I was late, everyone was still having their coffee, though I totally understand why it was annoying and always did genuinely feel bad about it. I would then make an effort to be on time as much as possible, but of course I would fall off the wagon a week later. It became almost folklore that I was always late, so even when I was on time people thought I was late.

The worst incident for me came when I was bawled out in front of the rest of the cast of *City Lights* (who were all sitting chatting and drinking coffee) for being late. I was eight and a half months pregnant and seven minutes late (I looked at the clock as I was being humiliated). Now, it may have been the straw that broke the camel's back, but I was utterly mortified as the entire cast and crew stood staring in disbelief at what was happening. I think all the years of dislike and frustration about me came out at that point, and I was left feeling lost and, for once, speechless. I have never, ever been so close to turning around and saying, 'Shove your f****** job up your f****** arse!' and walking out the door. In many ways, I still wish that I had.

I had to get on with the rehearsals, though, and I pulled myself together with a few kind words from Andy Gray and Johnnie Watson. I got home in a complete state. Bob was absolutely furious. He had suffered more than most with my lateness and would always be the first to establish my guilt and then tell me I was a prat for always being bloody late and give me a lecture about getting my act together. However, having seen me over years of my life in various states of upset through work and the way I was treated, he felt that the nature of the whole thing was about something else and, given my present pregnant state, he was ready for punching someone. He saw how miserable and scared I was and knew that the pressure of doing this job was having a pretty bad effect on my pregnancy.

From then on, I was in rehearsals on time every day. What was wonderful was that it did garner me sympathy (not easy in a room full of competitive actors), and even better were the days when one of the main actors was too pissed to get in on time and a member of the crew had to be sent round to their house to bang on their door and get them out of bed and into work! And another cast member went off to do a voiceover job he'd been told he couldn't do and then got stuck on a train from Edinburgh, holding rehearsals up for two hours.

The jokes about my impending delivery kept coming: 'You'd better not drop that wean before the studio next week.' And the advice: 'If you have it this weekend, you can be out in time for the studio.' I was in a complete state and actually begged Valerie Hood – my wonderful obstetrician – to induce me so that I could get into the studio to record the show. She refused, thankfully. On Saturday, 10 December, after the rehearsal run-through, I started to feel unwell and in a bit of pain. I called the hospital and they told me to hang on, as it didn't sound as if I was in labour. I did but by the time it got to about 8 p.m. I knew things were happening and we made our way to the Southern General.

Although we lived in the East End, I opted to go there because my Uncle Jim was head of obstetrics and a wonderful doctor. He advised me on who to go to and also on how to deal with my local GP surgery in Townhead, who'd told me I had to go to Rottenrow at the Royal Infirmary or nothing. The East End of Glasgow at this time was an area with many problems – beginning with poverty – and it felt to me that the people (particularly the women) were still treated like poor little uneducated urchins. I complained about this doctor and then fortunately got a really good female GP, who had no problem with advice or choice of hospital.

Anyway, off we trotted to the Southern (we had a car by this time), they decided to keep me in and I was taken to a labour suite.

CHAPTER 20

A NEW LIFE

It was a long night, of which I remember little. It's a series of flashbacks: being put in a wheelchair, undressed and put in a bed; countless examinations; Bob popping in and out for a cigarette (he smoked then); calls to the family; cubes of ice to suck on; kind midwives reassuring me; visits by doctors; the arrival of the anaesthetist as the labour progressed (thank God).

Fortunately, I never felt scared and I remained calm at all times. I genuinely felt in safe hands and was really glad of these more experienced and wiser heads around me. I didn't have a 'birth plan' and the best advice had come to me from Gregor Fisher's beautiful wife Vicky Burton, who said, 'Elaine, don't get caught up in it all. It's not a competition. As long as you and the baby are fine and well, then that's what matters.' My Uncle Jim was of the same way of thinking and that must have led to a less panicky approach from me. I didn't want to control what I couldn't and so gave myself over to it. Maybe I was in a dream state, but I felt fine and relieved to finally be at the stage of delivery (and it meant I could get to the studio to work on the Wednesday night; I was still worried about getting it wrong and being a 'bad girl' for mucking up the schedule).

My mother's words by way of preparation for childbirth were: 'It's the hardest day's work you will ever do in your life!' Well, thanks, Mum, but I have to say that I have had many a hard day in my life at rehearsals but I have never needed two epidurals to get me through it! Due to the joys of said epidurals, I never got to the stage where I was standing up in the stirrups shouting that my husband was not actually my husband and that his parentage was in doubt. I am of the 'don't suffer pain if you don't have to' school and have never once thought that the dentist shouldn't give me an injection and ought to just pull the tooth out instead, in case the drugs would harm me in the future. No, no, get rid of the pain first, please. I was glad to find out, however, that the epidurals became much 'lighter' in later years. When I had Hannah, there was much more movement and feeling, but still no pain – brilliant.

The labour went on through a change of shift and thanks to the dedication of Sister Young (who opted to stay with me even though her shift was finished), another epidural and finally episiotomy and forceps, Katie arrived! At 6.05 p.m. on Sunday, 11 December, Katherine Ann Morton was born. She was put on my tummy and into my arms and the full force of this little person looked into my eyes and into my soul. In that second, I realised that I hadn't been handed a baby, I'd been handed a wee person. I looked at her and said, 'Oh hello!' and was quite surprised that she didn't actually reply with anything more than a slightly curious look. She still looks at me that way. It was the best day of my life.

My body then went into a sort of shock and I threw up immediately and then enjoyed the best cup of tea and slice of toast that I have ever tasted before or since. Mum got into the labour room and was so overjoyed that she threw her arms around me and gave me a kiss. I think it's the only time she felt able to do that. She openly showed such emotion and love because, I think, she truly knew what I'd been through and understood what it meant. I felt that I had finally done something right and felt my mum's love and approval. My sister-in-law Alice told me that when she delivered her first son, Gregory, she was so out of it with exhaustion that she must have nodded off for five minutes and awoke to see her husband Frank draining his cup and munching a bit of toast. He turned to her and said, 'God, Alice, I needed that, I'm knackered.' Sadly, I can't print her reply to him.

Bob was bewildered and ecstatic. I later found out that he'd told my mum that her daughter (me) had been a complete star, though he never told me, of course. He went home on cloud nine and called everyone to let them know that his daughter was now on the planet and wrote a poem, for the first time in his life, about it. He confided to me later that it took days for him to believe this wonderful thing had happened to him because nothing that good had ever happened in his life before. I woke at five in the morning after everyone had left and gazed at this wee miracle lying in her crib. I whispered, 'I've got a daughter . . . I've got a daughter.' Nothing has ever bettered that feeling except the arrival of her sister, Hannah.

Having a baby strips you of all physical dignity. At the point of delivery, I felt more like an animal than a person, and that continued for days afterwards, as every nurse and doctor in the place seemed to be prodding, pushing or taking blood. I have never had my nether regions checked out so much and all bashfulness disappeared, to the point where I would simply roll over and show my arse to anyone who was coming into my room; pity the poor domestic who was just coming in to give me a cuppa. I would personally like to thank the woman who came up with the idea of the ice packs from the fridge that can be put in your pants to reduce swelling and the person who hit on the fact that a hairdryer is a great way to cool down and dry your stitches – aaaah, genius!

On the Tuesday night, the director Ron Bain and his wife Jen arrived in my room in the hospital with a beautiful gift . . . and the shooting script. It was bizarre. But against the wishes of my doctor and accompanied by Bob, two midwives and a rubber ring, I was in the BBC studio on Wednesday – just two days after giving birth – recording the Christmas episode, having left Katie in the hospital with expressed breast milk.

I arrived at the studio, where the crew all cheered and handed me a beautiful card and gifts for Katie; it was so emotional. Andy Gray and Johnnie had brought gifts too. As the wrap party was about to start at the end of the recording, one of the production team shouted, 'Are you not comin', Elaine?' I could hardly walk and was just so tired and mumbled, 'No, I'm going back to the Southern General.'

'What for?' he said.

'I had a baby on Sunday.'

'Oh right, so you did . . . well, see ya,' and off he went to the party. I watch that episode and can still see my eyes cross as I sit down such was the pain and discomfort from the stitches – I still don't know how I did it. But as all new parents soon realise, the birth is only the beginning of a long stretch of worry, fear, joy, love, responsibility and trepidation that never actually ends. As one friend remarked to me, 'The last thing you need at the end of a long, knackering pregnancy and delivery is a bloody baby.'

Back in the ward, I felt I could now get on with things and set about becoming a mum. I was amazed, thrilled and terrified by this beautiful wee thing that depended on my every move for her survival. I stayed the full five days after delivery (fortunately, I had a doctor who believed in some recovery and rest for mothers). Bob turned up and we nervously thanked everyone and headed for the car. We had a carrycot and I sat in the back with it for the journey home. It was terrifying; I refused to let us go on the motorway and made Bob drive at about 20 miles an hour for fear of any bumps in the road that could harm her. I was a nervous wreck. We got home into the flat exhausted. Katie immediately started crying for a nappy change or a feed or something and we went into panic mode trying to find a nappy among the many bags, flowers, gifts and assorted stuff that we were carrying. We stood looking at each other thinking, 'What the hell have we done?' I went to have a bath once we got her to sleep and Bob came in to find me in tears, wailing, 'I can't do this. I don't know how to be a mum.' He was calm and rubbed my back, telling me that of course I could and that I would be great at it and not to worry, I was just exhausted. He got me into bed for an hour's sleep before the feeding, changing and nursing started all over again. He later told me he was shitting himself too, but his ability to stay calm was just what I needed.

I was also breastfeeding, which I was finding very hard. I wanted to scream at all those women who'd lied to me. All those pictures of beatific, smiling mums and babies telling me how easy it all was. They lied about the pain of childbirth (if I just breathed properly, it would be fine – NOT!) and how easy it was to breastfeed. They don't mention the cracked nipples, the pain, the fear about giving the baby enough food, that you feel your tits are going to explode at any minute, the milking machines to express milk, the walking through a shop and hearing any baby cry and your breasts filling up immediately. I breastfed and am glad I did, but I just wish I'd known the truth and not constantly felt that I was doing it wrong. I wasn't helped by the army of other women telling me to just bottle-feed, because that's what they did. I think a lot of that was to assuage their guilt at having not breastfed themselves.

I had friends and relatives who told me to put whisky in the bottle to make her sleep or jam on the teat for sweetness, and I even saw one woman with a baby whose bottle had a digestive biscuit in the milk to make it sleep. One woman in our ward was actually giving her few-days-old baby bits of mince and potatoes off her plate, which was only discovered when doctors became concerned that the baby was losing weight. So there is a lot of conflicting information out there for a stressed-out new mum.

Breastfeeding is hard, and can be traumatic, especially if it doesn't work. Many new mums try and go through hell because of all the pressure to do the best for your baby by breastfeeding and feel like complete failures when it doesn't work out. I was in tears many times. But equally I have never understood why some women don't even try.

Anyway, I persevered. We lived in a top-floor flat, and as it was the dead of winter, cheerful strolls around the park weren't that easy. I did have a walk down to Duke Street, and I came back with over £17 in change. There is a tradition in Glasgow where people 'hansel' the pram of a new baby. With me being on TV, the birth had been in the newspapers, so people were coming up all the time to see Katie and put money in the pram. One wee old lady, who was obviously a pensioner, came up and put £1 in the pram. I tried to stop her and said, 'Oh no, that's too much.' She grabbed my hand and said, 'Naw, hen, don't worry, that'll bring me more luck than it brings you.' As I pushed the pram up the hill towards our flat, I noticed Bob and my sister Di standing at the window doubled up laughing. Apparently the sight of me pushing a pram was just too hysterical for words.

Mum was wonderful. I don't think I'd ever needed her or thanked her so much in my life. Finally she became my mum and acted like one because she knew much more than me and took to having a granddaughter around brilliantly. She told me that Katie had given her a reason for living and doted on her. Thankfully she had her own, flat by now, realising that Bob and I needed to be on our own, but she still had her room (there's always been a 'gran's room' in all of our homes since, and even though she is gone, her room in our house is still called 'gran's room'). She calmed me down, coped brilliantly and taught me so much. When she stayed with us and heard me getting up to feed Katie (while Bob snored beside me – I think he secretly loved the fact that I breastfed, as it let him off the hook), she would come in and take her, change her and let me go back to sleep. It was magic.

I became a bit of a 'Stepford Wife'. I had a desperate need to control things, mainly because the world terrified me. I didn't know how women coped and if I saw a woman with four kids, I felt like running up to her and shaking her hand and saying, 'Well done. How the bloody hell do you do it? I've got one and I'm going mental.' If I was out of my pyjamas by 4 p.m., I felt as if I'd run a marathon.

I coped with that first Christmas: about 14 people in our place for drinks, as well as Elaine and Peter staying with us too. They'd had a nightmare journey north as the Lockerbie disaster happened on the night they were coming up. That was a night of disbelief and of thanking our lucky stars.

I had a real need and determination to appear fine and in control. Maybe I was freaked out because I'd always had control over my life before and now this wee thing was exerting total control over me. I grieved a bit for the fact that my old life with Bob had gone. No more me, Bob and Charlie the cat. No more long lie-ins, staying in bed with the Sunday papers, or taking off for a run to Callander at a moment's notice. Going anywhere now involved a major logistical plan of action.

Bob went back to teaching, as I couldn't work and received zero maternity pay from the BBC because I was a part-time contract worker, so we needed the cash. I desperately tried to be the perfect wife and mother. My house was spotless (cleaner than she'd ever seen it, according to my mother). I was so paranoid about germs that I was cleaning all my worktops with Milton sterilising fluid. Bob would come in from work to find me dressed, Katie sleeping in her cot, dinner in the oven and me sitting with a book. He didn't know who I was and if he'd looked closely, he'd have seen that I was twitching slightly.

I started filming again for *Naked Video* when Katie was 11 weeks old. I was exhausted and so was Bob. He was teaching all day and then had to drive to our filming location so that I could give Katie her night feed. Mum was helping out but we talked it over and decided that Bob should be with Katie too. I was earning much more than he was, he wasn't enjoying teaching and it would let him start work on other freelance projects too. As I briefly mentioned in the preceding chapter, Tony Roper wanted to do a commercial tour of the hit show *The Steamie* and had asked Bob to handle it all. So as I filmed, he was booking a tour and making deals, with Katie in her wee rocking chair at his feet. He was, and is, brilliant with babies, maybe because he had to deal with so many of his wee brothers and sisters. I don't think we drew breath for a year.

I was back filming *Naked Video*, but the real story was the success that the one-off episode of *Rab C. Nesbitt* had enjoyed, and not just in Scotland, but across the UK. A series was commissioned, which was to be shot that autumn. So life was secure financially for a bit and we got to enjoy being a family, or adjust to it anyway.

I was asked to go on a trip to Nicaragua with Scottish Medical Aid, which we'd done a lot of benefits and fund-raising for. Our old political comrade and pal from Edinburgh, Des Tierney, was head of the organisation and put together a team to go: Charles Gray (then head of Strathclyde Regional Council and a powerful figure in the Scottish Labour Party at the time), John Rafferty (who ran the Volunteer Centre in Glasgow), Bishop Joe Devine from Motherwell (so yes, the actress and the bishop did go to Nicaragua) and head teacher Joan Brear (a political activist and an ex-girlfriend of Bob's too). Bob was actually the first to say that I should go. Katie was only seven months old, but he said that it was an opportunity that I might never get again and that it was only for two weeks. It cost a couple of thousand pounds to go, but we felt that once I had gone I could help inform others as well as raise money when I came back.

As ever, some of the cynics I worked with (whom I have to say I never saw put their hands in their pockets for more than a pint for themselves) started sniping about the cost and would we not be better giving the money to the charity. They soon shut up when they realised we were paying our own way, taking nothing from anyone and that the charity would only benefit in the end. I have always felt that if you do something as a celebrity for a charity, then the only people who should benefit should be the charity itself. I have to say, though, that the attraction for me was that it was the other side of the world. The question I was asking myself was, 'What kind of mother could even think of leaving her baby?', but eventually, after much discussion, I decided that I should go.

It was an amazing and wonderful trip. It was tough going, as we witnessed the widespread hardship and poverty the people endured – even with a caring and benevolent Sandinista government led by Daniel Ortega, who had fought so hard to rid the country of the US-backed regime that had ruled for years. It is always a shock for someone from the West to get a close-up view of a Third World country – everything we take for granted just doesn't exist there. But what does exist is amazing kindness and an ability to see how well and with what great dignity human beings can and do live their lives without all the mod cons. This was a political fight for the soul of Central and South America, and the Left throughout the world were doing all they could to support them. So every liberal in the USA, from Kris Kristofferson (whom I shared a lift with in the only decent hotel in Managua) and other actors and musicians to clergy and politicians, was there too. It was a fight against the might of the US government, who had imposed an embargo that stopped food and goods getting into the country. Nicaragua was in turmoil and struggling to overcome the many social problems it had inherited, and there was a civil war going on. It was dangerous at times, especially when we were in areas controlled by the US-backed Contra rebels.

We flew back via Toronto (as there were no direct flights) and I remember feeling really strange at suddenly being back in Western-style shops. I had just spent two weeks in a country that was chronically poor and predominantly rural, where doctors and teachers were being paid with a sack of rice and beans. I felt real shock at being back among such affluence, and in a matter of hours too. It was the stupid things like being in a department store that had 200 different pairs of tights and stockings on display, and I had just left a country where a single pair of tights was a week's wages.

Over the weeks and months and years after our return, we all did everything we could to send money, fund-raise and support the people of Nicaragua in such difficult times. It was a wonderful experience, but coming back to Glasgow and getting my wee girl back was the best present ever. I still don't know how I managed (or how Bob did) while I was away and she was so young. At times I just hope that she didn't notice, but I think in some profound way she must have and the way she snuggled into me in the car on the way home seemed to say that she'd noticed my absence. I just cried all the way home, full of exhaustion and elation at being back.

But adjusting to this new way of life was knackering. I had had little time to recover from the birth of Katie – as I had worked until the last minute and was back full time when she was only 11 weeks old – and we had a very demanding baby to deal with. Lack of sleep took its toll on both of us and, like most young couples, we took it out on each other (well, who else was there?). We were tired out and fully concentrated on this wee baby that dominated everything, so we gave little time to each other, and as a result we came close to breaking point. I started to sink lower and lower into depression, while of course showing a brave face to the world. I was still writing the weekly column for the *Evening Times* and doing other little jobs, but I felt alone, hopeless and a shit mother into the bargain – always telling myself it couldn't be post-natal depression because Katie was now ten months old.

I went back to see a counsellor I'd seen before Katie was born (in an attempt to help deal with all the fall-out from my parents' marriage) and though it was of some use, it couldn't lift me out of this fog I was in. But eventually the crying, the despair and exhaustion became too much and I went to see my GP. She was brilliant, explained that indeed I did have post-natal depression and put me on a course of antidepressants. I was reluctant but she told me they were not habit forming and to give them a try. So I did. Within a couple of weeks, I felt different, positive, with more energy. After about three months, I simply stopped taking them (having cut down over the weeks before this momentous decision), and I felt better – I finally felt like me again.

CHAPTER 21

NESBITT ... FOR IT IS HE

We finally got the go-ahead for *Nesbitt* and we set about filming the first series. The writing by Ian Pattison was just spot on: dark, tragic, irreverent, clever, near the bone, and above all very funny. His lines are so fantastic for an actor to say. In my opinion, Ian is to TV comedy writing what Jimmy McGovern is to TV drama – he's the real deal.

Any actor will tell you that the hardest part of our job is dealing with bad or not very good writing – as I am sure any writer will tell you that the hardest part of their job is dealing with bad actors who can't say their lines, but it's true. With good or great writing, the actor's job is made so much easier; just put the right stresses and emotion behind it and you're away. An actor has to work very hard to make terrible lines or situations believable, truthful or funny. We struck it very lucky with Ian. That is not to say that every line or episode was perfect (as I'm sure he would be the first to say), but his black-humoured take on life, combined with his intelligence – along with an incisive, humorous analysis from the perspective of those struggling against the odds in Govan – is comedy gold.

I have always thought that the scripts are even funnier than they ever were on the screen, and that is saying something. I can honestly say that I have laughed out loud reading the scripts and have had to get up out of bed (I like reading scripts in bed) as I was laughing so much. Poor Bob would have to endure nights of my saying, 'Oh, listen to this, it's brilliant,' or, 'I can't believe he's saying this, listen.'

The decision to shoot the series almost like a documentary was a great one too. The way that Ian writes and that style of shooting seem to work well together. I don't think we as a cast or production team ever sat down and decided on a style of performing; it just evolved, really. The only person who ever speaks to the camera is Rab and that is a great device. He gets to comment on life and the situations we find ourselves in but the rest of us have to play it for real and ignore the camera. Initially that proved confusing for me but my experience years before playing Rosa in the Dario Fo production stood me in great stead. Again, I realised that if I, or any one of us, even hinted that we thought what was going on was funny, then it would kill it. All of us have to believe in those characters and play it as if it is real.

There is nothing worse than watching actors do 'comedy acting' because they are in a sitcom and think to themselves that they have to put on the funny voice and costume and shout and wink at the audience. In Scotland we call it the 'Haw Maw' syndrome, which is when actors think, 'Oh, I am playing a working-class Glasgow character so I'll put on a cod, broad accent that you would never hear anyone in reality ever use, throw in a swagger and a wink and shout "Haw Maw" and the audience will love it.' Yes, it may work and get a laugh, but in my opinion it's the worst kind of laugh and is even worse (or more exposed) on TV. Find the truth, play the truth and the comedy will always come from there, in my opinion, and that's my approach. So for me Mary is always in a bit of a drama or even a *Play for Today*.

We had the same team as was involved in the pilot, headed up by the *Obersturmführer* that is Herr Colin Gilbert, whom you've heard much of in previous chapters, so we felt in safe hands. He is a very funny man and at his core very kind and compassionate, though years in the 'business of show' have no doubt toughened his hide. If you want good gossip then Colin is the man; the Comedy Unit is where gossip starts at the top and works its way down. He laughs like Muttley from *Wacky Races* and has that public schoolboy irreverence that is so funny. He was brought up in the business, as his mum was an actress and his dad the legend that is Jimmy Gilbert, who produced shows such as *The Likely Lads* and *The Two Ronnies*, so Colin knows a thing or two about egos, insecurity and talent. I think he may have had some idea of what he was letting himself in for with all of us, but who knows. He has a very laid-back approach and a dark wit, so the combination of him, Ian and Gregor was terrific for the programme. But when I thought of them discussing or arguing about things I tended to envisage a cauldron and scenes from *Macbeth*, with some dark arts taking place – thankfully I was never privy to any of that.

Gregor Fisher (aka Rab) is a terrific actor and though I would never call us soulmates, we work well together and have developed a respect for what we each bring to the series. Initially, I don't think I would have been his first choice as Mary; I think he would have preferred someone more experienced and well known, but then you'd have to ask Gregor that. During *Naked Video* I was very intimidated and a bit in awe of him. I think I was a bit too desperate for his approval and that never feels like a good position to be in. He's a very powerful personality as well as a very talented one. To this day I haven't really a clue what he thinks of me. But we act well together, have great laughs together and are professional in our approach to work. He has great instincts and a lot of wisdom as well as a great capacity to laugh. At times he can take himself a bit too seriously (who doesn't?) but when he laughs he lights up the room. If he 'corpses' or cracks up, it can go on for hours and that is just joyous for us all.

Those days on the set when we end up unable to speak for laughing make all the days in the pishing rain and getting up at five in the morning worth it. Trying to say some of Ian's lines with a straight face is very difficult at times. You try saying, 'I'll tell you what, I'm no' half missing a podger,' or, 'I had to smoke like a beagle in a laboratory to get aw they coupons.' Try and keep a straight face when Rab says, 'Oh Mary, Mary, hen, look, I brung ye mussels,' as he proffers a jar of mussels in vinegar for me to enjoy. He and Roper are like two naughty schoolboys when they get together, and they enjoy nothing more than setting each other off. Tony (Jamesie) also has a very acerbic, dark wit, so when we all get together (Mary, Rab, Jamesie and Ella) the scenes can take a while to get through, especially if Jamesie is attempting to heal wounds between us all by quoting lyrics from Sting. That scene from one of the later series (they have all now merged into one for me) where the four of us are sitting round the table while Jamesie says, 'As Sting says, "If you love someone you have to let them go,"' actually had to be re-shot because none of us could get our lines out and if one did, then the other cracked up.

Having Tony Roper on board as Jamesie, as well as that wonderful woman and actress Barbara 'Babs' Rafferty as Ella, has been the icing on the cake for me. With a cast that also included Eric Cullen, Andrew Fairlie, Brian Pettifer and Iain McColl, as well as a great crew who consulted with us all the way through (especially Julie in make-up, who created that fabulous Mary Doll look), it was a great show to work on.

One of my favourite episodes of them all, and it's from the first series, was shot in Fuengirola in Spain. We were all so excited that we were getting to go there to shoot it but then discovered that it was in March and that it would be shot out of sequence, so we couldn't sunbathe or get a tan. We were based in a beautiful place called Mijas just up the hill from Fuengirola and had a great time.

Bob, Mum, my sister Di and Katie came out for the second week of the shoot so the separation wasn't so bad. But in that first week filming before the family arrived, I realised that I'd started to feel happy again. I felt free and happy and not burdened by life. I had hope and I laughed a lot with fellow actors like Louise Beattie and Kate Donnelly, who were there for the shoot too. It turned out to be a seminal episode of the show and went on to win many plaudits and awards.

Ian captured an experience common to so many ordinary working-class punters: the package holiday in Spain (long before the excellent *Benidorm* series). The writing captured the sheer joy of being abroad for the first time (jumping on the beds and enjoying the view from their 15th-floor 'patio'; the desire to fit in with the beach life ending in Jamesie being carried off the beach with sunstroke and unable to move, having refused to wear sunscreen with his thong (long before *Borat*, by the way) in an act of macho Scottish bravado. This would be topped by Ella's wonderful riposte as she makes him scream by dragging her fingers down his skin, 'That'll gie him an idea whit a Caesarean feels like!' The send-up of the beach scene in *From Here to Eternity* with Mary and Jamesie was brilliant, and the whole show just captures the sheer madness that can ensue in the sea, sun and sangria when folks aren't used to it. The episode was completed by a magical final scene – that left most of us in tears – between Nesbitt and his Spanish counterpart, both howling at the moon together. Brilliant.

No one was prepared for the impact it would have. We thought it was good, but it was actually groundbreaking and got massive audiences when it came out. We got calls from people across the business, from Michael Grade to Lenny Henry, telling us how superb it was, and the show just got better and better. It was funny, dark, eccentric, painful, and, best of all, groundbreaking.

We also had to deal with the tragic death of Eric Cullen, who played Burney, which was a shock and a blow to all of us and the series. Both Babs and I were very friendly with Eric, and we were very fond of him too. He was like a wee mischievous brother and at times I did feel like he was my misbehaving son. He made us laugh, was very bright and caring to both of us and very good to Katie, my little girl. He would often just drop in for a cuppa when he was passing our house, or pick me up and drive me to location or the theatre when we were on the tour (I didn't drive at the time). He was very ambitious and making a lot of money from the deserved fame that he got from *Nesbitt*. He was doing pantos and public appearances all over the place and he loved it. He drove his big Mercedes with its personal registration and had bought himself a lovely house. He was like 'show business on wheels' at times, and addicted to the notice and fame to a certain extent.

Onstage he was very funny, though not the most disciplined of actors. If there was a sniff of a laugh, he was off, and bugger everyone else, which got him into trouble with the rest of us a few times. Andrew Fairlie, who played Gash, was a completely different type of actor, but funny too. I think that he had the most difficult job with Eric because most of his scenes were with him, and they did occasionally clash quite royally but would make up easily too. I think they were just so different in every way that it was inevitable.

Eric was controllable on a set while filming, but put him in front of an audience and his addiction to laughter – any laughter – would surface. We had a scene in the stage show where Mary, Gash, Burney and Ella are all standing at a bus stop. Eric had a line that ended with something like, 'Och, my da's talking sh . . .' and it was written like that, 'sh . . .', so that I could come in over the top of it and say, 'SHUTTIT you!' The writer had intended that the word 'shite' would not be said – a much funnier gag if you think he's going to say it then doesn't, eh? Well, not for Eric. Every night he timed the line differently so that he could say 'shite' and get a laugh of his own rather than the combined and better laugh from 'shuttit you'. Eventually I had had enough and he was called to Ms Smith's dressing room, where I asked him what he was doing. He of course pleaded innocence, but I told him in no uncertain terms that if he wanted to do it that way, then he should speak to the writer. I said that he should know that a headless chicken standing on the stage of the King's Glasgow would get a laugh saying 'shite' and that there was no great comic skill involved in getting it. He got the message and timed it better from then on.

On another night he upstaged Gregor in the final scene where Rab comes home to Mary and the family, which was actually quite an emotional and truthful scene. We played it very straight – which obviously bored Eric, because as he lay on the couch in front of us, he started looking around, picking his nose, you name it. The audience obviously noticed it (well, he was only four feet tall and tended to draw the eye anyway) and started to laugh during Gregor's big speech. I couldn't believe what he was doing and I could see the red mist descending over Gregor's face and knew that there was trouble lurking.

At the end of the scene, Rab had to chase Burney off as the music swelled and the revolving set turned. Well, this time the chase was real and many expletives were shouted as we started to move. Unfortunately they both forgot that they were radio-miked and the mikes were still up, so we all stood there waving as the set turned (á la *Sunday Night at the London Palladium*) and all we and the audience could here was, 'C'mere, ya wee bastard, you're supposed to be a bloody professional,' with Eric shouting, 'What? What? I never did anything, honest!'

To this day I don't know the details and in many ways I don't want to know what happened, or what went on in Eric's private life, but when the story broke that he was involved in child abuse or a paedophile ring, I was as shocked as everyone else. I was working in St Andrews and it was my landlady who told me that it was all over the papers. I duly went out and bought a *Daily Record* and there it was on the front page (he'd actually knocked Michael Jackson's abuse story off the front pages in Scotland, which would have pleased Eric in some strange daft way). I called him and found out that Dorothy Paul had very kindly given him space in her home away from the press. He was distraught and in tears. My advice was to get out of Scotland, to lie low, get a pal to drive him to a cottage in the Cotswolds and stay there until he could get legal advice and sort this whole thing out. He didn't go, he stayed and tried to fire-fight it, but the situation just seemed to get worse and worse. He was arrested and charged and had to be dropped from the series, as the case was pending.

More details emerged that seemed to indicate that he was involved in some very dark stuff with some awful, awful people who were eventually imprisoned for child abuse, though Eric never was. In subsequent conversations with him, I never got to the root of what went on but I do believe that Eric suffered a great deal of abuse as a young child (and young man) at the hands of these men and was tied to them through some sort of blackmail that they threatened him with. The more well known he became, the worse it was.

His illness (achondroplasia, which is a genetic bone disorder) meant that Eric had a great deal of pain in his limbs a lot of the time and he took painkillers constantly, which caused a lot of digestive problems. Due to a new baby, I hadn't seen him for a long time and I think Eric felt unsure how to react to his old friends and colleagues. He wanted to keep us all out of it. It's a testament to all of us that not one of us broke the silence and gave any stories to the press. There was much money to be made at the time. We didn't speak to each other about it, we just took a decision not to do it. We didn't know what the truth was, or what went on, and didn't know how to react, though we tried to keep in touch. He was taken into hospital for what was in effect a routine operation and died on the operating table. It was an awful end to a very tragic and terrible situation for Eric and his family.

When the funeral was set we all decided not to go. Again, we didn't speak to each other about it, and I wouldn't have judged anyone else for going but I am glad that we stayed away, not because we didn't care, but because we knew it would give the press the picture they wanted (i.e. the Nesbitts grieving for their son Burney) and I didn't want to be a part of that. I was very sad and upset but not for Burney, for Eric. He and his family had suffered enough from the media and I didn't want to add to their pain and grief.

Through all of that and through other dark times, the show endured and ran for eight series. It wasn't universally loved by the critics and got some appalling reviews from the self-appointed arbiters of taste, and still does to this day. But it has endured and is the only sitcom from Scotland to be featured on the recent programme *Britain's Best Sitcom*, as voted for by television viewers. When it came to an end, I think we were all ready for it to stop – I certainly was. I still loved the writing and the show, but felt that we'd all got a bit tired and all things have their day. We had collectively created something very special and to be proud of, and to my surprise the characters and the show are still held in great affection and regard by so many people.

Initially I think we all wanted to move on and do other things, even if we knew they weren't as good. We went on to do other shows, films, new series and all relatively successfully. Playing Mary may have closed some doors in my face as far as jobs were concerned, but it opened many more and gave me a passport to jobs like *Two Thousand Acres of Sky* that I would probably never have been considered for otherwise.

There were always muted soundings out to see if we wanted to go back and do more shows, but we were all reluctant and I think especially Ian. I had no desire at all to go back and continued to get on and enjoy my own life and career. I was having a great time.

I'd kept in touch with Pattison and was very touched that he took the time and trouble to call after the last series had finished to thank me for what I had contributed to the character and the show, saying that he felt that my contribution had always been underestimated and taken for granted. It was so good to get that sort of acknowledgement – which actually means much more to me in the end than all the fame or money. Knowing that the work I had done was valued was huge for me; it was something I had struggled with through all my years with the Comedy Unit, and I needed that sense of respect and value for the sake of my self-esteem. I ended the call in tears. But it was over.

Ian was a great supporter and when in Glasgow would come along to our shows or my stand-up and allowed me to use some of his great lines too. He told me he had been approached by Colin to do more episodes but was reluctant, as was I.

Then in 2008 I got an email asking me if in principle I would be interested in doing more. I said that I was unsure but could see a possibility of maybe doing a one-off Christmas episode if Ian felt that he wanted to and everyone else did. I still thought it was unlikely that it would happen. We then got news that a script had been commissioned and my heart sank a bit, as I really did wonder if it would work. We've all seen those TV specials of hit shows that just don't work and leave the viewer saying the dreaded, 'It's not as good as it used to be.' Nesbitt had gained a sort of iconic status as a comic creation and that was a worry, as expectations would be very high.

Anyway, the deal went through and when I got the script I realised that Ian had done a fantastic job of keeping to what was great about the show and moving the characters on: Rab now off the drink, a house-husband and 'born again'; Jamesie no longer chasing women half his age but chasing their mothers instead; Mary and Ella running their own cleaning business, House Mice; Gash remarried and living a nice middle-class life as far away from his father as he could get. I also wanted Mary to move on as far as her 'look' was concerned – the look that launched a thousand chips! I didn't want her to look glamorous by any means, but I wanted her to look more current – that is, more dye in her hair, better cut, etc. as well as slightly better clothes. Well, she was a businesswoman now. But that simply meant less BHS and more Primark.

My only problem was that I was doing *Calendar Girls* at the same time and had only two weeks in Scotland when I was available to film. The Comedy Unit did a great job in arranging the shooting schedule while I was in Edinburgh at the King's with the show. I was filming during the day with a car standing by to get me to the theatre by 6.30 p.m., but that meant I tended to be on first thing, so I was like a zombie by the end of the week.

It was very strange being back, and very emotional. Some part of me, until that first day of shooting, didn't really believe that we were doing it. But seeing Gregor, Colin, Graeme in design, 'Gorgeous George' in props and some other very familiar faces in the crew, it felt like I hadn't been away. As soon as I put the wig on, that was it; the voice was back to full pelt as we rehearsed the first scene (going to Gash's house for dinner) and that was that. But emotionally by the end of the day I was exhausted.

Doing the bed scenes with Gregor was hysterical: the sight of him in string vest and hackit pyjama bottoms pleading for a 'cuddle up' is not an easy one to keep a straight face with. I then had to say lines like: 'How can I put this so as not to offend, Rab? Naw wait, I cannae. See if I was on Fanny Island and there was nothing but fannies as far as the eye could see, and I saw a footprint in the sand and found out that it belonged to Rab "Two Cocks" Nesbitt? I wouldnae even take a loan of those two cocks to start a fire. Do I make myself clear, Rab?'

'Crystal, Mary Doll, crystal.'

However, due to my schedule and the need to get me to Edinburgh for the show, we managed to do the scene eventually, but Rab had to have his back to me so I wouldn't laugh. We still took about ten takes. The show aired over the Christmas period to four million viewers and didn't disappoint, by all accounts, so a new series is being written right now as I type.

Who would have thought that what originated from a couple of monologues on a sketch show, this wonderful Chaplinesque character, down on his luck, in bad suit, flapping trainers, string vest and bandage, would still be howling at the moon after all these years? Maybe, just maybe, it's because there are a lot of us still out there with him howling at that same moon.

CHAPTER 22

POLITICS

You will have guessed by now that politics is a big part of my life. However, I am not a showbiz 'luvvie' who has suddenly decided to pick an opinion about politics to get myself into the newspapers. If I weren't an actor, I would most definitely be involved in politics full time, fighting for a cause. Indeed, for many years before even stepping on a stage as an actor this had been my passion, so I guess I feel I have done my time and earned my right as a citizen to express my opinion. I just believe it's a way to make things better for the people who live here – and not because I think it will further my career.

I have always loved politics and political debate. Maybe it's being a Scot but it has always been a huge part of my life; my political beliefs weren't, and aren't, really about ideology but are simply based on a sense of what's fair or just for the society I live in. It has always been in part an emotional response, which still holds true today, and has been reinforced by my years spent campaigning. I love a political argument and would rather argue with a Tory to the right of Attila the Hun (and frequently have) than with someone who has no interest in or is apathetic and cynical about politics. Anyone who moans and complains yet can't be arsed to get out and vote, whatever their excuse, is the worst in my eyes.

I am a strong supporter of independence for Scotland and was heavily involved in the 'Yes, Yes' campaign for a devolved parliament. The vote we wanted was 'Yes' to our own parliament and 'Yes' for it then to have its own tax-raising powers. I had come out publicly to say that if we had a parliament then I would consider standing at some point in the future. It was part of a publicity drive to convince the voters that a new parliament wouldn't just be more jobs for the Labour boys and that every town councillor wouldn't automatically get a seat. There was a lot of cynicism around about who would stand for election and so they asked various people from different professions to say that they would stand: doctors, university professors and actors such as me. It got a lot of coverage, but a few days later Princess Diana died and all campaigning was suspended. Somewhere in that period, it seemed to get into the Scottish psyche that I was standing for the parliament.

To the disbelief of most Scots, we actually did something positive for ourselves: we voted a double 'Yes'. I had been doing a show in Stirling and the BBC sent a car to get me through to Edinburgh. I was interviewed by a lot of TV people on the night but in the run up to the result I just didn't have a clue how it was going to go. The Tories and the Unionists were set against it, seeing it as the slippery slope to independence, and naturally there had been a lot of fierce argument on the campaign trail. I realised that something momentous was happening as I was sitting being interviewed in a hotel overlooking Princes Street. It was the quiet that alerted me. The street was deserted. There were no fireworks, no daft eejits running up and down with the Lion Rampant hanging out their arse. Just peaceful silence. I imagined that all of Scotland was sitting in front of the TV quietly saying, 'Come on, Scotland,' almost afraid to hope for fear of its all being thrown away, as we have done so many times before.

I knew something different was happening, though, when Michael Brunson, from *News at Ten*, turned to me off-air and said, 'You are going to win it.'

'Are we? I'm frightened to hope.'

'Well, all our evidence says that you are going to get it.' I headed for the count and stood with my wonderful pal and great journalist and commentator Ruth Wishart in the Conference Centre in Edinburgh. We held our breath and when the vote came through we just couldn't believe it. We laughed, we cried, we cheered, and Scotland woke up the next morning more surprised than anyone. This would change the way our children thought and dreamed for ever. It would be a long road with many mistakes and cock-ups, but at least they would be our own cock-ups and we wouldn't spend our days blaming the English for everything. That sort of racist nationalism is something I hate. To be pro-Scottish does not mean you are anti-English, or anti-anyone, in fact. It felt, for me, like a big step towards maturity for our country.

So we got our new Scottish Parliament and our newly constructed building. I have to admit that I love it, even though it's in the wrong place (it should have been on the top of Calton Hill, which famously looks down onto the centre of the city). But I love the fact that it's modern design, that it's built on the site of an old brewery (how apt and funny) and that we have even got a special venue outside for people to demonstrate at; it's so Scottish to have a built-in area for a rammy! At the recent 'Homecoming' celebrations this area, complete with its ornamental pools, was apparently full of kids in their pants using it as a paddling pool and play area – fabulous. Well, it was hot. Don't think we'll ever see that at Westminster.

I hated the debacle over the finances and felt that it should never have cost what it did. It's a disgrace, actually. But could I just point out that all the costs were estimated by Westminster, as we hadn't had an election for the Scottish Parliament when it was given the go-ahead. And when it comes to costs, can we please remember that our Scottish collective taxes helped to pay for the Millennium Dome at £750 million, the hellish office block that blights the side of Westminster in the form of Portcullis House, which cost £250 million, and the Jubilee line, which most of us will never use.

My involvement and all the interviews and press caused much confusion for the voters. I got into a taxi one day after the first Scottish elections and the driver was chatty (well, it was in Glasgow, so it goes with the territory). I was going to a lunch with Alan Yentob and the big guns at the BBC. 'Awright, Elaine, so are you busy the noo?'

'Oh, yeah, runnin' about like the proverbial blue-arsed fly,' I replied.

'Oh, you'll be busy through by, eh? How are ye likin' it?'

I just smiled and said, 'Aye, fine,' a bit confused, about what he meant.

He then said, 'Ah voted for you, by the way.'

I said, 'No, I don't think you did.'

'Aye, Ah did. Ah'm out in Coatbridge, that's where you stood, wasn't it?'

I laughed and said, 'I'm sorry but I never stood as a candidate,' and he said, 'Aye, ye did.' This went on for a bit as he explained that he'd voted for Elaine Smith in his area and I assured him that it wasn't me and asked him what party she had been in, and he said Labour. I told him that I was a Scottish Nationalist so it definitely wasn't me, but that I knew there was a Labour MSP called Elaine Smith who was now sitting in the Parliament. He looked stunned and said, 'Well, Ah have to tell you that half of Coatbridge voted thinking it was you.' I have since met my namesake and she is a great woman and a very dedicated and hard-working politician; but I told her she was only there because she had half my votes.

Ten years on, there is more of a sense of self-confidence and less of a feeling that Scots need to move away from our country to fulfil themselves, and I think that can only be a good thing. The diaspora from Scotland is very much like that of the Irish, spreading across the globe, with many leaving to try for a more comfortable life and better careers, and I don't blame anyone for doing that. Scots who leave have many different emotions about their homeland. Some have a huge sentimental pull back to the 'Motherland' so they end up being members of Caledonian societies and are much more patriotic than most of us who still live here. You could see that this summer with the huge celebrations in Edinburgh for the marching of the clans during Homecoming.

Others want to deny they were ever Scots, lose their accents and pretend to be English, American, Canadian, South African or Kiwi – anything but Scottish. Some who have made a good life in London or elsewhere seem to have a sort of love–hate relationship with the country. Maybe it's a sort of guilt at leaving in the first place? It may also be that they no longer feel truly connected to what goes on in Scotland. I know from living in London that you hear little, or nothing, of life or politics in Scotland except through your family and friends. It must be quite alienating to leave and build a life in another country yet still have roots and an affinity with the place you were born and grew up in. I've also noticed that there is a lot of concern when discussions of an independent Scotland arise. They seem to put up more arguments against it than any English person I have ever met. It never surprises me when I hear London-based Scots talk of their opposition to independence. It appears to me at times to come from a place of fear and self-interest – especially if they are successful. Maybe not, though, maybe they just don't like the whole idea, which is the same for many Scots in Scotland, unfortunately.

It is one of the sadder aspects of our cultural scene that it has always been necessary to export our actors and that their creative ambitions can only be met by their leaving to work elsewhere. I believe that independence would help (as we might get more funding for the arts), but actors will always go where the good work is if they have the choice. I have heard successful artists express fears that the London galleries would just ignore them, seeing Scotland as just another country on the northern borders of Europe. I have heard successful Scottish writers – who sell very well in many European countries – express fear that they would be ignored by London publishers. Successful producers of national series for TV or plays in the theatre worry that London would no longer look at their work if we were no longer part of Britain. My argument is that London is always looking for product and good material will always shine through (the recent wonderful production of *Black Watch* by Gregory Burke being a prime example).

Another couple of great Labour supporters who are as Scottish as they come and live in London confided in me that their opposition to independence was mainly due to the fact that they couldn't bear to live in a Tory country and if Scotland and Wales left, they knew that England would vote in a Tory-majority government. When Sir Alex Ferguson was given a Scottish Hall of Fame award in Glasgow, he mentioned that he always feared becoming one of those Scots who lived in England and ended up hated by their countrymen or viewed as having sold out their 'Scottishness'. He felt truly welcomed back and supported by Scotland, which was great. But in my view it seems that you are more likely to receive great honours and awards if you are successful 'outside of Scotland' rather than staying here and working (never be a prophet in your own land). The last few years seem to have made it much more possible to live and work here as well as being successful outside, and yet we have an SNP-led government in power. I said to Sir Alex that Scots only ever turned on their own when it was felt that they forgot their old arse and got a new one. That made him laugh.

Poor Denis Law got a lot of stick for losing his accent, as did Lulu at times, and her becoming more Glaswegian when she returned home seemed curious to me. But for Denis I dare say it helped him be understood by his teammates and with life in Manchester. For Lulu it seems it was a requirement by the BBC, which felt it would help her Saturday night show on TV to reach out to a mass audience. I believe that the more people are exposed to accents the more they get used to and understand them. Unfortunately for Lulu, that enlightened thinking had not reached the corridors of BBC light entertainment in the '70s. We all know that we have to slow down or try to be clearer in the way we speak when we are abroad, but coming back from two weeks in Spain with a Spanish accent is just ridiculous.

The answer for me would be that Scotland should have its own flourishing media and cultural scene, but unfortunately, for now, it just isn't big or wide enough to accommodate actors who need to stretch themselves, and that's a great shame. So if Scots are going to have a career in England, they have to change their accents to get a job. There are very few visible Scotswomen on national TV, apart from Kirsty Wark on *Newsnight*, or Lorraine Kelly on *GMTV*, or Muriel Gray when she was a presenter. Many terrific Scottish actresses have had to drop their accents to get the top roles (unless it happens to be a Scottish part): Hannah Gordon, Siobhan Redmond, Brigit Forsyth, Isla Blair and Phyllis Logan to name a few. I am delighted at the success of John Sessions, Robbie Coltrane, Ewan McGregor, Dougray Scott, Douglas Henshall, and James McAvoy – all proud Scots, I am sure. But apart from their immense natural talent, I feel a degree of their success has come from their ability to lose the Scots accent too.

They are all great actors who I believe would, and will always, find success regardless of their ethnic origins. But the odds are stacked against them and that is frustrating at times. For me, the only way to remedy this is if we run our own broadcasting and media, and properly fund our theatres and galleries, thus giving filmmakers and artists more freedom to work where they want. But that still seems a long way off for now.

CHAPTER 23

THEATRE

My anus tends to clench when I hear an actor luvvie saying, 'I love the theatre, it's my life.' However, for me, I have to agree, and admit that the longer I have been in this business the more I have grown to like live theatre and the response from audiences. I wouldn't say it's my life, but that contact with the audience is just wonderful. We toured the UK for the first time in 1990 with the theatre production of *Rab C. Nesbitt* and it proved to be a fantastic experience. Being away from home was hard, especially being away from Katie, who was two by this time. *Nesbitt* was still very popular across the whole of the country and after the tour we started filming another series. I felt as if I was becoming Mary Nesbitt and that I would never get to do anything else. No one becomes an actor to play one role for ever; one of the reasons I've always avoided soap operas, much as I love them, is because I want variety in the work I do.

During filming, I started to feel really unwell. At first I thought it was just flu, but the pain was terrible, and it turned out to be the dreaded 'Oh, that's a sore thing' shingles. We were all pretty knackered from the tour and I think my immune system just gave up. We'd been on the road for months in cities and towns across the UK, and it had been such a success that we had to extend it by another six weeks. I guess it says a lot for our collective professionalism that we hadn't all tried to murder each other – although we probably came close a few times.

Fourteen weeks in a tour bus is all very rock 'n' roll, but we understood by the end of it why rock stars go mental and wreck hotel rooms. Another city, another hotel, another bedroom: it got to the point I couldn't differentiate between places – Doncaster merged into Leicester into Bristol, and one WHSmith store just looked like another.

Much as I loved *Nesbitt* and the high times and fame therein, there was also a downside from an acting point of view. Increasingly I felt straitjacketed by the role, even if it was a gold-lined straitjacket that brought many benefits. More and more I felt unchallenged and very uncreative. I didn't know what to do.

I was lying in bed, feeling lost and worthless, in lots of pain with sores all up my neck and face, with my doctor telling me that I needed to stop immediately. I never got to go to Blackpool to shoot my scenes because I was lying in my bed in agony. I realised also that I was very depressed and needed a change in my life. The bottom line was that apart from getting well again, I knew deep down that I needed to do something else – I needed to grow. I started to face up to just how depressed and restricted I felt. I hated the fact that I seemed to have no control over what I was doing. Although I may have felt hemmed in, I still didn't want to stop *Nesbitt*, because I loved it, but on its own it simply wasn't enough.

Although there was a great deal of recognition, awards and fame that went with the show, we were all on short-term contracts and never actually knew whether we would even be in the next series – and the show ran for 13 years. The public assumed that we were this happy band of actors on contracts all year round, with a guarantee of work and lots of cash, when in reality we certainly had the fame but few of us had the cash. Don't get me wrong, we weren't poor by any stretch of the imagination, but we weren't paid like the cast of *Friends* either. I was aware that the wrong word, in the wrong place, or a demand for too much money could result in the new series starting with an episode called 'Mary's Funeral'. It could end at any time – but that is the life of a jobbing actor.

So, I had to find a way of keeping going and developing. I had been very lucky up until this point, in that through shows like *City Lights*, *Naked Video* and *Rab C. Nesbitt* – as well as a theatre background with companies like 7:84, Wildcat and Borderline – I had established myself as a comedy presence in Scotland. The material seemed to strike a chord and resonate with the public. Why? I don't know. The essence of everything is timing, as we all know, and the timing of my link with the BBC Comedy Unit in Glasgow was very important. But what made a big audience actually like me? Who knows? If I knew what makes an audience like and relate to one performer and not another, I would be a very rich woman. But whatever it was, or is, I thank my lucky stars for it.

I was only 29 when I started playing Mary Doll and always wanted to do other things. Contrary to popular myth, I also had to find other work, as the money I was earning wasn't enough to keep us going all year; it was only six episodes shot over three months at most, so I had the rest of the year to fill. I wanted to know if I actually had an audience of my own and I wanted there to be productions touring Scotland that women wanted to go and see. Stories for, and about, them.

In theatre, the vast majority of the audience who buy tickets and sit there are women, yet the majority of the things they watch are stories about men, written by men, directed by men, in theatres and TV corporations run by men. I wanted to put on shows that spoke to women like myself, my sisters and my aunties. Over the years I had returned to the theatre to challenge myself. The theatres liked it, too, because a 'name' from telly in the cast helps sell tickets and gets some much-needed publicity, too. So, I went off and did things like *The Steamie* with Wildcat and Tony Roper and *Much Ado about Nothing* at the Lyceum in Edinburgh.

I had always had a bit of a pipe dream of doing something like *Educating Rita* or *Shirley Valentine* in Scotland, setting them with Scots accents and making the characters as real to a big commercial audience as I could. Yes, I could have shown off that I could do a reasonable Liverpudlian accent but I wanted the plays to relate directly to Scottish women's lives (I still have a dream to do *Blood Brothers*, by the way, but time is slipping). We had tried to get the rights for *Shirley Valentine* the year before, after Tony Roper and I went to see a touring production of it in Glasgow. Unfortunately, the rights were already out with another company. Tony wasn't sure whether this was right for me or what direction I should take either, so we didn't follow it through and I put the idea on hold.

But now, feeling ill and lying in my bed, I started to think that a Scots version would actually be a good idea. I had a sort of epiphany about myself and doing something for the Scots female audience, which I felt, and still feel, is poorly served by the programmes of most theatres. I needed a risk and to find out if I had an audience as myself – or would I for ever be Mary Doll Nesbitt? I talked it over with Bob and he decided to call Willy Russell's agent. He walked in from the office ten minutes later and unbelievably we had the rights for a Scottish tour.

A couple of years before we had created our small production company RPM, which meant that we had the means to set the show up and organise all the paraphernalia that one needs to tour a theatre company. Bob had previous experience of putting tours together and we'd put on my first show *Elaine C. Smith . . . Herself,* which had gone really well. We always started in Cumbernauld Theatre (my off-Broadway try-out). I'd got a band together, headed by the wonderful musician Robert Pettigrew, who had created the music and toured with me for *The Steamie.* We rehearsed in his Edinburgh flat, while his lovely wife Annie made cups of tea and their kids, Alice and Henry, ran about. (Henry has gone on to become a terrific actor now himself, and when I saw him in *Black Watch* I was so pleased for him: he was superb. He went on to perform in the West End in a production of *Hamlet* with none other than Jude Law.)

I put together some songs that I loved, from Michael McDonald to Dave Anderson and Bob Dylan, along with some stories and some characters, and hey presto! *Elaine C. Smith . . . Herself* was born. It was very much a 'my dad's got a garage so let's put on a show' sort of approach but everyone got paid well and I loved putting it together. I liked the sense of control over my own creativity and ability to find my own voice. A very pretentious title, I know, but it's what I wanted to do, to come out and show who I really was, what I believed in and thought about the world we live in.

It was also a risk, as there is always the chance that people completely love you in a certain role but can't stand who you really are and either don't turn up or shout 'shuttit' from the back of the stalls. I have loved some actors and then when I have heard their views on certain things I've realised that their politics are pretty right wing and I was put right off them. I'm sure there are a few who've felt that about me, and probably still do, but fortunately they were drowned out by the rest.

The show brought in a varied audience, as there were my TV fans (*Nesbitt*, *City Lights*, *Naked Video*, etc.), political fellow travellers and theatre lovers – a strange and eclectic mix – generally just punters who wanted a good night out with a bit of opinion thrown in. This was summed up in comments overheard by my husband in the men's toilets: 'Aye, she's good, but Christ I wouldnae like to go home to her with an open pay packet!'

But it had worked. The show was a sell-out and was really well received. So we had some experience under our belts, as far as putting a show together went. But doing *Shirley Valentine* was rather different.

Over the next few weeks we set about organising a tour of Scotland and were delighted at the response from theatres. The success of actors on TV does not guarantee a full house, though; in fact, I would argue that shoving someone from a TV show into a live theatre production is no guarantee of success. For me, I think it was a combination of things: the years of touring in good shows with Wildcat and Borderline, and other theatre shows such as *The Steamie*, helped, as I had a separate reputation as a theatre actor that the punters were prepared to pay their hard-earned cash to see live, so theatres were great for me personally.

We had no financial backing and everyone we contacted turned us down, so we took out a loan with our house as guarantee. Looking back on this it was madness, but we were so overcome with the enthusiasm to make it work. It was risky but we knew that we had good guarantees from the theatres that would pay for the sets, the lighting, the director and the costumes and would make sure the crew and everyone else connected to the show were always paid. We knew we might walk away with nothing, but as long as everyone else was paid then we felt it was worth it. We've always worked that way, put the staff first and treated them well – that's why we'll never be millionaires, but at least we can sleep at night.

We called the great man himsel', the wonderful and gorgeous Alex Norton (aka Mr *Taggart* and director of *The Steamie*), and he signed up as the director, and the tour was set for spring 1991. The sense of freedom that I felt was just immense, but the big question for me, and for every punter I have met over the last 30 years – is how would I learn the lines? To learn a whole two-act play, with only me onstage for two and a half hours, was a pretty daunting task. If I am honest with you, it felt like climbing a mountain at the time.

On top of all this, our daughter Katie was developing into a terrible sleeper and would refuse to go to sleep unless we were in the room with her, or were outside on the landing on the rocking chair. It drove Bob and me mad and the boredom was unbelievable. Just when you thought she was asleep and tried to sneak downstairs, a wee voice would meekly say, 'Mummy', and the whole rigmarole started again. I'm sure every parent will smile ruefully reading this. So it was during all this that I started learning my lines on the landing outside my daughter's bedroom.

I was determined to be at least really familiar with the shape of the play and where I was going in the text. I wanted to know the piece backwards, but I didn't want to be 'off the book', as it's called in the profession. It is a question that most people find fascinating, and to tell the truth all actors employ their own special way of achieving this. Some actors turn up on the first day of rehearsals with every line learnt, as it makes them feel secure and in control of the situation – 'if you're on top of your part, then that's all that matters', they think to themselves. The problem I have always found with that approach is that actors usually have a totally fixed idea of their performance, which makes them impervious to directors, their fellow actors, to the play as a whole and, worse, they seem not to give a toss about the most important aspect of theatre: the audience. All they care about is their 'bit' and getting it right. There's nothing organic about it and they end up separate from the team. It's like a good footballer deciding that he or she is going to play the way they want and to hell with the tactics or what the manager says.

I have worked on plays with actors who are 'off the book' on the first day of rehearsals and it's an awful experience. Their performances are generally set and never grow. They never communicate with anyone or care how another's performance will fit with theirs. They take their moves from the director but anything the other actors are doing is of no significance. It is so uncreative, almost stifling. For me it is the ultimate in selfishness. In my view, if they want to be onstage on their own then they should go off and do stand-up or a one-person show.

I would tend to be the opposite and possibly a trifle under-prepared – I like to put the work off until the last minute. I am ashamed to admit it but I have on occasion turned up on the first day of rehearsals having read the script once. I work hard when I'm there, but it does feel like a bit of homework that I've left till the last minute. I have got better as I have got older. I suppose it's partly because I take myself and my job a bit more seriously now. Preparation is everything in the end, as then you can really fly, though as I said, being over-prepared is almost as bad. So there I sat with my script every night for at least an hour or so. By the time we got to rehearsals, I knew the shape and some of the speeches, but I really felt I knew the play and who Shirley was.

We set the play in Bishopbriggs and changed locations to help it relate to the audience we were playing to, and all with Willy Russell's blessing. Alex was wonderful, though the actor in him did get carried away. It wasn't unusual for me to look up and find him a foot away from me, mouthing every word and every line. If he could have got away with it, I think he would have put the frock and the wig on and performed Shirley himself. My trusty philosophical and wise sound man John Harper was back in the game and it was so great to have him on board. One day during rehearsals he walked up to me and said, 'See when you get your BAFTA, Elaine . . .' I laughed and asked him when he thought that would be, and he replied, 'Oh, you'll no' get one fur years. Everybody looks at you and just sees you doing things all the time and takes you for granted, so you'll no' get one till you're about 70. But see when you do and you're hobbling up to the stage, you'll mention this play and what it did.' This was before we even opened at Cumbernauld. It was such a weird thing to say, but I know that he was quietly telling me that this was life-changing and that he felt the production was very good.

We rehearsed in Glasgow for around three and a half weeks and then got to Cumbernauld Theatre to open the show. Cumbernauld is what was called a New Town, built in the '60s and '70s. It was also the setting for the movie *Gregory's Girl*. It was obviously no longer a

New Town and is just called Cumbernauld, funnily enough.

I always liked opening my shows there. The theatre is out in one of the original villages that made up the town and has about a 300-seat capacity, with the stage on the floor and the audience rising up on three sides. It had great audiences, who forgave a lot but who were also discerning, as well as being glad that you'd made the effort to get to Cumbernauld in the first place. It's a great environment to find out what works and what doesn't in a show. You learn a hell of a lot very quickly. But it didn't stop me feeling a creeping terror at the mountain I was about to climb.

The technical rehearsal was a nightmare. Alex had decided that we should have a 20-minute lighting fade to go from a beautiful blue Greek sky to twinkling stars, but getting it right took for ever. He also endeared himself to our wonderful crew by insisting on real sand to create the beach. For me, the sand was lovely, as there was something so luxurious about being able to rub my bare feet in it. For the crew, it was hellish, as we were a touring show, so they had to invest in a giant hoover to get it up, then store the sand for the next show, taking it from theatre to theatre. That's as well as cleaning the stage every night. We got round the logistical nightmare it became by covering the set with a sand-coloured carpet and then putting real sand on top, so the effect was great.

Meanwhile I had dried up and forgotten my lines. Bewilderingly, several times during the technical/dress rehearsal, lines I had been doing no problem before just disappeared from my brain as I realised the enormity of what I was about to do – and I had to fry bloody egg and chips onstage at the same time. I was terrified and the look on Alex's face didn't help either. I was so scared that I had our trusty stage manager, the wonderful Christine Dinwoodie, outside the window on the set with the script. We had planned that if I had a total 'dry' I would walk over to the window and she would whisper the lines to me.

I sat in my dressing room hearing the audience come in (you can hear it all in Cumbernauld, as the dressing rooms are underneath the seats). I was wearing my throat mike when John came in with a worried look on his face. (He told me later that it was because he'd been listening in to test my mike and had heard me talking to myself and got a real fright. He said that there was something in my voice that he'd never heard before and he'd started to doubt if I could carry it off.) Alex Norton then came in with a large dram in his hands, looking stricken. He then proceeded to tell me that as a fellow actor he realised that he couldn't do what I was about to do. I could have punched him . . . Not what I needed to hear at that point.

But something always happens to me at this point – the point when there is no going back, other than to walk out to the audience and say, 'I'm sorry I just can't do this.' Like childbirth, there is a point when there is nothing else for it but to get that baby out! The desire to do it takes over and I am propelled to get it over with. So, I walked onstage, the lights came up, I said the first lines and that was it. I didn't drop a line, I never dried; I just focused on telling Shirley's story to an audience who didn't know the lines, or what should or shouldn't happen, and somewhere I was secure in the knowledge that I could do it. I came offstage to a wonderful reception from the audience and for the first time in my life I knew what it felt like to score a winning goal. I was like Ally McCoist in the wings, shouting with a clenched fist 'Yeeeessssss!' as I ran along to my dressing room.

There I found a half-pished Alex Norton, who'd dropped to his knees with relief, saying, 'How did you do that? Where did that performance come from? It was magic. In fact, I think I've just had a religious experience.' Well, he was half pished! I told him it wasn't religious, it was just his relief that it didn't go belly-up, but it felt wonderful. Alex and I now have a blood tie because of that show; no matter where we are, or what we do in our lives, we will always have *Shirley*. What a night, and what a relief, and that was just the bloody start.

We began the tour and audiences flocked to it (95 per cent women), and the response was amazing. I had dozens of letters from women telling me their life stories, of how the show had touched them and made them feel that they weren't alone with the feelings they had and their need to recapture who they were as young women before kids and marriage. I was really blown away by the amount of women who came backstage too, some of them in tears. Alex Norton and I did joke about how many divorces that show might have been responsible for. What was most amazing was that the hunch I had had about setting the show in Scotland did make it more relevant for them and it also seemed that there was a huge female audience not being catered to at all.

We got a car company to sponsor us, so I was driving around in a great vehicle – the only drawback being that it had a huge picture of me on the side with the *Shirley Valentine* logo. When I was in it, the car was fine and I forgot about it, but then I'd get weird looks from folk at traffic lights. We did most of the out-of-town venues (off-Broadway) before hitting the King's in Glasgow, as it's a 1,700-seat venue and we had risked performing there for two weeks. The theatre obviously thought we would sell out but it was a risk and the pressure was on. Typical of me, though, I decided that I wanted to do the whole first night for Women's Aid. So Bob set about doing it and we got the publicity out, hoping that it would be a good kick-start for the show's run.

On the opening night I was nervous as hell and stood backstage watching over the top of the set, where I could see the audience, and I was amazed to see them in the back row of the gods – right where my mum and I had sat watching Billy Connolly all those years ago. That's when the words of the fortune-teller came back to me; I wasn't doing stand-up but it was close. It was a wonderful night that I'll never forget.

But before I get too carried away with myself, there are always comments that bring me back down to earth. One took place in Aberdeen as two women passed my sound man, John, on the way out: one turned to the other and said, 'You know, Betty, I thoroughly enjoyed that, and normally I can't stand her.' The other was at the Ayr Gaiety Theatre when I was taking my final bow. I looked to the front row of the audience, where three or four old ladies were bending over and rustling and gathering up their shopping bags. One turned to her pal and said, 'Well, is that it, Agnes?' All that work . . . well, that's 'showbidness', eh?

CHAPTER 24

FAME . . . LIFE CHANGED

As I started to be more successful, especially on TV, I got to be recognised much more and, to a certain extent, was enjoying it, as most young actors would. It all felt new, and though it wasn't something I had particularly sought it was nice. I liked the fact that people were generally nice to you and bothered to come up to tell you that they liked what you were doing. It didn't stop some people from telling you just how 'shite' they thought you were as well; it was Glasgow, after all, and there is a great deal of pride associated with telling some jumped-up celebrity that they are rubbish.

But fame brings as many brickbats as it does plaudits and the trick is to make sure that the audience is who you stick with because neither the good nor the bad reviews are the truth. Hamish McColl, who directed *Calendar Girls*, gave me a great piece of advice when he said that a good review is as dangerous as a bad review, and it's so true. I have seen many productions where the actors come out preening because they've had good reviews. It drives me mad. I want to shout, 'Ye've not had a good review from me yet, so bloody get on with your work and earn it!' You can't believe the good reviews because when the bad ones come (and they will) it means you've got to believe them, too. The public are fickle and spot a phoney pretty quickly, so trusting your own instincts – and others whom you trust but are not in your pay – is vital. Family are good, as they will tell you the truth, even when it hurts.

I remember working on *Laugh??? I Nearly Paid My Licence Fee* when Robbie Coltrane came in quite shaken and told us that he'd been standing looking in the jewellers' window on Byres Road when a wee guy ran up and just booted him in the stomach and ran away laughing. Initially, he thought he'd been stabbed, but it was more the shock that someone would actually take pleasure in doing that that made us all so pissed off by it. Similarly, Gregor Fisher was standing in a chip shop one lovely summer's night, waiting in the queue with everyone else, when a woman came up behind him, put her hands between his legs and squeezed his balls and said, 'Aye, yer no' laughing now, eh?' He declined the chips and left. The ego of the Glaswegian knows no bounds and 'getting too big for your boots' is akin to a war crime in the eyes of certain punters.

I had a terrible time when Bob was rushed into casualty with a suspected heart attack. The nurses were great when they realised that I was a bit too visible sitting in the waiting room of the Royal Infirmary on a Friday night and took me into their room for a cup of tea when things got a bit too hairy with the natives. Bob was eventually given pain relief and admitted to a bed, but I was in a terrible state. I was standing in the curtained cubicle crying when a hand came through the curtain clutching a pen and paper. Someone said, 'We thought it wis you. He said it wisnae but I said it wis; gonnae sign that fur us?' I don't know whether they saw my tears, or my look of disbelief at what they were doing, or if they knew that my husband was lying in a semi-coma in the room, but if they did they didn't care. He could have been dead, but it seems that fame doesn't let you be a human being. I took the paper, signed it and turned away. They probably went off saying, 'Well, she was a bit sullen, eh? Didnae have much to say fur herself, did she?'

It is hard to write anything about critics and criticism because immediately it gives them a sense of power and importance. Basically we have four or five main critics in Scotland (i.e. they write for the papers with falling circulation – *The Scotsman* and *The Herald*, sometimes a Scottish section in *The Guardian* and an occasional review in *The Times*). These jobs, in the days when the papers sold many, many thousands, had some kudos and that is probably where their sense of power and influence comes from. It's a throwback to old Hollywood movies when you would see the producers waiting on the notices coming out and screaming, 'It's a hit', and knowing it would bring success. Those days are largely over. Yes, it is wonderful to be in a show like *Black Watch* but the Scottish critics don't really count as to whether the piece will travel or not. I have been in plays that the critics adored but no one came because the buzz wasn't there and the audiences didn't take to it. I have been in plays the critics hated and audiences loved and packed the place out. Gradually, over the years, I have realised that the audience will always tell you what really works, and generally we in the business are a bit behind them.

That is not to say that there are shows that are huge hits that I haven't liked: *Mamma Mia!* for instance – great fun if you love Abba songs, and a great jaunt, but, as a play, not very good in my opinion. But good luck to it, may it run and run. I feel quite sorry for critics now. It has never been a highly regarded job, generally poorly paid and in newspaper pecking orders the arts is seen as pretty low down, with current affairs, sport, features and even farming all deemed far more important. My beef is that what has seemed to emerge is a tendency to loathe you, the audience. They seem to hate the audience for making its own choices and decisions about what to go and see – maybe because it makes them redundant. They like to think that they have influence, and to be fair in subsidised theatre (all the arts council-funded stuff) they do, and they generally champion it. But it means there are too many artistic directors and publicity girls fawning over them, looking for a good review in the hope that their show is deemed a success and they can therefore justify their grants. They would rather have good reviews and a small audience, it seems, than their theatre packed to the rafters.

Now, before I am accused of being a philistine and only wanting the theatres full with potboilers and comedies, I would like to say that I am a huge fan of theatre when it works – experimental, mime, avant-garde, you name it, it's great. I am also a fan of people pushing the boundaries and doing obscure pieces that we, the taxpayer, fund. AND I want it all to continue to be funded and more. All my early work came from subsidised theatre; everything I know and learnt was with companies such as Wildcat, Borderline, the Traverse and the Lyceum, and I want them to continue to be funded. What we all want, obviously, is a packed theatre and an audience enjoying a show that moves, informs, educates and is driven with great writing, observations on life, humour and poignancy. And that it is both a critical and commercial success – that is the holy grail. No one sets out to make something bad, or rubbish – our hopes and expectations are all the same, but the relish, the sneering, the elitism and the outright snobbery of some of the critics in Scotland is out of line.

And with fame and success, their sights have turned on me in a vicious way sometimes and that can be very hurtful for all those close to me. It goes with the territory, I suppose, and everyone has an opinion. The rumours of the supposed amounts of money that I was earning for pantomime were legion. My friend and the great actor Peter Kelly told me that when he returned to Scotland to live, the figures that he was quoted about my supposed earnings were amazing, like footballers' wages. I just got tired of trying to say, 'No, I am not earning anywhere near that', because people didn't want to hear it. I started to laugh at it and say, 'Oh you're right, I'm earning a fortune and, to tell you the truth, I don't know how to spend it.' That soon shuts them up. The irony was, and is, that even now – and I am happy to say I earn a very good living and feel very lucky to do so – I don't earn what the greats like Rikki Fulton and Jimmy Logan were earning 30 years ago. But then again, I'm a woman and that makes a much better story.

But it does, as I've said, bring out a lot of jealousy and a lot of sexism, too. A lot of men think that a woman shouldn't have opinions, be funny, political or otherwise, and shouldn't be earning more than them. I'm not even a great beauty in their view, so they don't fancy me either. Women (and men) who are fancied by critics tend to get an easier time. In my case, they have also occasionally overstepped the line of what is good criticism.

I have had glowing, hellish and not very good reviews throughout my 30 years, and many have been pretty accurate and helpful, too. The only review I saw for *Little Voice*, by Shona Craven, made very good points about the set in the fire scene and my acting at the end, and she was absolutely right. Sometimes you can be so close to a production and so up against things timewise that things get missed, and constructive criticism can be really helpful. It's when reviews are vindictive and personal, as well as destructive, that they serve no purpose.

We have no awards for theatre in Scotland – they are all in the south and we are so small that we don't stand a chance – so they now have the 'Critics' Awards'. You, the audience, have probably never heard of them, but in the tiny world of Scottish theatre they have otherwise intelligent directors and actors scurrying to them, giving them an importance that is ultimately meaningless. They don't respect the individual, as they are generally failed writers, failed actors or people who couldn't walk on a stage and perform if you paid them a million quid. I loved the fact that they phoned our company and asked me to donate financially to help the awards get off the ground. I would have laughed had my jaw not actually been on the floor. Give to a cancer charity, hospitals – yes. But to fund a critics' award? Get a grip!

I have got to the ripe old age of 50 and am much more philosophical about the critics we have and see that they are just doing a job and trying to pay their mortgage, at the end of the day. I actually feel quite sorry for them; slogging away, pretending to themselves that what they do is of vital importance, having to go to watch shows night after night when I personally would rather have needles stuck in my eyes. The problem is the way that we are trained. Drama schools and universities teach us what is supposedly good theatre and mainly this means good writing. Now, we all love great narrative and good writing – and for an actor there is nothing better than getting great lines to say, as your job becomes ten times easier. But there is a tendency to forget that if the wrong actor is cast, with a bad director and a terribly designed set in the wrong type of theatre, then it can all go belly-up. But the best revenge in all this is just to keep on going, and that's exactly what I did.

I always tried to do other jobs that made me feel better and meant I wasn't stuck in a rut as an actor. They were scary and challenging but great for me to do. Just when the critics and sections of the public have put you in a box, it's great to go and do something to surprise everyone. I'd already done a Christmas show at the Tron for Michael Boyd, who was running the theatre. He asked me to come and do a Scottish version of French-Canadian playwright Michel Tremblay's *Les Belles Soeurs* translated as *The Guid Sisters*. When he had first approached me, I was filming and the wonderful Una McLean took on the role and was great in it. When a possible tour and trip to Canada was mooted, Una was unavailable and I was approached again. I had friends such as Elaine Collins in the show and thought that a production with 14 other fantastic actresses would hopefully be a great experience. It was and it wasn't; fame played a part in how I was being viewed at that time. I think I can safely say that at this point for a lot of actors my success wasn't seen as deserved – it had all come a bit too fast, too soon perhaps – and that was a heavy burden to carry around. But there was no bitching or anything like that.

With *The Steamie* and other shows with all-female casts (for example, *Calendar Girls*), I have had to endure the usual misogynistic stuff about the cast all hating each other and fighting. Why? Because they were women, of course. No one ever asks the cast of *Black Watch* (all male) whether they get on or not because there is an assumption that men will behave themselves and sort out their differences without any bitching. So, can I explode a myth here? Yes, women argue and discuss and disagree. Yes, there are people we like working with better than others – that is normal. But to assume that one sex will be worse than the other is just ridiculous. I have worked on many shows over the years where the behaviour of the men is bitchy, egomaniacal and violent at times. I have watched temper tantrums, guys not speaking to each other and sneaky, sly behaviour that undermines the director and the other actors, but somehow that is just seen as being an actor, not because they are men, and it drives me crazy.

The reason I found *The Guid Sisters* hard to do was that I had only ten days to rehearse with a cast who had already been together very successfully for around three months. There was little time to find my own version of Germaine, the lead character, and it was at a time when I was becoming more of a box-office name in Scotland. Understandably, I think there was jealousy and a bit of resentment amongst my peers and I didn't handle that all that well. I still felt uneasy with it all. I was desperate not to seem full of myself, or be disrespectful to other performers, but for some I realise that no matter what I did it wouldn't matter. Maybe they just wanted to believe that I had changed and was now totally up myself, probably because of some daft article they'd read about me in the *Daily Record* (whilst pretending they didn't read tabloid newspapers, of course).

When I saw the poster for the show, I was horrified because they had put a big production photo of me right in the middle of it; it was a great shot and would help sell the show and that's all that mattered to the theatre. They had taken on a 'name' and needed to generate income, so they'd moved the production from the 250-seat Tron to the 900-seat Clyde Theatre in Clydebank (which was at that point the Wildcat base) and so they needed to sell tickets. I eventually agreed to the photo being used, but asked that all the women's names should be on the poster too – and thankfully they were. I realised that a lot of the audience coming would be fans of *City Lights* and *Naked Video* and that they would have a certain set of expectations, particularly in Glasgow. They like you to do what they know you for, and take a bit of persuading if you do anything new. While this play was funny, it was set in Canada, in the '60s, with a very tragic undercurrent. So I was nervous about how the audience would react to it.

It's the story of a woman who wins a million Green Shield stamps and then asks her friends and sisters to come round and help her lick them, stick them in the books and listen to her brag about what she is going to buy with it, without even offering them a book to take away as a gift. What unfolds is a tale of jealousy, resentment and poverty, as well as the question of whether the Canadian dream of consumerism is the answer to everything, shared values and love being the first things to be sacrificed on the altar of consumerism.

Of course, the analogy with my own life was huge. Here I was in a fortunate position, a position most actors would love (money, fame and good work) and there but for the grace of God were the faces of 14 other actresses who could, or should, have been given that break too. Why was I lucky? Why had I been given this chance? I suppose it was like survivor's guilt. I felt unworthy and guilty about what I'd been given, and I had an audience wanting me to be Irene in *City Lights* or Mary Nesbitt. I was actually physically ill and trace my bouts of IBS (irritable bowel syndrome) back to this time. I don't think Michael realised how terrified I was, or, if he did, he didn't let on. He was just trying to get a show on in ten days that was selling out fast and I tend to give the impression of coping even when I am far from it. I felt he had too much on his plate for me to ask for help, and I floundered a lot, but was thrown several lifelines by the wonderful actress Ann Scott-Jones, whom I had long admired. She has a keen intelligence and gave me some quiet pointers that took me in the right direction, and she was able to read the situation well too. Her experience and help were invaluable to me.

So when we got to the first night, I was feeling less than confident; I didn't feel on top of the lines or that I had the support of many of the other actors, who, I assumed, would have enjoyed my failure as a sort of payback for the success I was having. I never felt disrespect for any of those women and genuinely tried hard to get on with them all, but there are always politics and vying for positions in any job, though I don't think I have ever felt more of an outsider in anything.

I got through the technical rehearsal and was in a sort of daze as we approached the opening. I was still 'drying' and forgetting lines, which must have been annoying for the team, who knew it backwards by this time, and I just didn't feel on top of it, or in control. I felt intimidated in the last, tragic scene where Germaine is left wailing on the floor in a sea of stamps, shouting, 'They're ma stamps, they're mine!' I felt embarrassed in rehearsals, as I always have when required to do some big stuff (be it comedy numbers or tragic speeches). I think it's because I believe that the audience is integral to the whole thing – the show is for them – to make them laugh and feel, not to make other actors amused or amazed by your skill. I have worked with too many folk who are wonderful in the rehearsal room and seem to fade in front of the audience, and the audience fail to connect to what they are trying to do.

I pulled myself together and approached the first night feeling out of my depth and unprepared. I stood in the wings waiting to come on with that terror from an anxiety dream when you are going onstage and don't fully know the script – and shouted my first line, 'Lynda' from offstage. The audience roared with laughter at the sound of my voice and I thought, 'Oh my God, what am I doing?' I got on, got through it, raised my game and even managed a few tears from the audience and myself in that final tragic scene. It worked. I also think many of the other actors saw for the first time what I was capable of doing (and the effect I had on the audience) and I gained a grudging respect. I felt I had to manipulate my route between being true to the audience and doing justice to the play, and I think we did it . . . though I found it difficult every night and never fully relaxed into it or felt in control of it until the end of the run. But in Canada it came alive.

In Canada, I was free to simply be a good actress. No expectations, no baggage, no TV persona. I also felt really on top of the role; I knew who she was and what the play was saying to the audience. I knew where the gags were and I knew how to play the truth of the real tragedy of the piece. We got to Toronto, a wonderful city with a terrible airport, jetlagged and tried to get our bearings. We were part of the Harbourfront Festival at the theatre there. We teched the show quickly and were on to a packed house the next night, and the reaction was amazing. We got a standing ovation. Michael Boyd ran into my dressing room at the end, shouting, 'Elaine, Elaine!' and lifted me shoulder high (I don't think his back has ever recovered). He knew that I had finally been able to give my real performance because I was free to do it. I was free from the fears and constraints that were imposed on me at home, but also those that I'd imposed on myself. I learnt a lesson that night: apologising for yourself gets you nowhere – do what you do and don't let your head get in the way.

Months later, at Elaine and Peter's wedding, I met the lovely and talented Gaylie Runciman, who was one of the actors in the show. We started chatting and I confessed to her how difficult I had found the whole job of *The Guid Sisters* and that I was barely coping at times. Gaylie said something I have never forgotten: 'Elaine, take the chances you've been given, rejoice in them and do it for all of us who won't get the chance; that's your responsibility.' I have tried to do that ever since, not always winning but trying.

Out of the blue, I got a call from Kenny Ireland, who was running the Lyceum at the time, and he asked if I fancied coming and doing a bit of Shakespeare. Well, all actors have to do it sometime and *Much Ado about Nothing* seemed the perfect one to do. I was aware that a section of the popular audience would avoid it like the plague, but it was a challenge and something I felt I had to do to grow as a performer. I discussed it with Bob and headed for Edinburgh.

So I gave of my Beatrice (as we say in actorland). We had a great cast that included Billy Boyd, Johnnie Watson, Tom McGovern and the wonderful Forbes Masson. Music was by Ricky Ross, of Deacon Blue fame, and it all had a fresh, youthful feel to it. It's a wonderful play and there was some great satisfaction in being back at the Lyceum doing Shakespeare in the city I had first seen it performed in and where I'd fallen in love with the idea of what theatre could do. I don't think that I was the definitive Beatrice, as too many wonderful actresses have done that before, and after, me, but I did a good job. It worked and I think I (and the production) breathed a believability, relevance and a sense of humour into her and the play. It was also where my friendship with Carol McGregor had its foundations. It was months later at the Scottish BAFTAs that I met her and discovered who her son was.

The *Nesbitt* team were having a works night out and we were pretty drunk. I do remember proposing marriage to Ally McCoist at one point on my way to the loo but there was a queue (for Ally, not for the loo!). We'd won everything apart from Best Writer (where in the politics of these events the votes went to Tony Roper for *The Steamie*, not that it was undeserved), and Eileen McCallum won Best Actress for *The Steamie*, which was hard for me, as it was for the part I'd helped create, but *c'est la vie* and she was gracious as ever in her speech, thanking me for being too young and beautiful to play the part on TV. Anyway, this lovely woman approached me to tell me how much she had loved my Beatrice and the whole show, which was great. She then talked about her charity work with the audio description of films and I said I would do anything to help. It was actually only when she left that I realised whom she meant when she said, 'I'm Ewan's mum.'

I started doing what I could for the Audio Description Film Fund and sat on the board for several years. We also had an amazing trip to Pakistan together for the charity Sightsavers, who do such amazing work throughout Africa, India and across the world. What we saw in the fight to save the sight of so many men women and children – and for free in many of the hospitals and schools in Pakistan – will stay with me for ever. We met living saints in the form of doctors and volunteer nurses amid poverty that I could only have imagined before. But what I have found, wherever I have been in this world, is that people are just people, struggling against the odds to try and have a good and decent life, and it is generally the poorest who are the most welcoming and generous.

It was exhausting, uplifting, upsetting and disturbing, especially as white Western women in a mainly Muslim country. But experiences like that make strong bonds and I am glad to say that we are still friends to this day – she and her lovely man, Jim, are just simply good people.

CHAPTER 25

STAND-UP . . .
ELAINE WITH ATTITUDE

The success of *Shirley* prompted the then director of Mayfest, Paul Bassett to ask us to do something else. He had an idea of doing another *Shirley Valentine*-type of show such as *Educating Rita*, which is still a play I would love to do. I didn't feel it was right – it felt too similar to *Shirley* and I wanted to do something more fun, I wanted to sing again with a band and to do something funny. It just felt right. Looking back I realise how brave and naive I was, all at the same time. I just forged ahead and did things because I wanted to do them and worried about them later. I had never written any comedy before, but thanks to a year of writing for the *Evening Times* in Glasgow I had found a voice.

I had never done stand-up either, but had always been relatively good at talking to audiences at fund-raisers and gigs, especially if I had things I wanted to get off my chest, and I could be funny while ranting . . . usually at my own expense. I've noticed that in the years since I only want to do, or write, any stand-up when I have something to say about the world and the madness of our lives. So the theme, 'How the hell did I end up in this job?' was the question of the hour. Bob and I agreed to get a show together and do two weeks during Mayfest in the old Fruitmarket in Glasgow.

I started writing about what I knew – my life in Lanarkshire, wanting to be Doris Day, my parents, celebrating New Year, dieting: anything and everything about my life. I had masses of material and once I started I couldn't stop, but obviously I didn't know whether it was funny or not, so I phoned my friend Kate Donnelly. I first met Kate when she was with the comedy team the Redheads with Libby McArthur, Peter Mullan and Peter Arnott. They were funny, political and very hip at the time. We were doing the *Nippy Sweeties* at the Fringe back at Hill Place, where I had last performed in *Sexual Perversity in Chicago*, and they were in the same venue. I thought she was really funny and a great performer. She then joined the *Naked Video* team for a series, when she did her great 'Georgina' character, a sort of posh Glasgow 'It' girl with a waspish turn of phrase. We got on well and I really trusted her opinions and instincts, as well as the fact that she wrote her own material, something I'd always been scared of doing up until now.

So armed with all my writing, I ended up in Kate's living room in Partick doing a wee show for her. She was fantastic, saying that she thought I was really onto something special, pointing me in the right direction, as well as giving me some great new gags. She seemed to get what I was doing and we developed a kind of comedy shorthand. We took some of the material to Philip Differ at the Comedy Unit, whom I wanted to script edit, but he was working on *Only an Excuse* for the BBC. He was positive and praised the fact that I had come up with so much new material and gave me some great pointers on keeping the routine topical and fast-paced. The next thing to do was pick songs, and a few of the Wildcat songs of old were just perfect, but I also wanted to give my audience a good time and let this great soul band I'd put together play. So we decided on a medley of Stevie Wonder and James Brown soul classics to round the night off.

We had no cash but knew that with the guarantee from Mayfest they would pay everyone working for the show; we were confident, given the success of *Shirley Valentine*, that it would sell. We hired two dancers and a ten-piece band with some superb musicians, headed by the musical genius and all-round mad bastard Kennedy Aitchison – who came in just towards the end of our rehearsal schedule. So there it was: I had a band and I sang my favourite songs while telling the story of my life so far and how a girl from a small mining village in Lanarkshire had ended up as an actor in a hit TV show.

We had instant success; a sell-out show for 14 nights at Mayfest and a run at the Fringe in Edinburgh, followed by a small tour that ended with its being co-produced and shot by Wark Clements (Kirsty Wark's then production company) and televised by the new boss at Entertainment in BBC Scotland, Mike Bolland. It went out on New Year's Eve – a night when all of the nation is watching – and it actually changed my career. I don't think I was prepared for the impact of how it would elevate my profile. As the show had sold out in most venues, I think I assumed that the majority of people had seen it. Never underestimate the power of the TV, especially a show going out at New Year, and it can make or break a performer. I wouldn't have been the first good performer to bite the dust after a Hogmanay performance in Scotland, as memories of Chic Murray and John Grieve, or Robbie Coltrane came rushing back. Brilliant performers who didn't quite catch the wave I was riding post-Hogmanay show. Having Kirsty Wark's production company behind us helped a great deal. Her husband (Alan Clements, who is now at STV) was great and had set about getting the whole thing into BBC Scotland. Mike Bolland, who was in charge of the Light Entertainment Department, was a Scot but had been London-based for many years, so he really didn't have a clue who I was, apart from *Nesbitt*, and I had felt a little like the new girl explaining myself. Thankfully, he had come to see the stand-up and got what I was all about and we had been commissioned to do the show.

The day of the recording arrived and I was terrified. I had a weird feeling all day about it during rehearsals. Fred MacAulay came in to do the warm-up for us and went down really well and then they announced me. I walked onstage to great applause, started to speak to the audience and realised that my mike kept cutting out. After a couple of minutes I asked the audience if they could hear me, and they shouted, 'Naw!' I had to leave the stage and Fred, thank God, came back on, as we laughed at the fact that I had to go off and change my mike.

I got into the wings in a complete flap ready to get my mike changed, only to discover that they didn't have a spare pack. They had a hand-held mike, which I only used for songs, and I knew that it would get in the way of my doing my routines if I used it. So there we were, in front of two thousand people, seven cameras, a band and an army of BBC production staff and no bloody mike! The sound supervisor

(Mick Wild, who had worked with me on everything from *Naked Radio* to *Nesbitt*) saved the day. He doctored one of the BBC mikes to our frequency (so we didn't have taxi drivers' call-outs coming through as I was talking) and off we went. By this time, the audience had been waiting a good 20 minutes and I think Fred had run through all of his best gags – twice – so he was a total trouper and I can't thank him enough for that.

The upside was that all my nerves left me, as I was so bloody furious that I'd been left in that position. All these people who were supposed to look after me and I didn't have a backup mike, and no one had checked. I was raging and actually the show went well, though we did have people leaving before the end to get their buses home as we'd run on so late. They were lovely, though, and kept waving to me as they left and saying 'Sorry' to me. After it was all over, I slept for a week.

A few weeks later I saw a rough cut of the show and I thought, 'That's it! My career is over.' I wasn't allowed into the edit to help choose what should be in the show. We were cutting a two-hour performance down to forty minutes, so we knew a lot of material would have to go. As usual, I always think that other folk know better than me so I waited to see what they had chosen to put in. I watched the tape and burst into tears as, in my opinion, they had cut all the wrong bits out and kept the material that only really worked in the theatre and not as well on TV. I didn't know what to do. I knew that if I went on and said what I thought I would be dismissed as the Diva throwing her weight around.

So I called Mike Bolland, who was sympathetic, listened, agreed with much of what I was saying and then, thankfully, got it re-edited with all the points that I'd made. He was the boss, so he had the power to ensure it was done correctly – so the next cut was much better. It still had flaws and, as ever, I thought I was rubbish and shouted too much but, all in all, we were happy. The show aired on Hogmanay and the reaction was absolutely fantastic. We got a huge audience and a terrific response. At last it seemed that people were noticing who 'I' was and not seeing me simply as a character and that felt very rewarding. Why was it such a success? Well, like everything else in life, I think it was timing: it was just the right time for a woman to come along and say what she thought about the world from a female perspective, with a Scots accent. Yes, it had been done in England (I was a total admirer of Wood and Walters, and French and Saunders) but no one was doing it commercially in Scotland. Dorothy Paul – who was a great influence on me – was of a different generation and, wonderful though she was and is, there was room for something that spoke of a newer Scotland. While Dorothy spoke of life in the '50s and '60s in Glasgow, I wanted to speak of the '70s, '80s and '90s in Scotland.

The show was from a woman's perspective obviously, so initially I was taken far less seriously than any male comedian. It was also from a working-class woman too, so it was not the life story of the cognoscenti in Scotland, and certainly not of the journalists and employees of TV companies, who tend to hail from the middle class. In Scotland at that time, I think it was still a surprise that a woman could be funny on her own and have plenty to say about the state of the world, and that she could make men laugh, too. Have you noticed that no one tells Billy Connolly that his comedy is only really for men cos its from a man's perspective? It's taken as read that his is a perspective for everyone – even though most women have never been in a shipyard in their lives, or spent their evenings in the '60s in the company of pubs full of men.

Connolly has also suffered from that sort of class prejudice in Scotland. When he started he was loved by the huge working-class audiences that flocked to his shows in the Pavilion and the Apollo. The TV companies in Scotland only really noticed him after his interview on the Parkinson show – until then he couldn't get arrested in TV land. So not only was I a vocal 'oik' with a working-class accent and background, I was also a bloody woman. Fortunately, humour shines through most of the time, though I have had to endure the usual taxi driver comments like, 'Aye, it's mainly women that like you, isn't it? You don't really like the men, do you?' This, because I dared to make a comment about some of men's idiosyncrasies, or just generally pointed out that they are occasionally stupid arses. They seem to omit from their memories that I also do the same to women! It's often said to me as if making women laugh was somehow inferior to making men laugh and by way of an insult. I have to say, for me, making women laugh is much more flattering, particularly given the puerile stuff that most men these days seem to see as funny. For every Eric Morecambe and Eddie Braben piece of classic comedy, there are a hundred 'nob' gags parading as humour around the comedy circuit.

Making other women laugh is a huge compliment, because women can be so judgemental of other women anyway. I freely accept that I don't make all women laugh and for some I am too common, too working class and too opinionated, but fortunately at the time of *Elaine with Attitude* I was, for thousands and thousands of women across Scotland, someone they related to. I was giving their lives a voice. Of course, I didn't know that at the time: I just wanted to tell funny stories and paint a picture of life in the '70s, but it seemed to strike a real chord.

I've never thought that any of my limited fame or popularity was based on amazing talent – I wish it bloody was. What I am is a good communicator at a time in Scotland when it is required. My audience, fan-base, whatever you want to call it, responds to that. I think it's because there are so few places in Scottish life where women see themselves reflected back. Where do we see ourselves? Where do women get to just hear each other and speak to each other in our own voices and accents? Nowhere, really. If there are Scottish voices, they rarely talk about Scotland; they just have funny accents and come from Scotland if they are on *Newsnight* or *GMTV* or *Loose Women*. I am not knocking that and I am genuinely glad that these women do well. I just wish we had our own programmes here, shows for women who live here, by women who live and work here too. Much of my popularity is because I just do that, I hold a mirror up to women's lives in Scotland and generally I make them laugh about it, too. I also try (and mostly succeed) to make men laugh at the madness of us 'burds' and also a little at themselves.

Making people laugh is a very powerful weapon, too. It breaks the ice, the tension, can puncture pomposity and cut right through a lot of the seriousness that people attribute to situations in life. And I can't help but see the funny side of things. I was on *Panorama* for the first time a few years ago. It was before the Parliament in Scotland had been granted and as I was part of the Yes/Yes campaign at the time and was asked if I would speak in the debate. They staged it in the old Royal High School building, with David Dimbleby chairing it. It was a very tense, bitter debate between the Unionists, led with the most pompous and terrible acting that I have ever seen in my puff, in the form of Donald Finlay QC and those supporting a Parliament. I was called to answer questions from my own side and then to be questioned by the ex-Scottish Secretary, Sir Malcolm Rifkind. David Dimbleby turned to me after my own side had finished and said, 'Well, Elaine, I am now going to throw you over to Malcolm Rifkind', and before I knew it, I said, 'He'll need to be a helluva strong man to catch me!' and the whole room burst out laughing – including Malcolm Rifkind. Afterwards he told me that it put him completely off his stride because he had laughed so much.

Anyway, the struggle and risk that was *Elaine with Attitude* changed everything. It ended up being produced as a video, a DVD and a best-selling book, and all because I had shone a humorous light into the lives of working-class women. I was a bit of a pioneer, I suppose. But I am the first to say that I wasn't trendy or even cutting edge, as far as comedy was concerned. But with that show my life changed yet again.

CHAPTER 26

HANNAH AND ST ANDREWS

I went off to do a play called *Shades*, by Sharman Macdonald, at the Byre Theatre in St Andrews, which had been a hit previously for Pauline Collins in London. I had loved Sharman's other play, *When I Was a Girl I Used to Scream and Shout*, and jumped at the chance offered by Maggie Kinloch to be in it. The fact that my mother was to be played by the fabulous Kay Gallie (whom I'd worked with in *The Guid Sisters* and *The Steamie*) clinched the deal. It wasn't great money and I had to live in St Andrews – which is a nightmare to get to from the west of Scotland. The good news was that the Old Course Hotel (very expensive) was sponsoring the show and I got a week in a gorgeous suite there courtesy of the management. I then rented a room in the house of a friend of the theatre, and an aspiring actress, Ruth Smith, who was great to me.

It was a play about the dominance of a mother on the life of a young boy (loosely based on the life of the great Scots actor Ian Charleson). The main thing was trying to find a young boy (or two, as they had to be alternated). We found two lovely boys, one of whom, Jim Webster, has gone on to have a great career as an actor himself. He actually played Billy in our production of *Little Voice* last year. The play went well, but due to budgets and other constraints, it wasn't the best of productions. Sharman did come to see it and seemed to like it and did bring her children with her – one of whom was a ten-year-old Keira Knightley. She wanted them to see Crail and the other beautiful fishing villages of the East Neuk of Fife near St Andrews, where she'd spent a lot of her own childhood. It was a great summer and a lovely place to be. The worst part of the stay was the breaking news about Eric Cullen splashed across the front of the *Daily Record*.

I managed to get back to see Katie start her first day at school, which was my main priority, and Bob and she visited as much as they could. It must have been the sea air or something, but I returned from St Andrews pregnant with what was to be our beautiful second daughter, Hannah. I'd learnt a lesson from my pregnancy with Katie and set about ensuring that I was actually going to have the time off when she was born. Fortunately, she was due the following May and I could plan to have the whole summer off, which I did. I worried about having another baby because I didn't believe that I could love it as much as I loved Katie. My love for her was all-consuming and I worried that there would be nothing left over for this new little life that was coming to us.

My pregnancy was again scarred by morning sickness, but this time I was better at dealing with it. I kept going into false labour and had a few trips to the Southern General. We later found out that Hannah had the umbilical cord around her neck and that was what was giving me the pains. After another visit I had some reflexology from a nurse who was pioneering it as an aid in birth (and I was a willing victim) but nothing happened and I was sent home. At five in the morning I was up and washing my clothes and changing the beds, as I couldn't rest, and started repacking my case. Bob was teaching and after dropping Katie off at school left me to get on with my cleaning. I started ironing, for some reason, and was standing in front of the TV when the terrible news that John Smith, the then Leader of the Labour Party and probably the best prime minister we never had, had died of a massive heart attack. I was getting really bad back pain and my manager Lynne turned up to find me bent over the ironing board in tears, saying that I was fine. She called Bob at school and he and I were at the Southern again by four that afternoon.

Hannah was born at 8 p.m. that night. It was a wonderful birth, a light epidural applied, so no pain, and I was singing along with my Bonnie Raitt CD as Hannah came into the world. Again I threw up immediately after she was born, but we were blessed with another healthy, beautiful daughter.

Hannah was the calmest baby ever, maybe because I as a mum was calmer and more prepared. She slept through the night from three months and brought even more joy into our lives. I found out that you don't love one child more than another, your heart just gets bigger to make room for the next one, whom you love just as much. I did feel incredibly lucky in the weeks following her birth. Somewhere I knew that I wouldn't have any more children and that was it finished. At times I got very melancholy at the passing of a certain phase in my life and a terrible feeling that there was only cancer and death to come – it must have been a premonition.

I started getting offered interesting bits of work, too. Annie Griffin, a very talented filmmaker, got in touch and asked me to come and do a project for Channel 4. It would be a series of short films on the 'Seven Deadly Sins' and she was making one called *Wrath*, which was loosely based on the Gallagher Brothers (of Oasis fame) and explored in a really funny way the anger of young men and their rage at the world. It was shot like a documentary and I was to play the mad Scottish mother of the lead character played by the terrific Paul Kaye of 'Dennis Pennis' fame. It was great fun to do and I really loved working with Annie.

She had based her company (Pirate Productions) in Glasgow and set about doing another series for Channel 4 called *Coming Soon*. I loved the whole idea of this and the way that she worked. For two days she brought the actresses that she wanted for the project together to improvise ideas and script and it was there in that hotel room in Glasgow that I met Julia Davis, Jo Scanlan and Vicki Pepperdine: all fantastic actresses and comedy performers, who it was a real thrill and pleasure to work with. We later did more improv work around this avant-garde theatre company from London coming to tour Scotland, with a cast that included David Walliams, Paul Kaye, Omid Djalili and Ben Miller. It was a great project, which sadly ended in a lot of fall-outs and madness at the end of it all, but it was really well received and a piece of work that I loved doing.

CHAPTER 27

NOTHING LIKE A DAME

Pantomime, the great theatre art form that I am proud to say we Scots (and big Scots too, a wee panto gag for you there) in particular do so well, has played a huge part in my career. It's quite odd for me to realise that I have become a star in pantomime because until I was actually in a production of one, I'd never sat down and watched any of them. I obviously knew of the huge stars of the genre in Scotland like Rikki Fulton, Jack Milroy, Stanley Baxter, Jimmy Logan and to a lesser extent those great women performers like Una McLean and Dorothy Paul – though unfortunately they were never given the coverage or credit for successful shows that their male counterparts received.

At drama college and while at Glasgow University, it was obvious to us as students that this was an art form that was kind of looked down upon. I may be being unfair, but my memory and experience have left me with a feeling that other forms of theatre were seen as much more serious and credible. In fact, variety in general rarely got a mention. I have since learned that being popular is never a good thing in the Arts as you get no subsidy, no help and are generally dismissed as an artist because the punters turn up to see you.

When I was at college, it seemed that the search for new writing and what was going on in the English stage, particularly London, was what was seen as 'good' theatre. So at the age of 18, I was incredibly open to all that received opinion and took it on board because I didn't have anything to counter it with, as I'd never been to the theatre. It was only later that I got angry about the way that variety was treated and the absolute snobbery applied to it and anything working-class Scots at the time. So, what I am trying to say is that at the beginning I was a bit snobby about the whole genre. And panto and I didn't get off to a great start, either.

My first one was at Motherwell's Civic Theatre, which you would think was a nice start for me. There was a lot of local press about my coming home, etc. but to tell the truth I'd only done a few shows professionally so I hadn't actually been away, but it was a good angle for the local journalists. This also wasn't a Christmas show in subsidised theatre, where I think I would have preferred to be. It was in the commercial sector and it was widely known that actors did commercial panto because they got well paid. Even doing a Christmas show on minimum wage earned you more because anything over eight shows a week you had to be paid again, so it was a lucrative thing to do, as well as great experience.

But for the money you were paid, you had to work, and not six shows a week, as I had been used to. No, no, no, it was two shows – sometimes three – a day, every day. I didn't know what had hit me, on so many levels. The star of the show was Phil McCall, a very good and well respected actor, but who'd become a household name from an advert for a famous brand of soup: 'Pea and ham? From a chicken?' So of course that had to be in the show at some point, too. Phil wrote a lot of the show too, mainly made up of routines that had been performed over the years by various companies and turns. The songs had to be popular too: 'Memory' from *Cats* and another few pop classics, you get the drift? His wife Kate, who'd been in TV and stage management for years, directed the show. In all, it was a piece of light entertainment to give the folks some cheer at Christmas – nothing wrong with that, eh? I hated every minute of it. I'd come from Wildcat, where we all mucked in, were paid the same wages and contributed. It was a bit chaotic, but it felt vibrant and alive. This felt staid.

When my agent called me, she said that they wanted a feisty, different, more relevant Cinderella. The description was that they wanted an 'Elaine Collins type who could sing'. Elaine was the original Lucille in John Byrne's huge hit *The Slab Boys* and her portrayal of the cheeky, sassy Lucille had won plaudits everywhere. I didn't know her at this time but had seen her work and thought she was superb. The thought of creating something new and original was great, but the reality was that the script had two scenes with a feisty Cinders who got a few laughs, but ended up as the straight 'Oh I wish my prince would come' girl doing a duet of 'Then There Was You' with a 42-year-old soprano from the Ivy Benson Band in thigh-length boots! The lesbian sub-plot lived on in the 'pantoland' of the '80s, not helped by the fact that as an alto I sang a lot lower than the Prince – the kids must have been so confused.

But I did make a good friend in the singer Catherine Kerr, who was playing Dandini; we were blood sisters after a hair-raising drive from Chelsea Girl in Argyle Street in Glasgow to make the matinee in Motherwell. We got there two minutes before curtain up; the stage manager was far from pleased. As Cinders, I looked more like Snow White because of my dark hair and an odd costume designer so that when we got to the ball on the first night (with me in a hellish wig and in a frock with no sleeves in it), I looked like Elsie bloody Tanner! By the end I was exhausted, traumatised and very ill with flu and kidney stones, so the thought of doing panto ever again did not appeal. The fact that I have now been a panto star for so long is quite strange, looking at how it started and how much I hated it.

But the following Christmas the wonderful Morag Fullarton from Borderline Theatre asked me to come down to the Magnum Centre in Irvine and do a new version of *Cinderella* written by Tom McGrath. They had a great fun and quite irreverent approach to panto and used young, talented actors such as Phyllis Logan, Robbie Coltrane and Gregor Fisher, and were a company that all young actors wanted to work with. But this time it wasn't to play Cinders but the Fairy Godmother and the Wicked Stepmother. It was a great challenge, though at the time I didn't realise that it would mean that I would have to be in every scene (and changing from one wig to the next behind a curtain in the wings, so how I didn't come on in the wrong wig, God only knows).

I was getting to meet and work with more actors, too, and that was great experience. Generally you learn more from watching other actors (the good and the bad). This cast had a young Hilary Lyon (still a friend to this day), who had just come out of drama school,

Freddie Boardley, and Billy Johnson as Buttons. Billy had got a lot of coverage after a very funny cameo part in *Gregory's Girl* (he was the guy being taught to drive). He had been working on the crew of the film, I think, and got offered this wee part to save money. He looked fantastic as Buttons but on the first night his nerves got in the way when he shouted to the kids, 'Hiya, kids, I'm Buttons, now when I shout, "Hello, Buttons," I want you all to shout, "Hello, everybody." Will you do that for me?' I was listening on the Tannoy in the dressing room and thought to myself, 'That doesn't sound right.' But he then proceeded, oblivious to his mistake, to shout, 'Hello, Buttons,' and all the kids started to shout back, 'Hello, everybody' with confused looks on their faces apparently. Billy couldn't understand what had gone wrong and kept up the shouts until he got onto the next bit of the script. My dad, who was in the audience, thought it was the funniest thing he'd ever seen in his life. Billy then compounded it all by coming out to do the song sheet at the end with me, saying, 'Oh, boys and girls, I'm that upset. Cinders is away with the Prince and I always fancied Buttons, didn't I?' to a huge laugh from the adults and confusion from the kids. I came off the script and said, 'You fancied Buttons?' Billy laughed and said, 'Oh, I mean Cinders, I fancied Cinders,' and we got on with it.

But though the long drive to Irvine and back from Glasgow every day was hard, and it was two shows a day for not a lot of money, I loved it. It was a hard slog, but a great laugh and it was new in taking the form of panto and playing around with it in a clever way, but still entertaining the audience. I felt much more at home.

The following year I was really happy to be asked back to work at Borderline on Alex Norton's *Peter and Penny's Panto*. His show had made its way into Scottish acting folklore for its take on the panto genre, its irreverence, and for a cast that included Phyllis Logan, Gregor Fisher, Elaine Collins and Terry Neason – as well as Jimmy Kennedy as Merlin. Jimmy was a lovely man and lovely actor whom I had only worked with once, in my first TV play.

The cast included Katy Murphy, Kevin McMonagle and the man who would end up as a colleague and friend from then till now, Andy Gray. He makes me laugh, and like all great comics from Laurel and Hardy to Tommy Cooper, his real skill is to make himself the butt of most of his jokes, and his ability to laugh at himself is just wonderful. He was the first person to ever actually speak to me, as himself, off the script onstage, and it was hysterical. You have to have your wits about you. In the training and development of actors it is an unwritten rule that you never come off the script, or out of character. But when you do, it can be hilarious and cause complete hysterics; in the business, we call it 'corpsing'. How can I explain to civilians the sheer daftness of trying not to laugh onstage? Well, remember when you were at school and the teacher was really strict and you were sat next to the guy that kept saying things under his breath and making you laugh and you were terrified of being caught? That's what corpsing feels like. And Mr Gray takes such pleasure in making you corpse, it's like a badge of honour if you can hold your own and even get him back (which I have thankfully managed to do over the years). But his sheer cheek and bravery about it was really shocking to me at first.

I went off to do the Lyceum the following year for their Christmas show. It was hard work and a bit joyless.

I then headed back to the Tron to do another version of *Peter and Penny* and reprise my role of the Govan Fairy in Michael Boyd's production. This time I got to work with Kate Donnelly as well as Paul Samson, the hysterical Jimmy Chisholm and the lovely Bob Pettigrew. By this time I had a one year old at home so that was pretty tough going with the schedule. But smaller theatres tend to have a shorter run and that gets you through and then you also got a couple of days off around Christmas and New Year – unlike the commercial sector, which at times had shows on Christmas Day too. It was a great show and I loved being in Glasgow again, doing something that was packing them in but that still gave a lot of nods to great variety routines and the story.

Billy Differ – who was general manager of the King's – came to see the show and loved it, and as a relatively young man he said that he would love to have something like this on at his own venue, or at least bits of it included in their shows, but he knew there was no chance. The rules for panto were very strict, and basically women didn't get to be funny in them – that was left to the guys. I always took Katie and her friends to see the King's show and had noticed that with the retirement of the likes of Rikki Fulton, there was a dearth of real Scots panto stars. Gerard Kelly had done a fantastic crossover from TV and is actually one of our few legitimate stars of pantomime to this day. He is the definitive Buttons or Wishy Washy of the last 20 years. Andy Gray and Alan Stewart have also done well to keep the genre alive, but in the mid-'90s things had become tired and a real reinvention was needed. This is not unusual for panto, it's something it's done since the Italians invented it with *commedia dell'arte*, but it tends to go into a new phase only when the old is no longer working.

When I went to see Glasgow King's pantomimes with the likes of Les Dennis, Christopher Biggins and a very young Amanda Holden, or even the great Cannon and Ball, it was obvious that panto was a bit lost in the city and needed to do more. Worse, the audiences were deserting it, especially the middle classes. They were heading to the Citizens or the Tron and looking at Christmas shows that were cleverer and more relevant to the audience. The King's, with the wonderful Pauline Murphy, was looking for a new way forward. They called in Kelly and Ron Bain to have a talk about where to go and what was wrong – and apparently my name was brought up.

I'd been offered the King's Edinburgh panto (for a tidy sum) the year before and had had to turn it down due to the fact that I was held to an option of a comedy pilot written by Bob Black for the BBC. It was a great idea about a woman who runs a lonely hearts agency and had great performers such as Louise Beattie in it as my sister, and a very young and lovely Kevin McKidd as my secretary. There were high hopes for it, but when I saw the pilot I realised that it needed a lot of work (not least from me) and didn't think it would go to a series.

I was doing Davy Kane's brilliant play *Dumbstruck!* (again directed by Michael Boyd) at the Lyric, Hammersmith in London. In the bar after the show I found out from a BBC executive who'd come to see the show that the BBC in London had no intention of commissioning the show, though they were being far from straight with the producers in Scotland, who seemed to think that it still had a chance and so held me to my option. When it finally was axed, it was too late for me and I lost the panto job, and sadly the house that we were hoping to buy from its proceeds. We'd seen it, our dream house, around the corner from where we were then living. It was an old Victorian detached house and we loved it, but for us it was too expensive and the only way we could have risked it was with a panto wage, but it wasn't to be. We thought it lost for ever when we heard it was sold, but the old Scots saying is true, 'Whit's fur ye won't go by ye.' The house must have had our name on it, as a year later it came back on the market. By this time, I'd been offered the role at the King's and had news that another series of *Nesbitt* was on the cards, so we could actually afford it. We live there to this day.

Not doing Edinburgh proved to be a good move. Much as I love the place and the theatre, the panto they wanted me to do was much more of the old-school variety and I don't think I would have been happy doing it – it might have put me off for good. What attracted me to Glasgow was that they were into reinvention of the form. It would have a full script written by Bob Black, so no inserting of old routines and no narratives. They wanted to marry the old with the new, and decided that the Ugly Sisters would be women. They asked me and my friend and sparring partner Ella in *Nesbitt*, the wonderful Babs Rafferty. From the music done by Hilary Brooks and the choreography by the terrific Stuart Hopps to the direction of Alex Norton and the poster design, everything was different. No longer the smiling photos of top-of-the-bill turns on top of cartoon bodies, but an actual paid-for photograph with the entire cast in costume.

The feeling was that if panto was indeed dead in Glasgow, then it was dead everywhere. The council, who ran the show and funded it, didn't skimp on costs, believing that the people of Glasgow deserved a top-class show on a par with the West End and for that they had to be applauded. So we set about creating, or attempting to create, magic. There was a fair bit of resistance to the news that the cross-dressing was going in the new show. Babs and I were playing the Uglies, John Leslie and his brother Grant Stott were the Prince and Dandini. Women playing the Dame was certainly not approved of by the old guard and they made their feelings known quite publicly. I have always felt that the ability to play the Dame in panto has little to do with your sex and is more about the type of performer you are. I have seen men be awful Dames, and some women, too. But the ability to talk to the audience and come out and say 'I'm going to make an arse of myself, come along with me and watch' is what works. The reason that it had always been men in the role was that they were, and generally are, the comics – there are so few women comics even now, and it stands to reason that the big comedy parts go to the popular comics of the day. So, for us, it felt like a revolution.

Amongst the younger generation, the 'lesbian sub-plot', as I call it, (i.e. the Prince being a girl singer and proclaiming love to another girl in the form of the Princess) was looking more and more ludicrous. The whole tradition was a hangover from the Victorian era, I think, where it was simply there to give the men in the audience a chance to see a bit of leg and thigh. The cross-dressing part of the Dame was also there to allow the big male star comic of the day to put on a frock and do his act. I was pretty daunted by the whole thing and the weight of responsibility on my shoulders to make it work. Kelly had a solid track record in panto and was playing Buttons, so the knives, if there were any, would be out for me as top of the bill. But it worked brilliantly and set the route for many of the pantos across Scotland in the following years.

The real seal of approval came when I got calls from the great Jimmy Logan and Rikki Fulton to say that they were wrong and that it did actually work. Dorothy Paul also loved it, though added that, in her opinion, it wasn't a panto. She was right, it wasn't panto as it had been, but the time had come to move on. Audiences were up and a friend (who had left the King's for years because she hated how old-fashioned and irrelevant it all seemed and had taken her kids to other Christmas shows) told me we had 'saved panto' for her. I was exhausted, though: twelve shows a week, two kids back at a new house with a kitchen demolished and all of us living on a building site, alongside a husband who didn't realise his wife would basically be AWOL for two months. Then there was Christmas in the middle of it, and I felt the need to control it all, running up and down Sauchiehall Street in a big coat and hat to hide the hellish panto hair flattened by the wearing of ten wigs a show and the panto glitter everywhere. I had to get the presents, the food and have everyone over to the house, on my one day off, too – what an idiot.

I finished the run and took to my bed depressed and knackered, unable to process what I'd just been through. I had felt slightly constrained playing an Ugly in the show and maybe that contributed to my unhappiness, as it just didn't feel right. I loved working with Babs but the 'turn' in me felt hemmed-in by the part, as well as the script. I think that these parts are better played by men and that takes the curse off it for me. I missed the ability to interplay with the audience and I do believe that there is a difficulty in women playing the Ugly Sisters. All the humour is based on how ugly and awful they are and in the most sexist of ways. I think in these times it makes audiences a bit uncomfortable. They are the butt of the gag but never able to get their own back, unlike the part of Dame, who has more control of the humour and takes the piss out of herself.

But the whole experience toughened me up and I did feel I wanted a crack at something bigger and was ready for it. When I was asked to return the next year to do *Sleeping Beauty*, I discussed it with Bob and we decided to go ahead but be better prepared. At least we knew what we were in for. Now when I do panto I go into a sort of training. You sort of have to miss out on all the real Christmas fun that everyone else is having, so no nights out or parties. I don't drink apart from a glass of champagne on Christmas Day or Hogmanay, I take lots of vitamins, have acupuncture or massage, when I can fit it in, I eat and sleep well when I can (usually a wee bed on the floor of the dressing room) and finally do the shows. I do make my dressing room look like Santa's Grotto and I'm partial to a fairy light at the best of times, so Christmas for me is a gift.

Bob Black created the wonderful Dame Nannie Be Good for me and I loved her. I can safely say that she is my all-time favourite Dame. Sadly, Kelly was off to do the panto in Edinburgh and it was decided to go for Johnnie Watson as the sort of Buttons character. Johnnie also brought his TV persona from the hugely popular show *Only an Excuse* (a great routine as his alter ego, footballer, womaniser and all-round wild boy Frank 'Where's the burds?' McAvennie). We also got Babs Rafferty back as my arch-enemy, Carrion, who ironically turns out to be my sister. We also had a very young, and hugely talented, Billy Boyd in the cast as Norvil (pre-Pippin in the *Lord of the Rings* trilogy, so we could afford him). He and I did a fantastic duet of Stevie Wonder's 'True to Your Heart', which I loved doing.

Unknown to me, a young Geordie lad from the then Queen Margaret College in Edinburgh had come to sit in the audience. The visit to rehearsals had been arranged by my old chum (and head of drama) Lynn Bains. She had huge hopes for him, as she had never had a student before who was such a good actor and singer but who wanted only to be a producer; he loved theatre but he wanted to be the guy running it. Usually, actors fall into directing or producing after realising that they are not going to make it, but not this guy. His name was Michael Harrison and he has gone on to become a huge part of my life and career, though I never met him on that day as he sat in the audience. He remembers it all vividly, but I was busy trying to remember my lines. He is now a much sought-after West End producer and has co-produced all my theatre tours in Scotland, too. He is a wonderful guy, passionate and enthusiastic about theatre, as well as being a great businessman. But then he was just a 22 year old who was daft about panto – and always had been, according to his parents. Four years later I was back doing *Sleeping Beauty* again, but with Mr Harrison now installed as the director.

I was asked by Pauline Murphy to go and meet this young man who had asked to get to direct the panto for the princely sum of £1. As a producer, her eyes obviously lit up at the thought of saving cash. I wasn't sure, as he seemed to have so little experience, but agreed to go and meet him, as Pauline seemed to really like him and thought he could do it. We met for lunch and on my way to the restaurant I got a call from West End impresario David Pugh. He was in New York and about to open his production of *The Play What I Wrote*. It turned out that he'd had Michael working with him for a year on a bursary programme to train up young producers and he wanted to tell me how great he thought he'd be for the panto. I met Michael, loved him and that was that. He was just magic to work with – tough and kind with fantastic ideas, great passion and intelligence.

After my first *Sleeping Beauty*, though, I returned to do *Aladdin* the following year and my first Widow Twankey. But I decided that three years of no Christmas at home with my family was quite enough and took the next couple of years off. Much as I loved it, I still wanted to do other things and didn't actually want to simply be a panto star. In retrospect I realise that that is no bad thing, but at the time I still felt that I had other things to do and didn't want to get hemmed in.

I must have had a premonition that I would need the time because that following Christmas my mum was diagnosed with breast cancer and was actually having a mastectomy when I would have been onstage in *Cinderella*. So I was taking my mum to a theatre of a different kind. I remember leaving Mum in hospital to take Katie and her pals to see the panto. It was the last place on earth I wanted to be, especially with the worry and the horrors that our family had been facing. But sitting there in the stalls, listening to the kids cheering and people laughing, watching the lights and action, I realised that for half an hour I hadn't thought about cancer and death. In that moment I realised that that is what panto and theatre could really do. People came in their thousands because they got to gather in one place (unusual these days, with the demise of the churches and the busy lives that people now live), experience something daft, funny and joyous together and for a couple of hours forget about the horrors of the world. I sat listening to the beautiful voice of Katherine Igoe as Cinders sing 'When She Loved Me', about her mother, and I was hosed out my seat in floods of tears. I lost all my actor-like opinion and snobbery about panto in that moment. That doesn't mean that I don't get upset and angry if it's a shit show, but I know what it can do for an audience and that's what we should all be aiming for.

I went off and did other things in theatre and TV, and had a bit of a life too, but ironically even though I was not in the panto there was an assumption that I was. It had been so successful and, I suppose, it was so unusual for a woman to be in the position of headlining that it was burned into the consciousness of the public. I haven't done a panto for five years now but still get asked by taxi drivers if I'm at the King's this year. I don't know why they bother with a publicity budget. Anyway, I returned to do another two pantomimes with the wonderful Nigel West (who'd been directing many musicals in the West End, including *Chicago*) and then another two with Michael Harrison.

I haven't been able to face one since the death of my mother, but I am teaming up with my mate Michael Harrison to do panto at His Majesty's Theatre (HMT) in Aberdeen for Christmas 2009.

CHAPTER 28

ELAINE . . . THE CAR CRASH

So things were going well in my career and my life in general. I had two children, a husband that I loved, a growing business and Mum was more settled and happy and enjoying her life, as was Dad. Television-wise things had altered. *Nesbitt* had finished after eight series and luckily my New Year show had been hugely successful, so BBC Scotland came back and asked me to do a series. Through my naivety, stupidity and inexperience, I thought I should do something completely different. I didn't want to rest on my laurels and not push myself, wanting instead to be creative and clever. Nothing wrong with that, I hear you say, but classically I forgot that the TV audience were just getting to know me as Elaine, and in retrospect I should have done something more along the lines of my Hogmanay show. But I was desperately trying to prove myself. All my influences were shows from the States such as *Seinfield* and *The Larry Sanders Show*, though I did love *French and Saunders*, Julie Walters and Victoria Wood. I forgot that none of these shows or comedians were actually the favourites of Scottish audiences – so my comedy references were sound and good, but out of touch with the majority of the Scottish mainstream.

So, I wanted to do something a little cleverer and a bit leftfield, and was genuinely excited at the thought of it. My enthusiasm brought everyone along. I truly believed that we would be able to do something great and that the audience would love it too, combined with the added wish that a network in London would pick it up. I learnt a valuable lesson, though: don't take your eye off the ball and concentrate on what you really are good at. Unfortunately, I got carried away with what I thought we could do.

We put a great team together, who bought into my vision: Rab Noakes to supervise the music and put a band together; Sarah Lawrence, a producer I had worked with on the children's series *Hubbub* and who had a wealth of experience in London on shows like *Wogan*; my trusted pal the writer Kate Donnelly was hired as the script editor and built a team of writers as well (Ricky Brown and Sanjeev Kohli); and Julie Dorrat-Keenan (from my *Naked Video* and *Nesbitt* days) came in on make-up. We employed a good designer, a sound studio director in Justin Adams and an acclaimed film director in Annie Griffin.

The BBC were wary, and Mike Bolland was a bit perplexed, to say the least – but my enthusiasm and the support of the team pushed things through. The idea was to have a Larry Sanders-type show with a real show going on in the studio and then cutting backstage to characters played by me interacting with Elaine the host. We had good guests such as Deacon Blue, Eric Bibb, Michael Marra and Raul Malo, the front man of The Mavericks, who'd had a huge hit with 'Dance the Night Away' and were on a UK tour at the time. One of the best things to come out of the show was that I got to go to the SECC and duet with Raul. I sang 'Blue Bayou' with him in front of a 10,000-strong crowd who couldn't quite believe it when I walked out onstage. It was magic

Kate and I wrote together, we commissioned writers, we had a good team, so were set to go into rehearsals. We moved into offices, budgets in place – all set to go. A week before we started our producer went on a skiing holiday, fell badly and tore her cruciate ligament so badly she had to have an operation, which meant several weeks off work. We were up shit creek. None of us had the skill, or experience, to put this together but we also didn't want to sack Sarah and get someone else. She was a single parent and was determined to do the show, though she had many reservations about what we were doing. She just didn't get it and looking back I don't blame her. My ideas were a difficult thing to comprehend and it needed someone who totally got what we were attempting to do. The audience themselves, however, wanted something more mainstream and, in retrospect, they were right.

Had I done my show on Channel 4, out of the glare of BBC Scotland's prime-time audience, we would have been allowed more experimentation. I envy Peter Kay and the backing he received to produce *Phoenix Nights* – had that series been put on BBC1 at 9 p.m. I'd argue they wouldn't have done another series. Finding a niche audience and having time to build up a following is the right way to approach a new series. Failure in the full glare is not really an option. But that's what happened. The show went out, the first episode actually looked good and went down quite well, audiences held up but it didn't exactly set the heather alight, and no one knew that more than me.

It was like watching a car crash. It looked good, we worked really hard, but our inexperience showed all the way through it. I took it really badly, as it had never happened to me before – I had always been associated with success and here I was in the middle of something that I, more than anyone, knew didn't work. My ego took quite a blow and I just felt exhausted, depressed and burnt out. I turned down all work offered and just stopped. I remember sitting alone at the top of our stairs in our house without even the energy to cry, with no idea what to do next. So I did nothing. I knew I had to regroup, work out what I wanted to do and take it all on the chin. I just felt stupid, like I had blown it.

My friends and family were very supportive because they knew how hurt I was, but they also knew that things hadn't worked out the way I would have wanted. Sometimes failure hurts your family more because they are the ones that have to deal with the punters telling them that they thought my show was shite. Kate phoned to apologise and I will never forget her for that. I couldn't understand why she needed to, but she said that she felt she had let me down and her inexperience and timidity as a script editor had resulted in not cutting a lot of the monologues. It was only when she saw it on TV that she realised that all the monologues were too long. The truth was that it was our inexperience, too, in asking her to do a job that she hadn't done before. It was our belief in her and enthusiasm that had carried us through. And I don't regret that either.

A new friend walked into my life at that time, and she is a friend I will always cherish. It's hard to meet your idols and then to go on and have a good, honest friendship with them, especially for me, and to this day I admit I am still a bit in awe of her. Helena Kennedy, as a human rights lawyer, activist, campaigner and true leader in the fight within the justice system for equality for women, had been a heroine of mine for a long time. I'd read her book *Eve Was Framed* and loved her TV show *Blind Justice*. Here was an articulate, intelligent, good-looking Scotswoman, who was there at the sharp end, doing us proud. She is a true icon for the feminist movement. At one point, I was asked by *The Scotsman* whom I would have as the first Scottish President (if we were ever independent) and I said Helena Kennedy QC. I later found out that her sister had seen it, posted it to her and that she had it on her fridge.

I did a programme for Radio 2 where I got to interview her. Unfortunately she was in London and I was in Glasgow, but we got on great and later she sent a card to say how much she had enjoyed the interview. Just after we had set up our press conference for the TV show, Bob and I went for a coffee in Sauchiehall Street and as we sat talking Bob looked out into the street and said, 'There's eh . . . eh, Helena thingmy.'

'Who?' I said, and at that moment she looked and spotted me too, rushed into the café; we fell into an embrace and have never stopped talking since. Bob says Helena is the only woman who can actually talk more than me (and a lot more intelligently, I'd like to add). So that was a positive thing to come out of a very difficult time, almost like a sign not to give up.

I learned a lot about my inner strength in the aftermath of the show. I learned that ignoring your audience is a silly thing to do – always take them with you and get your ego in check. In true Smith style, I licked my wounds, I pulled myself together and regrouped, concentrated on my family and decided to take time off until I could think straight. I genuinely thought that it was maybe time to give up. We went on lots of holidays, not big exotic treks across the world but weekends away with the kids and a summer holiday in Majorca. The best trip of all was to Center Parcs in Nottingham, where no one knew me and I could cycle around with my daughters quite happily. It was great. I started to feel the wind in my face and and to feel alive again. Looking back now it is actually one of the shows that I am most proud of doing, even though it didn't work. It was one of the most adventurous and creative things I have ever done. It just wasn't properly executed and we didn't have the expertise to carry it off; it was ahead of its time and tried really hard to do something different. It was back to the drawing board, because our biggest crime had been to do what we wanted as opposed to what the audience wanted.

I had been determined not to be pulled back into a 'Haw Maw' style of show (i.e. 'Wasn't it great when we all lived up a close?'), but I think I tried to leap too far and the lesson for me was to always to take your audience with you on the journey, rather than alienate them. Don't get me wrong, I enjoy all the old-school variety stuff, if it's done well and with great heart. There is nothing more relaxing or enjoyable than watching a great comic (or performer) do even the oldest gags in the book really well. Peter Kay is a wonderful example of an old-fashioned style of comic, with great skill, timing and ideas all mixed together with a new twist, and that's where it works best. My dilemma was that one part of the audience wanted me to always be Mary Nesbitt, and the other part derided me for it (as well as the critics), and the truth is none of it was accurate. I wanted and still want to do comedy with a Scottish accent that is good, true and, above all, funny.

I got a call from John Tiffany, who was then the literary director at the Traverse in Edinburgh, asking me to come in for a few days to do a workshop of a new play by the wonderful writer Kate Atkinson called *Abandonment*. I had read her award-winning book *Behind the Scenes at the Museum* and loved it, so I jumped at the chance and we had a great couple of days together. John was fab and Kate was just so funny, unpretentious and refreshing as a writer. A few months later they came back and asked if I would agree to do the play for the Festival, with a great cast including Patricia Kerrigan as my sister, the wonderful Sheila Reid as my mother, and the lovely Michelle Gomez and Kath Howden, too.

I had already committed to doing another stand-up show, so once more I'd be undertaking two roles in one period in Edinburgh.

I had started writing again with Kate Donnelly, and Alan de Pellette had contacted me with a view to working together. So I put together a new show called *Hormonally Driven*, which described the plight and madness of women at that time and tried to solve the age-old question asked by many a man (and woman) for many a year: 'Why are women off their heads?' It was the first time I had really gone out on my own to do a show without a backing band. It was proper stand-up – an hour on my own, in a 200-seat sweat-filled room at the Gilded Balloon at the Fringe.

We managed to alter some of the performances to fit in with the schedule of the Traverse show and I ended up doing them both successfully. What is it about my need to prove myself? There I was back at the Fringe, walking through the Grassmarket during the evening from one sold-out show to the other, doing my lines on the way.

For both shows I decided for the first time not to read any reviews and it was great. I got told, of course, that the notices were good but made a decision not to read any until the whole thing was over (and actually I still haven't read them – it is a great feeling). I started to trust my own opinions about what was good, or bad.

Hormonally Driven was a great success and sell-out, with the biggest accolade coming from my old friend Andy Gray, who actually came in to see the show. He has real comedy 'chops', so I was scared about his being in the audience. But it proved to be a wonderful thing, as he was so kind, thoughtful and considered in his comments and told me he thought the show was great and that he was really proud of me. I couldn't believe it, high praise indeed. It got better when I was stopped one day outside the theatre by Melvyn Hayes, star of *It Ain't Half Hot Mum*, who told me that he had seen my show and thought it was the most professional, complete and funny show in the whole Fringe – talk about being chuffed to bits.

CHAPTER 29

THE REALITY OF CANCER

Mum's independence and her single life allowed her to have a lot of good laughs and great times. She enjoyed her life more and more with her friends, whom we dubbed the 'Golden Girls', as they were all blonde, divorced and in their 60s. In a weird twist of fate, Mum and Margaret, the mother of my pal Elaine Collins, had met when we were doing a show together and had struck up a friendship. These women with two daughters called Elaine born months apart became friends 30 years later. They embarked on many holidays to the costas of Spain, Cyprus and Tenerife, as well as trips to Paris and London. Mum had a great social life, and finally managed to buy her own flat in Motherwell, which she just adored. Though the children and grandchildren always came first according to Stella, she was finally having a good time.

Apart from my daughters, she now also had Jack – her first grandson, delivered by Diane on 13 January 1998 – and then Harry, who Louise produced in 1999. Again Stella loved it because he was in Motherwell and just down the road from her flat. Then came her beloved granddaughter Tess a year later.

Stella was forced to retire much earlier than she would have liked. She wanted to work at least part time (she loved it and it kept her active) but because she was 65 they would not allow it. Losing this valuable stimulus left Stella low and she became very depressed, especially after a very nasty bout of chicken pox, which seemed to take her months to get over. Because her sister had died of breast cancer she'd been quite diligent about going for her screenings. But at that time they only took place until she was retired at 65, which was a really strange decision, since the highest risk of developing breast cancer is actually between the ages of 60 and 70. The screening programme has now been altered to cover this age group, but too late, unfortunately, for Stella. Her last mammogram had been when she was just over 64, so hitting one more year now took her out of the loop.

At 66, she started feeling unwell and had actually gone along to her doctor with a lump under her arm. The GP told her that it was just fatty tissue and to try and lose a bit of weight. She didn't tell us of this visit, as she had complete faith in her doctor and assumed that she was fine. Stella went off to Cyprus on holiday with her friend Helen but had a miserable time. She was off her food and felt tired all the time, as well as feeling guilty that she was spoiling her friend's holiday. When she got back, she went to the doctor again and was told it was probably a bit of depression and a tummy bug.

I remember seeing her when she came to the Traverse in Edinburgh during the festival when I was doing *Abandonment*. She had been on another wee holiday to her favourite spot in Brighton, where my Aunt Margaret, her sister, lived. Their relationship seemed to have strengthened and deepened after both their marriages had failed and the bonds of sisterhood grew. Margaret had finished her PhD by this time and had toured the world for a year with Paul McCartney, tutoring his daughter Stella for her A level English (my mother always felt that she had a psychic bond with her idol, Paul McCartney, and the fact that he'd called his daughter Stella confirmed that for her). On her return, she was lecturing at Sussex University, so therefore had decent holidays and entertained my mum regularly. Stella always came back renewed and refreshed but on this occasion, at the theatre, I was shocked to see her looking pale, tired and in obvious pain.

She had found sitting for so long difficult and had a terrible pain in her hip. Her mood wasn't helped by the fact that she was sitting next to two Edinburgh women who had decided to slate my performance. A damning 'That Elaine Smith can't act for peanuts' was their response to my subtle and underplayed performance, which had been widely praised elsewhere apparently. Ach, you win some, you lose some, but

I think if Stella had felt better she would have decked them on the spot. But it's a lesson for us all: always beware who you might be sitting next to in the theatre when you sound off about how rubbish you think someone is – it might just be their mother.

She continued to feel unwell and we urged her to go to the doctor again, as it appeared that she had all the symptoms of gallstones. As I picked her up to take her to the hospital to be checked out, she got me to sit down and told me that she had found a lump in her breast. She had noticed it due to her weight loss. I asked her why she didn't check and she said, 'Oh, well, when you're fat, you don't look at yourself.' It was the saddest thing I had ever heard, but I knew that her reply represented the feelings of many older women who were overweight, and the self-loathing they applied to their bodies. I was so angry, I said, 'Well, Stella, I am no skinny thing and at times there hasn't been a pound of me hanging the right way, but I look at my body every day.' My head was in a spin and I was thinking that the stomach problem and the weight loss were obviously 'secondaries' and that it was definitely cancer, while pretending, of course, to take it all in my stride and retain a calm exterior. I was going to be doing a lot of that in the coming months and years.

It turned out after the exam that she did indeed have very painful gallstones, which I was ecstatic about. So the next obstacle was the breast problem to get out the way and we'd be out of the woods. She'd gone back to the same doctor as before, who'd realised the link between the swelling that Stella had come in with five months earlier and this new lump and so fast-tracked her into being seen for a test. I had a terrible feeling about this, a real bad dragging in the pit of my stomach. I hoped against hope that it wasn't what I feared but couldn't get rid of the feeling that this was something really bad.

I went with her for her tests at Monklands Hospital in November 2000, for what turned out to be the worst day of my life. Well, until then. I could feel death breathing down my neck as I sat there waiting with her for the results. I kept going to the toilet, thinking I was going to throw up. I watched other women emerge in tears and I hoped against hope that we wouldn't be getting the same news as these poor women. 'Oh, not us, please. But, then again, why not us?' We were called in and Dr Dermot Murphy was sitting there with a kindly look on his face and directed all his comments to Stella. He said, 'I think you know what I am about to tell you,' and Stella smiled faintly and said, 'Yes.' She got a bit teary and I said, 'Come on, Stella, we're fine,' and took her hand while wanting to jump up and shout at this man to stop. I hated him and the words that were coming out of his mouth but could do nothing but sit there.

He then went on to tell us that they suspected that she had a tumour in her breast and they wanted to do a biopsy to make sure, right there and then. We'd bumped into Dr Iain McKenzie as we sat waiting, and he recognised Stella as the sister of his colleague Jim McGarry, as he'd been the consultant in charge of my mother's sister Magda when she had died in the same hospital of bowel cancer years earlier. He was lovely to us and had obviously gone in to ask why Stella was there, found out and decided to stay. When the news was given, he returned and did the biopsy himself. It was the start of a level of care and attention that was wonderful. They obviously knew that the cancer was advanced and that the pain in her hip was connected, but they were calm and caring and asked us to return a few days later with my sisters, basically to let us digest the news.

I left her to get her tests and ran outside to phone Bob and my sisters. I was actually quite hysterical; I couldn't catch my breath. I was on my own, keeping calm for Stella but silently screaming inside my head. It all came out and I arranged to go to my sister Louise's to tell them, as they were both at work. I went back in with a calm face and took her to X-ray, where they wanted to see if it had spread to her lungs . . . Oh, great.

At no point did she ever feel sorry for herself, though, or really show her fear, and that's what I was scared of more than anything. Her fear was something I thought I couldn't handle. She only got emotional as we were walking up the corridor when she said, 'Oh, Diane's baby, I don't want this to upset her and harm the baby.' I was in complete shock. When I got to Louise's house, I stood in the hall with my brother-in-law Jimmy, saying, 'I can't do this. I can't go in there and tell my sisters that their mum has breast cancer and it's serious.' But I did, and it was awful. Diane was four months pregnant and their boys were young so the thought of their gran not living, or Mum not seeing them start school, was just too terrible to contemplate. Stella arrived, having left me to break the news, and a strange normality and calm took over. She came home with us and we planned our next visit to the hospital.

The meeting with Dermot was actually great. The shock had gone a bit and we just wanted to get on with the operation and treatment. I just had this real desire to get the cancer cut out. We left and went to a restaurant for lunch. For three days, she'd had nothing but calls and kindness from friends, family and others who had heard the news and wanted to see if she was OK. I said, 'Well, at least you know now how much you are loved.' She smiled and said, 'You know, for the first time in my life, I think I do.'

'Well, we'll be with you all the way, Stella.' And we were.

The whole thing had understandably a bad effect on me. I secretly wished that I could run off to London or the States and then I wouldn't have to deal with the awfulness. I had this overwhelming feeling that I was never going to be free because I had to take on the role that my dad would have taken had they been together. I was in the middle of preproduction for my show for the BBC, I had two young kids and my mum was about to have a mastectomy. It was the best performance I have ever given, though, pretending to her that I was fine and in control. But in reality it was all too much.

On the day of her operation, I was with her and was allowed to take her down to the doors of the operating theatre. I smiled, told her I loved her and that it would all be fine and that I'd be there when she woke up. I was a blubbering wreck as I left the hospital and went into St Augustine's chapel (where my brother-in-law Paul had been a priest) and lit candles, cried and prayed like I never had in my life – and I still don't believe in God – but it seemed the only thing to do. I knew I had to keep strong myself and actually went and had a massage, which I cried all the way through, but it helped.

I went back to the hospital and this was the worst bit so far. As I walked up the corridor to her room, I could see all the tubes coming out of her, and the blood, and I wanted to turn and run away. She was still out cold and the lovely nurse assured me that all had gone well and that 'Dr Murphy had done everything he could.' That didn't sound good. What did it mean? Just at that moment, Dermot appeared still in his scrubs and asked to speak to me. He said that he wanted me to prepare and for the rest of the family to do so too. He had found cancer in 16 of the 17 lymph glands and had kept going for a long time. The tumour hadn't been as big as they'd thought but the pain in her hip was due to the fact that the cancer had travelled to her bone. She wasn't to have chemotherapy, as it would be a bit pointless, but she would be put on Tamoxifen and when I asked how long he thought she had, he said two to three years. She was only 66 years old.

When Stella was told this same news three days later (while sitting up in bed, looking great), she said, 'Great, I'd have liked longer, but I'll take that.' I was amazed at her. Where was the fear and wailing? She was strong, stoical and just thought that she would get on with it. Part of her loved being the centre of attention, too. Her room was full of cards and flowers; she'd got to know the intimate details of all the nurses' lives, which she regaled us with at visiting times, and thought the whole place was a marvel. She was on a real high and that did help us to cope.

I remember driving home from the hospital one night and getting hysterical in the car (sorry if you were in a car on a December night watching a wailing woman at various traffic lights en route to Glasgow). I was actually talking out loud. I am not religious at all, but I called out to my gran and to my mum's sister, Eileen, and begged them to help us. I started shouting at them and telling them that I'd never asked them for anything, but at that moment 'They needed to walk with us and help us through.'

Mum came back to live with us, and my Aunt Margaret came up to help, as we were producing and filming my TV series, as well as it being Christmas – great timing, eh? I put Stella onto a completely organic diet with copious amounts of vitamin C and aloe vera. I wanted her to cleanse her immune system, so that it could fight the disease that was still left, along with her drugs. I have great memories of Mum with Margaret, making batches of soup every few days. They were like witches making magic potions and loving it. Her faith in medicine and her attitude to the disease were amazing. She was fortunate in being cared for by the team at Monklands Hospital (her cancer care nurse, Elaine Ferguson, and her new friend, Isabel Bagwell), whom she grew to love. She thrived and, within three weeks, she seemed to get a new lease of life. Maybe it was because after years of worrying about the terrible things that could happen, they had actually happened, and it seemed to release her.

I was a basket case, of course. I'd recorded six shows in twelve days live in front of an audience in the Citz. We had realised that I had to go back to basics and that my comedy and stand-up worked better out of the studio and in front of an audience – more of a 'live event' feel. We got a really good TV director whom I had worked with and got on really well with while filming *Hubbub*. His name was Tom Poole and he'd also worked on lots of shows with Cilla Black and Frank Skinner. He was great to work with and a very calming influence on me, which was sorely needed. The whole team pulled around me too, as they knew what I was going through. I was lucky in having Kate, Allan and Christine Dinwoodie, as well as production manager Heather and producer Sarah Lawrence, who all put in loads of work to keep me upright and performing.

The show went well and we had some fab guests, the best of whom was the legend that was Edwin Starr. Getting to duet with him on 'Stand By Me' was a total thrill. In the middle of the rehearsals, I genuinely thought that I was having a heart attack and was rushed off to the doctors. I was strapped up to the old monitors but given the all-clear, the doctor telling me that I was stressed and that drinking copious amounts of coffee and not eating weren't helping but my heart was fine. At the end of the recordings, I took to my bed. My mum had gone home to her flat and was feeling great, as I lay in bed terrified, having panic attacks and convinced that I was going to die at any second. It was awful, made worse by my mother walking in wearing a beautiful coat of mine that she'd borrowed, with her hair and make-up done, looking wonderful and telling me that she'd never felt better in her life. She was euphoric. I could have chucked her out the window.

Kenny Ireland had made good on a deal we had struck when I was at the Lyceum doing *Much Ado about Nothing*. I had said that I would come back to the theatre if he ever did my favourite musical, *Guys and Dolls*, and let me play Adelaide. Bob was totally against it, as he felt that I was too stressed and knackered. He thought I was mad to go and put myself through a gruelling rehearsal period and performance schedule for eight weeks and for £350 quid a week. On one level, he was right, but I knew that I needed to get back to the safety of being with a company of actors in a good show, and with Andy Gray in the cast playing Nicely Nicely I knew I would laugh every day and I did. I laughed in a way that I thought I wasn't capable of and we rekindled a personal and professional friendship that I thought we would never regain. We had both grown up a lot (me more than him, of course) and it was a joyful experience for us. It was a huge hit for the theatre and the joy of standing in the wings watching Andy do 'Sit Down, You're Rockin' the Boat' every night was fabulous. I think we recognised each other's abilities – when you go off and work with other much lesser or little talents, you learn to appreciate those who can actually do it in this business.

Stella was also well enough to come and see it, which was just great. I was still prone to panic attacks and actually had one in the middle of 'Sue Me' with Tom McGovern one night. As I was singing, my brain was thinking that I was having a heart attack again, but working out that I was near enough the Royal Infirmary in Edinburgh and that there would hopefully be at least one doctor in the house. Yes, I was quite mad.

Andy had worked on the first series of *Two Thousand Acres of Sky*, which I had loved watching. It starred Michelle Collins and Paul Kaye and was written by American Tim Prager. It had a great cast of Scottish actors such as Tom Watson, Monica Gibb, Andy and my dear pal Sean Scanlan. I loved Tim's writing and its sideways, off-beat humour – a great counter to the straighter 'shortbread tin' version of Scotland depicted in the popular *Monarch of the Glen*. It was about a London family who ended up living on a remote Scottish island and their struggle to make a new life there. One of the casting people came to my show and I told them how much I loved *Two Thousand Acres* and that if they were looking for an actress to even play 'Woman at Bus Stop' I was happy to do it. A few weeks later I was at the Women of Influence lunch in Glasgow and Michelle Collins was there. We ended up getting a photo taken together and I said how much I loved the show and that I was a friend of Andy and Sean. My agent got a call a few weeks later, and I went to London to meet the producers, Tim and Michelle, for a coffee and, hey presto, Mrs McGowan was created. It was a great part, playing a mother (of the lovely Jenny) who is an embittered and angry woman in the village who resents the newcomers. I did it for two series and it was one of the best jobs I have ever done. Good writing, a great cast and filming in the beauty of the Galloway coast in Portpatrick and Port Logan.

We were blessed in that Stella's condition remained stable for a couple of years and she enjoyed her life on many levels. It is a cliché, but everything seemed to mean so much more to her and she found another level of energy. We decided to buy her flat for her to relieve her of any money worries at the same time as Bob and I were buying our wee but 'n' ben in Dunkeld, a beautiful place in Perthshire where we had for years enjoyed family holidays. Stella came to see our flat after we'd bought it from my actor pal Monica Gibb, whom I was working with at the time on *Two Thousand Acres of Sky*. Stella beamed as she sat there and said, 'You are all going to have such happiness here.' Indeed, she loved her visits to Dunkeld, as well as her visits to Portpatrick and the set of the show. Curiously, her illness brought out the best in her; she found a wisdom and a compassion that she hadn't known were there and found belated joy at the birth of her last grandchild (Tess).

Stella rarely moaned or complained about her illness, as if it were a sort of badge of pride. Her tears were for others, not herself, and she showed great courage and leadership to other patients in their fight with cancer. Her attitude got her through all the hard times, as did her love for her family and love of life. I suppose there is a wish we all have that we'd like to be at our own funeral and hear what people say. Well, for Stella's surprise 70th birthday 'do', we did just that. Over 100 people, family and friends, were there for a slap-up meal and speeches at one of her favourite haunts, the Avonbridge Hotel in Hamilton. Her daughters all spoke, as well as her son-in-law Bob, and the affirmation she received was something that we all deserve at some point in our lives. It was like the wedding party she never got. She looked beautiful, had a wonderful time and the love and attention that she got that day sustained her for another year. Both her consultants came and agreed that she was indeed a walking miracle.

Only in the last six months did her quality of life suffer, and even then she just got on with it and kept going. Although she got very tired, she still enjoyed her family, friends and a wee jaunt to the theatre, or Asda. The cancer had now spread to her bones and so she was suffering increased pain in her ribs and back. She woke one morning and couldn't move her legs. We called an ambulance and got her to Monklands, where they knew what was going on and immediately got her transferred to the Beatson at the Western Infirmary for a course of radiotherapy, which left her really tired but in much less pain and able to walk. Steroids and other pills gave her more respite and she came back again to stay with us.

Her determination to be healthy enough to go on one of her regular trips to Stobo Castle in March (I took her there on trips as a regular treat) was a great motivation for her, and it actually became a place of peace for us all. If there is a heaven, then for Stella it was Stobo Castle. When I go there now, I still feel as if I'm going to visit my mum.

Her four days with Isobel and her daughters were something they will all cherish. Although reduced to walking with a stick or Zimmer frame (or as her granddaughter, Hannah, called it, her 'Zoomer'), her pleasure at everyone being together in such a lovely relaxing place was there for all to see. She laughed, she gabbed, she ate, she drank and she danced and sang. The sight of her in front of the TV watching *Fame Academy*, dancing with her support to the wonderful Al Green song 'Let's Stay Together', still makes me weep.

Three weeks later she had a massive stroke, and it is the family's one huge regret that she was on her own when it happened. For some silly reason, we all thought that she should have some time in her own home to enjoy her brand-new bathroom and kitchen. She'd had it put in before Christmas and had been all excited about doing it and it gave her a focus too, as buying things always cheered her up. She now had a carer in place, who bathed her and made sure she was eating, my sister Louise lived down the road and we were on the phone constantly. My sister Di, who was holidaying in Dunkeld, had phoned Stella and spotted something odd in her voice, but also that she was confused about where she was and who was with her. Di called Louise and she decided to go to the house and she found her slumped on the sofa with her *Herald* crossword in hand. She called an ambulance and then me, and in a blur we were in Wishaw General in the emergency room. Stella had had several strokes and was barely conscious but started to come around when I spoke to her. My voice seemed to stir her somehow.

We stayed with her as she came in and out of consciousness, and she recovered enough to be moved into the ward. The emergency ward is not a place that I look forward to ever being again – overworked, harassed staff, beds too close together and little privacy afforded to the patients or visitors. The worst episode was when, as we sat with Stella, I could hear a guy visiting a patient in the next bed and, having spotted me there, slagging off my column in the *Sunday Mail*, my dad and my family. I eventually had to tell him that the piece of material between the beds was a curtain and not a wall and that if he was going to slag off my family he should maybe keep his voice down at least. He just looked stunned as he realised that I wasn't actually on the TV at that point and was a real person with real problems, the same as everyone else.

My mother's treatment – though life-saving – was confused at times. This was the hospital where she was treated with chemotherapy for her breast cancer but, for whatever reason, no one seemed to have picked up on the fact from her case notes that her right breast was now missing. Accidentally they proceeded to put the drip into that arm – an arm with no lymphatic system. Through her haze Stella kept trying to pull the drip out and we couldn't work out what she was doing. I had to leave, as I was filming *55 Degrees North* in Newcastle, and as she'd recovered slightly my sisters told me to go. I was only a couple of hours away if anything happened and the medical team did feel that she was doing OK. Leaving her was appalling and I was numb on the journey south. I don't know how I said a line, but the team and the director, Sue Tully, were just so supportive, as well as my fellow actor Andrew Dunn, who was just so kind and understanding. It all felt surreal.

It was only 12 hours later when Louise noticed that Mum's arm had swollen to double the size and fluid was pouring out, and then it dawned on her that Stella was getting no fluid or nutrients. We felt awful but were in such a state that it is forgivable, I think, but that's when you want the medical team to step in and make your loved one better again. She was moved into a ward where the staff were lovely, but again overworked and stressed. One of us was there every mealtime to make sure that she was fed, and to ensure she was changed and washed.

It became clear that even though Stella was recovering and able to speak and communicate, something serious was going on. Her body was breaking down and the cancer was definitely in her brain, causing little mini strokes all the time. But she was able to tell us that she wanted home and out of the hospital (which is a natural wish for any of us who find ourselves away from familiar surroundings). She kept raising her eyes heavenward when I asked her if she was all right in the hospital and was able to say a definite yes when I asked her if she wanted to come home. When I said, 'To your house, or my house?' she answered, 'Your house.' So we set about getting her home, even as the doctors told us that she was very ill and there was little hope of any recovery. In truth, I could feel it. I can't explain it, but I just knew this was it while hoping against hope for another Lazarus-like recovery, like so many Stella had produced over the years. But when her sisters (Margaret and Joan) arrived and I saw the three remaining McGarry sisters together, I had a feeling it was for the last time.

Then a strange thing happened; when one of the cancer care team came up to speak to us (I had asked for all chemo to be stopped, as it seemed pointless to put Stella through any more discomfort), the woman introduced herself as Elizabeth McGarry – my grandmother's name. In that moment, I knew the game was up. Everyone (the hospital, the social care team, Baillieston Health Centre) worked extremely hard to get Stella home and, I have to say, overall, the NHS did a fantastic job in supporting my family and caring for my mother. On 27 April, she got her wish, and went home to die.

I had visions of some more weeks together and being able to take her for walks in her wheelchair and even a wee trip to her favourite resort of Portpatrick, but sadly I never got to do it, as things were moving too rapidly. Glimpses of Stella did return – as displayed on a day when we all thought that she was in a bad way and the doctor told us that things were very grave, only to be met with a request for a Tunnock's pie, gravy, beans and a trifle. The wonderful Dr Harper looked at us, laughed and said, 'But what do I know?' Bob returned from Tunnock's in Uddingston with her goodies. She ate the lot. She was able to brighten up and chat for short spells and was able to tell people that they were wonderful and that she loved them.

I had to head off to see *Thoroughly Modern Millie* in Manchester as I was contracted to do the four-week run in Scotland, taking over the role of 'Mrs Mears' from Lesley Joseph. I was able to do it with the help of the rota that my sisters and I had drawn up. We had fantastic help from the local health centre in the form of Dr Harper, our GP, with visits four times a day, headed by the wonderful nursing skills of Helen Glassford and her team. I was in a sort of netherworld when I was watching the show, but luckily I got to see my friend Gwen, who had driven from Morecambe to see me, and she was a great comfort. As I left the theatre I buckled, saying that I didn't think I could do it . . . I didn't think I could watch my mother die. Gwen, who had nursed her own mum (the lovely Nessie), assured me that I could and that I was strong enough. I arrived back home still in a daze and found Stella in good form.

To my amazement, she was still in no pain, even though we knew that the cancer was all through her body. She didn't need any painkillers. I was on more bloody medication to try to get rid of the constant tension headache that I seemed to have. Her medication, although we had the morphine at the ready, was paracetamol – I kid you not. Stella asked me about the show and said that she still wanted to see it with her pal Isobel. I told her that I was sure she would. I brought her a cuppa and saw her gazing off into space and asked her what she was thinking about. She said, 'Life.'

'Oh,' I said, 'and what have you come up with, Stella?' She held me with a very determined and steely gaze and said, 'If it's like this, I want to die.' It took me completely by surprise. I took her hand and replied, 'Well, if that's what you want, Stella, don't you worry about us, we'll be fine.' She then looked at me: 'I'd like to get better as well,' she said. Laughing, I answered, 'Well, you do that if you want to, we'll be happy either way.' I walked out the room and burst into tears. My sister Di was amazed, saying Stella never spoke to her like that. But I knew that it was because of our relationship that she did. Stella regarded Louise and Diane as her daughters, and children, and I have to admit that I envied them that role. I was more like a mother, sister and daughter all rolled into one – and sometimes the weight of that was unbearable.

She had a couple more chats and a few more ice lollies, which she seemed to like, and seemed in good spirits. She slept really well that night and I realise now that she had made a sort of a peace with herself, or that's what I like to think.

The next day she didn't seem to want to eat and slept a great deal. My daughter Katie told me that as she was going to bed, she went in to say goodnight to her. Stella turned and said, out of the blue, 'Everybody's been wonderful. Bye, darlin'.' Katie never got to speak to her again.

I was sleeping in the spare room with a baby monitor and was awakened first by what I thought was Mum snoring. As I stirred, I heard our dog Stan whining at the bottom of the stairs, at the door of her room, and he sounded as if he was fretting. I then realised that the noise I could hear was something else. It was like a deep rattle in her chest. As I entered the room, her eyes looked fearful and I said, 'Mum, Mum,' and she couldn't respond. I suspected that she had had another stroke and called for Bob, who phoned the nurses, who were there within minutes.

A doctor arrived who was on-call and gave her the only morphine that she had in her illness. We thought that was it, as her pulse slowed down and the nurses looked grave. But just as we dissolved into tears she stirred and we realised she wanted to stay for a bit longer. She hung on semi-conscious for the day, surrounded by us all. We spoke to her, sang to her, held her hand and kept telling her how much we loved her. We had candles burning and my brother-in-law Paul (the priest) came in and did prayers for the sick for hours at a time. He was wonderful and there was something comforting about having him there for Stella – a woman who had spent so much of her life feeling like she had betrayed her family and her church. I am not a believer at all, but I found his presence, kindness and compassion a great comfort at a truly painful time in our lives and for that we will always thank him.

We all took turns to sit with her, as there was something awful about the thought of her being on her own, though my friend Ann, who works in a hospice, told me that I shouldn't get upset if she died when we weren't in the room, as the pull from us would be too strong. Whether that was true or not, we will never know, but it does seem that that is what happened. We were all knackered. Louise was asleep on the chair in the room and Diane was on the floor. I went into the living room and Mum's favourite movie, *Some Like It Hot*, was on TV. Suddenly, I just felt that enough was enough and I wandered out into the garden with a cigarette (I don't smoke, but Andy Gray had left them at our house). I looked up at the sky and called on my Aunt Eileen and my grandmother to come and take her. She'd been through too much.

I was tearful when the nurses arrived, who were all amazed that she was still alive. For some reason, I decided to go and iron a clean nightie for her, and in the midst of this I heard my sister shout for me. The nurses had turned her and obviously Stella thought that we were all out of the room and made a really strange rasping sound. Louise said, 'Mum, it's all right,' and Stella said, 'Elaine.' It was the last word she ever said. Helen, the nurse, quietly told her to 'get your sisters'. We rushed back in and held her as she opened her eyes; eyes that said, 'I'm sorry, girls, I have to go.' A tear ran down her face and she was gone. And that's how I felt. I never wanted to view her body afterwards, or go and sit with her. For me, Stella, my mum, was gone. My sisters and I wept for a bit and then went out and poured ourselves a drink and toasted our mother. It was the most surreal feeling in the world. So normal and mundane, everything was the same, yet changed for ever.

For the first time in years, we all crashed out in the same bed and felt like three wee girls again. When we awoke the next morning, the realisation dawned that our mother had left us. It was unbearable, and yet we were also full of relief that the ordeal was finally over. There was a feeling of disbelief throughout the day, as if it was New Year or something, with so many people coming and going from the house: the funeral directors; my mum's body being taken away; the phone ringing constantly and all the family around needing food and endless cups of tea. I didn't feel sad, I just felt weird, a bit elated and odd.

Telling our children that their beloved gran had died was just terrible. Katie was amazingly centred and calm; I think she was prepared for what was going on and at an age where she could understand. She told me once that as the oldest grandchild she also felt like Stella's youngest daughter. She was in the middle of her Higher exams at school and had to keep going in. She did, and passed them too, which was a testament to her and her gran. It was more difficult with Hannah, as she was only ten and had been very close to Stella. When Stella was staying with us during her illness, I would often find Hannah up in bed beside her and chatting, drawing or watching TV. I think she had a sense that she wouldn't have her gran for long. When we told her that Stella had died, she went into the room where her gran had been and lay on the bed and wept. I went in to sit with her while she was watching TV and the weirdest thing happened to me – and I promise you that this is true . . .

Hannah loved cartoons and was watching *Flower Fairies* on the Cartoon Channel. I sat cuddling her, looking out the window at the beautiful cherry tree that was in full bloom in our garden. I was in a daze, thinking, 'But where has my mother gone?' I remember asking, 'Where are you, Stella?' Then a voice from the TV said, 'Can anyone tell me where Stella is?' And the reply came, 'I'm right here.' I stared at the telly and saw a little cartoon fairy with a giant 'S' on her chest. I said quietly to Hannah, 'Have you seen this before?' and she replied, 'Yes.'

'And was there always a fairy called Stella in it?'

'Yes, why?' asked Hannah. I laughed out loud. It would be so like my mother to get in touch through the medium of light entertainment.

The next few days running up to the funeral are a blur of flowers and cards, amazing kindness and compassion, as well as a raft of strange emotions that I'd never experienced before. It was like the build-up to a wedding or something. Bob went into 'producer' mode and got all the music, photos and printing of cards done for the funeral. I had stupidly said that I would like to speak and Bob just said, 'Absolutely not – you've done enough.' I felt that I had to do it for her, but he was right, I was in no fit state, and it was a relief to have it all taken out of my hands. I also got to know who my friends really were and their thoughts and kindness will never ever be forgotten. My female friends were wonderful: Kate Donnelly, Kath Benham, Anne Lamond on the phone from Canada talking me through everything, Angela, Christine, Lynne, Rhona – all supportive.

I opened the front door the day after Stella died to my dear and wonderful pal Helena Kennedy (yes, the Baroness herself), complete in her Old Bailey lawyer suit. She'd been so worried about me and that she wouldn't make the funeral due to her trip to Australia that she'd got on a plane from Heathrow and turned up just to give me a cuddle. She cried with me, listened as I pored over every detail of what had happened and was simply there for me, exactly what I needed. I think I felt that the funeral would bring some sort of closure. I didn't realise that although it was the end of the illness, it was only the start of the grieving.

The day of the funeral was beautiful, and we did Stella proud. I wanted everything to be perfect and so was madly running around getting suitable clothes for Katie and new shoes for me. We all gathered in our house dressed in black, with breast cancer brooches and flowers on our lapels. There was a feeling of disbelief and the nerves I felt were terrible. It felt like the nerves before a first night, but this was a show I didn't want to perform in.

Andy Gray arrived with another very funny actor pal, the lovely Barrie Hunter (they seemed like Praetorian Guards, showing up to protect me), and they just looked so tall and strong as Andy swept me into his arms with a 'C'mon, baby, you're fine!' Bob had been in touch and they'd agreed to come and help as ushers, as we knew that the crematorium would be packed.

The hearse carrying Stella's coffin was blanketed in beautiful pink flowers and there were wreaths saying 'Mum' and 'Gran' – all arranged by Louise. As I got into the car with Louise, Diane, Katie, Jimmy, Brian and Bob, I said, 'Well, the only good thing about today is that we will never have to do this again: bury our mother.' I was just breathing and no more, I think, when we got to the crematorium. My cousin Claire saw me and said that she was really shocked: the only way she could describe it is that I looked stricken; and she was right, I was. I didn't want to be there. I wanted to run away.

The service was beautiful and Bob had done her proud. His brother Paul conducted the service, Bob did the eulogy, Jimmy, my brother-in-law, read a poem and our Uncle Séamas did a reading. We picked the music that Stella loved, ending with one of her favourite singers, Brenda Cochrane. She got to know Brenda when we worked together on a show about her life called *Just for Joe*. I wrote it, Nigel West directed, and Bob produced it, and it had played the Festival in Edinburgh and subsequently toured across Scotland. Stella saw it several times and loved Brenda's singing. She would have done it live but was abroad touring at the time. There were many tears shed for her and many laughs, too – well, she would have wanted that – and it brought her alive again for all the people who turned up.

On a lighter note, my sister told me that a neighbour of Stella's had come to the funeral and, later, when she was in getting her hair done, Louise said, 'It was a lovely service, wasn't it?' and the woman said, 'Well, it was a bit sad at the start and I wasn't sure, but it brightened up a lot at the end.' Louise could have hit her: what did she expect, a bloody variety show? Our mother had died and we were devastated; the fact that we could raise a smile was a miracle.

The meal afterwards provided a great relief for us all and we got gloriously drunk, helped by the man in charge of drinking, Andy Gray. He had been wonderful in getting Hannah to come out to the Bothwell Bridge Hotel, where we all were. She had refused to come to the funeral and went to school instead and then went to her friends. I think all the talk of the funeral had freaked her out a bit and she refused to discuss it. She and Andy have always had a great connection with comic books and graphic novels, so he called her, saying that he had some comics to give to her, and so convinced her to come and see us all. She was brought out to the hotel (the last place Stella had been out to the month before, to see Hannah be a flower girl at the wedding of our babysitter, Claire Hayes) and I think she felt relieved to see all of us back to a sort of normality, laughing and joking and drinking. I got to bed eventually after having witnessed Andy, Bob and Barry sitting with a guitar in the room in which she had died, surrounded by cards and flowers, singing 'Clementine' for Stella. She would have loved it.

The next morning I boarded a train for Newcastle to rehearse for the part of Mrs Mears, where my opening line was 'Sad to be all alone in the world' and my big number was 'Mammy' – ironic or what? How I did it, I don't know. A new life without my mother on the planet and I didn't know what had hit me. It is all a blur, the hotel, the rehearsals – and learning the lines was so hard because my brain was too full of shock and grief. But I kept putting one foot in front of the other, as there was nothing else for it.

The following Tuesday I opened the show at the King's in Glasgow. I stood looking up into the gods of the theatre that my mother had loved and begged her to help me, and she did. The round I got on my entrance was little to do with the show but to tell me that they knew how I was feeling and that they were with me. I played for two more weeks but could tell you little of it.

CHAPTER 30

GRIEF

The truth is that the sense of loss that you suffer when a loved one is taken from you is never ever over. I am reduced to tears as I write this and it's now four years on since Stella died. You simply have to learn to live with the grief and the fact that your heart lies in a place that you didn't know existed. Much as with the birth of your children, where your heart swells and grows to accommodate even more love you didn't know you possessed, so with the death of a loved one, your heart duly seems to shrink and move to a very strange and unfamiliar place.

Here's the thing about grief: before it happens to you, you really think that it's something you have to come to terms with and eventually you'll get over it. Well, that's certainly what I thought – and the world that we now live in makes us believe that getting over the death of someone close is just like recovering from a broken romance, but it's not.

My experience with a broken love affair has been that initially you have a lot of pain and distress, you cry for Scotland and can't stop thinking about the rejection and the pain. You want them back at any price because you can't live without them and then, lo and behold, a few months later, you wake up one morning and realise that your heart isn't broken any more and you are willing to get on with life. I realise that it is much worse than that and, believe me, in my younger days I had plenty of occasions where I was chewing the carpet over my broken heart. But in the main you get over it.

Now, I am not a stupid person and I know that the grief that comes with the death of someone close is much deeper; but somewhere, because it had never happened to me, I didn't or couldn't really know what real loss felt like. I said all the right things to people who had lost someone close, like 'You'll learn to live with it but you won't get over it,' I sent cards and flowers, but I couldn't fully empathise with the absolute raw emotion that comes out from within you at that critical and tragic moment.

Yes, we all have to wake up in the morning and 'get on with it', as they say, but the feeling of absolute apathy about everything in the world: not caring how you look (and not even noticing); having conversations with people that an hour later you can't remember; wanting to change your life, job, marriage or house completely and then realising that you haven't got the strength; crying at the drop of a hat or losing your temper over a broken hairbrush; ignoring your kids because any demand is just too much; basically just walking around in a fog – all of that is what loss does to you. I now understand the madness that is real grief.

In that first year after Mum died, there were months that I honestly don't remember. I met a friend who talked about the lunch we went for that summer and I was shocked to realise that I couldn't recall even meeting her. I couldn't make any decisions at all, and I don't know how Bob kept our business going, because he had a zombie for a wife. The truth was that for a long time I just wanted to die. Going on with my life seemed like a betrayal of my mum. I felt that I had no right to a life of my own and a part of me wished that she had given me permission to go on without her (but she never did); maybe she thought she didn't need to and that I would do it anyway.

A few days after she died, I stood in front of my own girls and said, 'Listen to me, when I die I want you to go on and have the best life you can have, don't waste a minute thinking about me. Just know that you are loved completely by me and that you have nothing to regret, and get out there and have the best time possible.' They nodded and walked off, believing that their mum was a complete nutter, and I guess I was. They were wonderful, my girls, because they knew that I was mad with grief and they so protected me. They put their own grief and sadness on hold because mine was so overwhelming, and I really regret that. They were frightened to talk about their gran in front of me in case it upset me and I thank them for it but hate myself at the same time for taking up so much space and not allowing them to express what they were feeling. We are fortunate in that we can talk about it and I have apologised and thanked them for being so patient and understanding, and gradually their own sadness has come out in different ways over time.

Everything in the world changed for me. I didn't know whether I wanted to be an actor any more because the world of celebrity had always made Mum happier than it actually did me. Finally, Stella, the wee girl from Bellshill, was Elaine C. Smith's mother and it gave her a feeling of status that she had never had and she dined out on it. Her daughter also had a degree and was a teacher, which made her feel that she was as good as the rest. Not only that, her other two daughters, Louise and Diane, ran a really successful hairdressing business – so through her children she felt like a success. But with her death, I felt it was all just pointless. The charade of show business, all the egos – the drive, the determination, the sheer enthusiasm for it had gone. In my opinion, you can't be a performer if you don't feel anything, and I felt nothing but grief.

I got very upset with people if they didn't acknowledge what had happened because it was so massive for me, even though I'd done it myself in the past to others. And that's because until it happens to you, you can't really know. I always say to people to not even worry about or project how they will be in that situation, because when it actually happens it is so devastating there's no point in wasting time now.

I received a lovely card from a friend who had lost her own mother and in it she said that she felt so sorry for me because I had a hellish road ahead. I remember thinking that that wasn't true, that the worst was over; the cancer, the death itself and the funeral brought a sort of relief and closure. But she was right, the worst is learning to live without them. I remember speaking to people a few weeks afterwards and seeing that they thought I wasn't myself but couldn't understand why. One friend who I hadn't seen for ages asked how I was doing and when I said, 'Oh, pretty rubbish. My mum died six weeks ago,' he replied, 'Oh, I am sorry to hear that, what age was she?' When I said 71, he replied, 'Ach, well, a good innings, eh?' and went on drinking his pint. In that instant I knew that his parents were both still alive. He has since lost his dad and I now see a look in his eyes that was never there before; he's joined the 'Death Club' and realises that a good innings means nothing when it's your own mum or dad – the fact that they are no longer on this planet changes everything. But it's like having a baby. No matter how many folk tell you it's a life-changing experience, you can't know until that wee thing is there and then you realise, oh my God, this is what they meant. My life will never be the same again. So it was with me and Stella's death, my life felt over.

Even though I had this wonderful husband, these beautiful daughters, two sisters who had gone through what I had and meant so much to me, the only thing that kept me going was that I didn't want them to go through what I was going through now. Two things helped move things on a bit for me in the healing process. First, I saw a photo of myself and realised that my face had actually changed, as I had cried almost daily for a year and that had to have an effect on how I looked. I realised I didn't look like me any more and that was a real shock. The other was a dream in which my mother appeared raging at me and said, 'Right, lady, you give yourself a shake and get your arse in gear. Do you think I fought so hard to stay here for you to lie down and throw all of it away?' I woke up laughing out loud. And, yes, I did think I was going mad. I walked downstairs to where Bob was and he said, 'What are you laughing at?'

'Well, I have just had a total sherricking from my mother.' He looked at me with a look that said, 'Well, I've been waiting on this, she's finally lost it,' but he said tentatively, 'What?' I explained about the dream and he said that maybe my mum was right and it was time to get my act together.

So I got myself back to the gym and attempted to recover. I worked and got on with things, we got through the first Christmas and attempted to get some balance back into our lives, although part of it had been ripped away for ever. The next hurdle was Mum's birthday, made more difficult because she shared it with my sister Diane. We couldn't avoid it, as it was also Di's 40th birthday and she was determined to have a big bash, not just for her, but for the family, to keep their spirits up.

The night went well and we all had a great time, considering, though I did notice that Di was very thin. We then went off for a girly weekend to Stobo Castle and I noticed just how tired she was.

Unbeknownst to us, she'd had some blood tests done and, on our return, she got called to the hospital. Within 24 hours, we got the devastating news that she had a potentially fatal blood cancer called multiple myeloma. We were shocked that our healthy marathon-running sister could be struck down with this out of the blue. We were knocked sideways and the grief we had for our mother was put to the side as we concentrated on Diane. The only saving grace was that Stella wasn't there to see it, as it would have killed her.

It's not for me to go into the details of Diane's illness, as it would be wrong of me to talk about her story in this book. All I can talk about is the effect on my family and me; although we once again had to pick ourselves up and get on with it, there was a feeling that the grief would never end. We were given a huge ray of hope (which we believe was Mum watching over us) in that my other sister, Louise, was an exact stem-cell match for Diane. We had won what felt like the lottery, yet we were still grieving for Stella too.

On the first anniversary of her death, the three of us drove up to her favourite spot in Dunkeld and started the real process of letting Stella go. We scattered her ashes on the River Tay, read an Alice Walker poem and started to set her, and hopefully ourselves, free. We all kept some of her ashes to be with us in our homes, but the rest we let go in the Tay, and in a way it felt like the first real step to getting on with our own lives. Well, in a way we had to, as we had a tough fight ahead of us.

The following months were rounds of hospitals, with many ups and downs and terrible anxiety – and some horrors, too – but the transplant worked. Our family is one of the lucky ones that have benefited from the research and dedication of those who fund-raise and work in science and healthcare. These people gave us the light back into our lives. They gave us hope. My sister, as I write, is well, happy, watching her kids grow up and back at work. It's good for all of us to know that, as time goes on, the treatments for a variety of cancers are actually working in many, many cases.

CHAPTER 31

THE TRICK IS TO KEEP BREATHING

I don't feel like I started to really breathe again for about three years after Stella died. Oh, I worked and functioned. I went straight into directing a one-act play that Bob had heard Tom Courtenay perform on Radio 4 called *A Limited Run*. It was basically a tale of God in his kitchen dealing with all the requests that came in from down here on Earth. It was funny, moving and poignant. He'd set about getting the rights and asked Andy Gray if he wanted to do it and he said yes – well, we all knew it was only a matter of time before he played God anyway, he'd been practising for a while.

How I did it, I don't know, but it gave me a focus and something to get my teeth into and it stopped me from thinking about Mum for a while. I loved, laughed, cried, got pissed and kept going. I've now managed to write a column for the Scottish *Sunday Mail* every week for the last five years, which has been a great discipline for me to learn, and I got so much support from Allan Rennie (the then editor), and some great comfort from the staff and the readers. On the first anniversary of Stella's death, I wrote a column about grief and I have never had a response like it. I had women stopping me in the street in tears, thanking me for writing about my mother's death because they thought they were alone in the way they felt. I got hundreds of letters from people across the country, from young men who'd lost their wives to daughters who'd lost mothers or fathers. It was heartbreaking, and these people had nowhere to put all that grief and emotion because we as a society just can't handle it. I realised I was far from alone in trying to deal with the madness of losing someone. But somewhere I still felt that I couldn't breathe.

Helena Kennedy spotted this in me quite early on and invited my family to her house in Cape Cod. I was resistant at first, as she had her own family and friends there and had just lost her own dear mum. Though she was very sad and felt her loss keenly, she kept saying that it was different, as her mum had been 93. But at the end of the day, it's your mum, isn't it, regardless of age? Ian Hutchinson, her husband, is quite the most brilliant, dedicated and compassionate man I have ever met. He is a consultant at Barts Hospital in London, specialising in facial cancers, and so was able to explain so much of my mother's treatment to me when I was confused about what was going on, and it was invaluable to all of us at that time. They both made us so welcome and, together with the sun and the unique light beauty of Wellfleet and the Cape, it did make me feel a bit physically better.

I met Jon Snow there for the first time too, as he's an old friend of Helena's, and he made us laugh so much, my kids just thought he was the best – and I even managed to beat him at tennis. It was the holiday that we all needed, but returning to Scotland was so hard, as for the first time I realised that there was no mum there to ask all the questions about our trip, as she always had.

I started to get more creative, especially when I got sent a fantastic short story by a very talented writer called Denise Mina, who sent me a lovely note out of the blue, saying, 'We've never met, but I feel like I know you. You live around the corner from my Auntie Betty and you gave her advice about football shorts for her grandson one day when she met you in a shop in Shettleston Road. Anyway, I believe Mario Puzo sent Marlon Brando a copy of *The Godfather* cos he thought he'd be perfect in it. So I am sending this story called 'Ida Tamson' to you cos I think you'd be wonderful in it.' It made me laugh out loud.

I duly read the story and loved it. It was the story of a Glasgow grandmother left to bring up her two grandsons after the drug death of her daughter (a situation all too common, unfortunately). It was pretty bleak subject matter, but the character was so funny, truthful and brave and actually got to win in the end. Normally in stories in this genre, everyone is bleak or gets defeated in the end, so this was really refreshing. I called Denise, we spoke for an hour and our company purchased the rights of the story for TV.

We weren't really up to speed on all things in the drama world, but we went to all the TV companies and other production companies in Scotland and, though my name and Denise's got us meetings (and nice comments), nobody seemed to get it at all. Television is full of fashion trends and if you hit at the right time with the right type of drama then it will get made. But there is so little money available that unless it fires up the particular producer, or a head of department, then there is no way it will get made. That's what happened to us. Denise also attempted to get things off the ground through her London contacts but nothing happened. So we had a great story, a great writer and me to play it – but that was it.

Denise then called a few months later to say that she'd been asked to do a play for Òran Mór in Glasgow, run by my old pal, the one and only Dave MacLennan. Òran Mór (Gaelic, I think, for 'the big song' or 'gathering place') is a converted church at the top of Byres Road in Glasgow, owned and run by the amazing Colin Beattie, a Glasgow publican and all-round good guy. He bought the church, commissioned stained glass by Alasdair Gray, got him to paint the ceiling too, and turned this place into a bar, nightclub, brasserie and function suite. It's beautiful and a fantastic venue for bands.

Dave MacLennan knew him and went to him with the idea of a lunchtime theatre programme called 'A Play, a Pie and a Pint'. A great idea, giving a platform to new and veteran writers alike to write a play lasting under an hour and charging £10 for admittance, as well as a pint and a pie (or a quiche and a glass of wine, if that's what you'd prefer). My sister Louise was queuing to get in and overheard one wee old woman say, 'A pie and a pint? I don't think I could drink a whole pint, Betty.' Louise explained that there was an alternative and that they shouldn't panic. It was a great idea and has now been running for around five years and has attracted writers such as Liz Lochhead, Peter McDougall, Alasdair Gray and more, as well as the talents of actors such as Davie Hayman, Robbie Coltrane and many more. So that's what we decided to do for staging *Ida*.

I contacted Morag Fullarton (who was directing *Taggart* at this point) and asked her if she was up for directing it, and she agreed.

Jon Morrison and I were cast and it was wonderful to do. It packed the place out (so much so that many people paid to stand and simply watch the play and never even got so much as a pie!) As Ida, I wore all of my mum's old clothes and even used her bag and shoes; I think that way I felt that she was there with me.

Our company flourished, doing sell-out tours of plays such as Jim Cartwright's *Two* and *Little Voice*. I helped produce the pantomime at the King's; wrote and performed my sell-out Christmas stand-up show at Òran Mór for two years, but I still couldn't breathe. One day I realised that I was holding my breath because I was simply waiting for the next disaster to happen, and as Diane started to recover, I became more and more aware of that. I knew that I had to give myself time, but after three years I knew that it wasn't right. I didn't want to forget Stella, but I wanted to feel that I had the right and the ability to go on and live a good and full life without her.

I started doing yoga around the same time with the wonderful Rowena (daughter of my friend Vicki McKenna). Of course, yoga is all about the breath and halfway through the first session, when I started to really breathe deeply, I just couldn't stop the tears. I kept crying with every breath. I'm sure Rowena thought I was going mad. But I had started to release the breath and with that all the grief and fear.

Counselling has taught me that what had happened to me was a sort of 'interrupted grief' – the loss of my mother and then the fear and worry over my sister and the thought of losing her had kept me in a sort of suspended place, waiting for the next bad thing to happen and scared to move. It took a lot of work and many hours of howling at the moon to get to a place where I was ready to start living my own life on my own terms.

CHAPTER 32

CALENDAR GIRL

In the middle of all this searching for a meaning to my life and my emergence from the abyss, I got a call from David Pugh – well, it was actually Michael Harrison who called me in my dressing room at His Majesty's Theatre in Aberdeen during the tour of *Little Voice*. He told me that he'd been speaking to Pugh, who'd asked him if he thought I might be interested in doing *Calendar Girls*. Bob had already said that he didn't think I'd be interested but that he should call anyway, and Michael thought that the money would be low and I wouldn't do it anyway. They were both wrong. I said a very quick 'Yes, I'm interested.'

I had seen the film and enjoyed it very much. Initially I had resisted going, as I thought it all sounded a bit clichéd, until I realised that it was actually a true story. I vaguely remembered all the fuss around these WI (Women's Institute) women taking their clothes off for a calendar in aid of raising funds for Leukaemia Research, but little more than that – though I loved the actresses in the cast. Mum had gone to see it, adored it and pestered me that I should go to see it. So, one afternoon I duly took myself off to the cinema and I really enjoyed it. I thought the storyline got slightly lost when they went to America, but I knew that it was for the US market, so that's sometimes the price you pay. I laughed, I cried (and enjoyed a great performance by John Alderton) and I left the cinema feeling uplifted, thinking to myself that if that was what the stage show could do then I wanted to be a part of it.

David Pugh and I had first crossed each other's paths when he came to see *Elaine with Attitude* at the Queens Hall in Edinburgh.

We'd apparently met with Phil McIntyre during the *Nesbitt* show at the Hammersmith Apollo but much drink was taken and I remember little of it. He wrote me a lovely card saying how much he'd loved my show and hoped that we could work together one day. I wrote and thanked him and that was that. David then went on to have fantastic success as a producer with the plays *Art*, *The Play What I Wrote* and more recently *Equus* (with Daniel Radcliffe from *Harry Potter*) and *God of Carnage*. We'd exchanged a few phone calls over the years, but we'd never actually met again. Eighteen years later he came back and offered me a job, and it was the right job – better late than never!

He called me and said that he needed a piano-playing, singing actress and would I come and play the part of Cora. I said in principle that, yes, I was interested, but that I'd like to read the script, which duly arrived the following day. The only person cast at that point was Lynda Bellingham, who I thought was a great choice for the role of Chris. Her public persona and popularity from being the Oxo mum, as well as starring in various TV sitcoms and dramas, and as co-host the hit daytime show *Loose Women* was, from a commercial point of view, just perfect. His idea was to mix the cast up with the popular and the serious, which was equally a great idea. I read the script, thought it would work – though Cora was a small part, she was onstage most of the show and a good part of the ensemble, which was exactly what I wanted. It came just at the right time for me.

The stress of being the lead actress in productions as well as being one of the producers had taken its toll on me and I wanted a bit of an escape from all the responsibility. In the past, when that pressure has become too much, I have escaped into a good solid company of actors either at the Lyceum, the Traverse or the Tron theatres and it has always helped me to recharge my batteries and get some perspective on who I am and what I am doing. In Scotland, I just feel too visible and exposed at times. And that familiarity does breed a bit of contempt in certain quarters. I used to warn companies when they asked me to do things that they could say goodbye to good reviews for the shows as the agenda about me from certain quarters would bring them a lot of flak.

Anyway, *Calendar Girls* came when I felt I really needed to spread my wings a bit. I was about to turn 50. My close friend Evelyn had died suddenly, having gone to bed with flu and never woken up. She was 52. Two weeks later, my cousin John, who I'd grown up with, died from an aneurism three weeks before his 50th birthday. All of it seemed to be telling me to get out there and have an adventure, to live life to the full and take a risk. So I said yes to *Calendar Girls* and, believe it or not, I didn't really worry about stripping off. I just felt secure in the fact that it would be done well, with taste and humour, and if actresses like Patricia Hodge and Siân Phillips were doing it, then so could I.

I liked the fact that this was a great story about real women in a small village and how they turned a terrible loss and tragedy into something wonderful and positive for the rest of us – raising a couple of million pounds into the bargain. The fact that these ordinary women of all shapes, ages and sizes had taken society's obsession with female nudity and turned it on its head was just fantastic. The idea was that we would rehearse in London, move down to open and run in Chichester for four weeks, and then tour until mid November. If it went well then there was a chance of its going into the West End, and that was certainly David Pugh's and Dafydd Rogers' aim, but we had a lot of work to do before we could even think about it.

In July 2008, I flew down to London to meet the rest of the cast, who by this time I knew to be Gaynor Faye, Brigit Forsyth, Patricia Hodge, Siân Phillips and Julia Hills. I had to meet them, take my kit off and get my photo taken doing it! David had the idea for the photo that would make it look very like a calendar and would also reflect the spirit of the original women, headed by the fabulous Angela Baker and Chris Stewart. They were always determined that the calendar and the movie (and now the play) would not just be about the stripping, or the nudity, but about the issue of transforming a great loss into a celebration of life. I finally met David in the lobby of the Covent Garden Hotel with Gaynor Faye and we hit it off straight away. I have always been a big *Coronation Street* fan so had known and liked her as an actress and had actually followed her career through *Fat Friends*, *The Chase* and also her stint on *Dancing on Ice* (where she was the inaugural winner). She has a great likeability factor as a performer, but I also knew that she was a talented writer too – better still, she loves a laugh, so we sat gabbing till the wee small hours.

We headed with David to meet Lynda Bellingham and Patricia Hodge at his favourite haunt, J. Sheekey's, where we had dinner and discussed his ideas for the upcoming photo shoot and the tour in general. The next day we were taken to the photographer John Swannell's house in north London, as his kitchen was going to be used for the photos (yes, it was actually a real kitchen in the shot that was used). I was introduced to the wonderful Julia Hills, who I had admired for a long time, as we were contemporaries on the comedy scene in the '80s. We both started in sketch shows (me in *Naked Video*, Julia in *Who Dares Wins* with Rory McGrath and Jimmy Mulville) and she'd then gone on to do huge sitcoms such as *Two Point Four Children* and *Dad* with the hilarious Kevin McNally (now married to my old pal Phyllis Logan). I then got to meet theatre royalty in the form of the dame that is the 'Queen of Wales', the amazing and beautiful Siân Phillips. I had been a huge fan of hers since the days of *I, Claudius* on the BBC and, of course, knew her from her very famous marriage to another hero of mine, Peter O'Toole. Poor Siân had just got off a flight from the States, having finished a run in Broadway of *Dangerous Liaisons*, so she remembers little of that day except a lot of coffee, a lot of hellos and having her photo taken with her kit off!

But it was a pretty weird first meeting. We all trooped into the kitchen in our dressing gowns, said hello to the photographer and crew, got our props (things like knitting, sunflowers, buns and me with a copy of *The People's Friend* to strategically hide my bits), put a fixed grin on our faces and kept eye contact all the way through the shoot (we didn't look below each other's necks when speaking to each other, as we didn't know each other well enough to have a peek and, well, it's rude to look, isn't it?). It went well and we then all went our separate ways, only to meet up two weeks later in rehearsals. It was quite bizarre, actually. It all felt very new and strange, and I was definitely out of my comfort zone, but as the saying goes: 'I said I could do it when I wrote in.'

As I left Glasgow that Sunday night before rehearsals, I had real second thoughts and worried about what I was doing. I had given up another tour in Scotland and a TV show for this. What if it was a disaster? I was very lucky in that Jon Snow had offered me his flat in lovely Primrose Hill for the duration, as he was combining a holiday with covering the Democratic Presidential Convention, so thanks to him I didn't have to stay in a hotel. I was in north London and rehearsals were near Kensington High Street, so I had a bit of a trek on the tube in front of me every morning and in 30-plus degree heat I wasn't looking forward to it. I couldn't sleep that night and was up around 7 a.m., determined not to be late on my first day. I left really early to ensure I found the place OK and ended up arriving an hour early, boiling hot, with my make-up running down my face, feeling sick with nerves.

I sat in a nearby coffee shop with my script – feeling like I was going to vomit – and decided to call Andy Gray, who almost fainted when he heard I was an hour early – 'un-bloody-heard-of' – so he knew I was really nervous. He was great and calmed me down while knowing exactly how I was feeling. I noticed a very attractive young guy sitting at the next table and just knew he was an actor, then spotted him reading the script. He turned out to be an actor called Carl Prekopp, a great guy, who played the photographer in the show. He was then joined at his table by another actor – a lovely Geordie called Gerard – who was playing Lynda's husband, Rod. I just couldn't speak to them. My head was full of that insecure rubbish of 'They won't want to speak to me, I'm just a wee Scottish actor who they won't know and I'll make an arse of myself.' Weeks later Carl asked me why I hadn't spoken to them, as they had thought I was obviously too up myself to speak to them, and he burst out laughing when I told him that I was too nervous.

Hamish McColl was our director and I just loved him instantly. He has great comedy chops, is hugely bright and funny, and loves to laugh (not one of those comedy horrors who only like to laugh at jokes they've made themselves!). He also has a huge heart of mush and our mutual love of Eric Morecambe made him my kind of guy. But he had a job and a half in front of him, with seven very strong-willed actresses (with roughly 100 opinions between them), producers wanting a hit show and a writer (Tim Firth) who was jetting between London and Hollywood every other day.

So with introductions over and me finally out of the loo (nerves, dahling), we all sat around the big table for the dreaded read-through. It went well, there were laughs, cheers and tears, but I felt there was something missing – it just didn't feel complete. I felt we had a lot of work to do on the script but kept my mouth shut (for once) and carried on. My part was small, with a few wee laughs here and there, but all the comedy was weighted towards the main characters and Marie, the head of the WI, played by the fantastic Brigit Forsyth. It felt a bit odd for me, but it was what I wanted, wasn't it? To test myself, to be part of a team and not to have the responsibility of being the lead and all the angst and pressure that brings.

It turned out to be Brigit's birthday, so some of us went for a glass of champers to celebrate, though we were too knackered to do much else. I returned to the flat exhausted, wondering what the hell I had done. It was very strange, though, as I was suddenly back to a single life and buying meals for one in Marks and Spencer's, or Tesco's, on the way home, tired and bewildered at where I was and exactly what had possessed me to take the job. It had seemed like a good idea at the time, but there was many a night when I went home tearful, wondering if I had made a huge mistake, leaving everything and everyone I loved behind, and for what? A play?

Fortunately, Lynda also lived in north London and offered me a lift every day, so Brigit, myself and Lynda had many a laugh and a good gab on our way into rehearsals. It helped break the ice and any feelings of isolation – it always helps to discover that everyone else is shitting themselves as much as you. Lynda had a lot of pressure on her, playing one of the main characters, and her profile was so high that much of the publicity centred on her. I have to admit that I didn't envy her, as I know what that feels like.

I flew home to Glasgow that weekend for my 50th birthday feeling a bit lost and odd. I had planned a big do months before but, with my timetable and the loss of too many people close to me, I just didn't have the energy. As ever with big events like that, everyone else has a great time and the host ends up wiped out, so I told everyone that I would maybe do something later in the year and that I wanted something quieter. My daughters took me out for lunch, which was just great – when did they get so grown up? My sisters had arranged a day of massage and facials and hairdos at their salon, and then we were all getting dressed up and heading out for a posh meal that night.

My wonderful brother-in-law Jimmy picked all of us up and we headed to our house to pick up Bob as planned. We went into the house, where he was surprisingly very excited and shouting, 'Come and see what's arrived.' I thought he meant another bunch of flowers (as they'd been arriving all day), but as I walked into my kitchen I could see people through the French doors in the garden. There were fairy lights on the trees and about 40 of my friends and family shouting, 'Surprise!' in unison. I had been set up by Bob and the kids, but it was great. I was in tears, of course, as I saw Dad and Andy Gray, Lynne my manager, Kate Donnelly, Kath Benham, Chris and Brigid, Margaret and George (my daughters' surrogate grandparents, who've been a constant in our lives for the past 25 years), my old friend and make-up artist Julie – whose husband, John, is a fantastic chef and did all the cooking for the party. I couldn't take it all in.

The champagne flowed and then the inevitable sing-song started, but in our house it's always a bit different, especially if you have the one and only Kennedy Aitchison there to accompany everyone. He is such a wonderful player, and if you keep plying him with drink, his playing gets better and better. We also know a lot of folk who can actually sing, too (after you shut me up), but the evening was topped off by a couple of songs from the truly fantastic Ricky Ross and Lorraine McIntosh from Deacon Blue – top that for a cabaret! They have been comrades and friends for almost 20 years now and are just great people, with much compassion and grace, and always love this kind of party!

As I stood there watching all these pals having a great time and singing along with Ricky as he played 'Dignity' (one of Deacon Blue's massive hits from the '80s), I felt so lucky and proud to be part of this family, to have a husband who would organise all this and to have these great friends. And I missed my mum. I then had to head back to London the next day (leaving my hubby to clean up) and not feeling the best, I can tell you.

Rehearsals were not easy from day one due to the aforementioned pressure on the show to be a success, combined with the added knowledge that some West End theatre productions were sold out before the first week of rehearsals. Getting it right was always going to be a slog, especially as my character – as well as Gaynor's character,

Celia – needed a lot of work, there being a huge imbalance between them and the characters of Jessie, Ruth, Chris and Annie. It brought Gaynor and me closer together, too, as we realised that we were both in the same boat and felt rather under-used. We were both onstage a lot but said little for huge passages of script. This had fortunately been noticed by David Pugh at our first run-through, and when we met for lunch he told me that he had spoken to Tim Firth to get rewrites done. This duly happened and, after that, the script changes, rewrites and reshaping came in thick and fast and actually continued to come in right through the rehearsal period. Both Hamish and Tim were very open to making things work and although under a lot of pressure, would listen and realise just when things weren't working, but there was so little time.

The rest of the cast seemed to be doing brilliantly with their characters. Julia's Ruth seemed miles ahead of us all. Ruth had the best through line of all the characters at this point and Julia was just so good at it, and so funny. Siân was simply amazing – she did her big exit speech, where she decides to do the calendar ('No front bottoms'), so brilliantly, complete with putting on of coat and scarf, and that I wanted to applaud. It was quite brilliantly done. I wanted to hand in my Equity card there and then, as Siân could do the 'proper acting'. When I told Siân that, she roared with laughter and said, 'It's all just smoke and mirrors, dahling.' She is quite the most amazing woman in every way.

Lynda was storming ahead with her role, as was Patricia Hodge. I was quite in awe of Pat, having watched her play the beautiful English rose in so many TV dramas and shows (*The Life and Loves of a She-Devil, Hotel du Lac, Rumpole of the Bailey*). She is very determined and knows what she wants in rehearsals, discussing things in detail, which intimidated me a bit at first, I have to admit. I didn't think we would be soulmates but surprisingly, as the saying goes, one should never judge a book by its cover. For Pat is a passionate, funny, warm, joyous and loving woman with the dirtiest laugh, and an ability to burp that would make a docker proud. Ah, you can take the lass out of Grimsby . . .

One scene where Cora plays the piano and reveals a bit of her past just didn't work, though. I tried it different ways but couldn't get it to work. She was supposed to be the daughter of a vicar, who was the church organist and loved the blues, but it came across as too arch and the music that I was playing seemed wrong. Hamish agreed and said he would talk to Tim, as he felt that the scene itself was in the wrong place too. I felt that Cora should hear the blues when she played hymns in church and with Steve, the musical director, I came up with the idea that she would hear something like 'Stormy Weather' playing in church. So, one lunchtime I grabbed Hamish, played it for him and Tim, and they both agreed. Tim went off and rewrote the scene and, although it was modified slightly over the lifetime of our production run, it really worked.

I had also decided that Cora had enjoyed her life and had always wanted to be a singer in a band, wanting to be Chrissie Hynde or Debbie Harry, and that gave me great scope for the costumes. A mixture of hippy, grunge and country and western, added to henna-coloured hair and black eyeliner. When Emma Williams (our costume designer) brought in an over-the-shoulder, black velvet Indian bag – complete with bejewelled elephant on the front – as well as the dreaded purple Crocs for shoes, I knew I had Cora!

The rewrites and changes left us all feeling a bit unsure, and with so much to do to get the show on there was little time for real discussion or character development. The central piece of the show is the calendar shoot itself, where the six women meet in the village hall to do the deed. Hamish decided that this should be funny, cheeky, sexy, fast and brave. It did all of that and more, but getting there was a logistical nightmare. The idea was that the audience would see the set-up and then the actual taking of the photo – so the nudity was only actually for a few seconds and no one was ever totally exposed. But the audience should see the finished shot as the flash of the camera went off.

We rehearsed it all with our clothes on throughout, but the day of the actual nudity was getting ever closer and it was like the big elephant in the room that none of us spoke about except in hushed tones. Getting our kit off in front of each other was actually worse than doing it in front of an audience! It seemed to take weeks of rehearsal to get it right. We had to feel really secure in it so that when we got in front of an audience we were in control. It was like a dance

– a wonderful piece of choreography – and I have to say that in 304 shows it never failed to have audiences cheering.

Lynda broke the tension by taking her top off one day when we didn't expect it. There was a scene at the top of the hill where Chris tries to persuade us all about nudity and that you can be naked without showing off all your bits and so takes her top off to demonstrate. We had rehearsed this fully clothed and then one day Lynda simply did it and was standing there topless. We all gasped, laughed and applauded her for doing it and getting it out of the way. Then it was our turn. I didn't actually feel too bad, as my shot was at the piano, so though I had to be naked, it was my back that was exposed to the audience and that felt fine, it wasn't full frontal nudity, and actually as the tour went on I got braver and braver and eventually didn't care, so sat there with the 'crack of my arse' showing too – ach, who cares! I think my disrobing was quite liberating for many of the women in the audience of the not-so-skinny, 14–16 size, and it certainly freed me up a bit.

The tyranny and fascism of size and weight of women in the Western world is so oppressive. I would like to say that I am immune to it, but I am not. I have been hung up on and have struggled with my weight since I first dieted as a size 12 at the age of 15. I was, of course, reared by a woman who'd been on a diet for thirty-five years and was eventually, of course, four stone heavier than when she started the bloody diet. The only thing about cancer that Stella liked was that she could get into size-12 trousers again – how warped is that? But for a woman who wasn't thin like Patricia, Siân, Julia or Gaynor, or average like Lynda, to take her clothes off was seen as brave. The number of women who called me brave during that tour was amazing; but, for me, 'brave' is saving someone's life, or climbing a mountain, or sailing round the world – not a plump 50-year-old woman getting her kit off. But it was liberating and I felt beautiful, too, and I even had a lovely gay man in the audience in London tell me that he felt so uplifted when I took my clothes off that he wanted to take his off too – I'm glad he didn't, but I got his point!

Hamish gave us good warning and told us that 'Kit-Off Day' would be the following Friday. There would be minimal crew there in the room and though I tried to get him to strip off with us as a sign of his solidarity and support, he refused! We all knew that it was now or never and actually got a real insight into what the real Calendar Girls must have felt. They later told us they all had to have a glass of wine to calm the nerves. We didn't get the chance unfortunately, as we were at work. Hamish was so respectful and kind, and when the moment came we all just did it and pissed ourselves laughing while getting on with the scene. There was a sort of giddy excitement about us all, and when we finished we all collapsed laughing and cheering and needing a bloody drink. But we'd done it: we felt great and not exposed at all.

Our difficulty came with the opening in Chichester, because the seats there are on three sides of the theatre, so feeling exposed seemed to be the order of the day, much as Hamish and the team tried their best to protect us. So for a few lucky (or unlucky) folks they got a bit more of a view than they bargained for. The move to Chichester was strange, but a bit of an adventure too. I'd never been there before but had heard that it was a beautiful place, so I decided to drive down through the heart of the English countryside to see it for myself. Joan Blackham, one of the actresses in the company, had told me Chichester was beautiful and typically English, and then remembered that she'd read somewhere that I was a nationalist and said, 'Of course you might not like it, being a Scottish Nationalist.' I burst out laughing and said, 'When you go to France or Italy, do you take an aversion to the beauty of it because it's not English?' I then explained that being a nationalist had nothing to do with hating another nation, but about believing in your own – and wanting it to be better – and if that meant wrestling powers away from a centralised powerbase like Westminster then so be it. I think she understood.

Anyway, I rented a beautiful little house on the outskirts of the town which had views over the fields around it. The town itself was lovely and the theatre was definitely part of 'actorland' folklore. Walking down the corridors left me in no doubt about that, as production shots of Sir Laurence Olivier and Derek Jacobi and other great actors stared out at me. It was a very sophisticated theatre audience, slightly up themselves for my taste, but hey ho! We were on in the main house while Robert Lindsay, Diana Quick and many other great actors were rehearsing in the smaller Minerva Studio attached next door. A lot of money had been spent on this facility, which had a bar and restaurants too, so it was a lovely place to be, even if I thought to myself, 'Why can't Scotland's National Theatre have facilities like this?'

I did feel a bit alienated while there, though, as it had the atmosphere of playing to the Tory Party conference at times. This ageing, settled, deeply conservative corner of England felt as foreign to me as any part of France. I couldn't believe how many elderly couples were there together, which was so unlike the East End of Glasgow where I lived, as there are very few men there in their 80s cutting about the place in good health. The average life expectancy for men is about 68, if you are lucky and the drink and poverty don't get to you first. A life of affluence and good genes seemed to have helped the men of Chichester, anyway. It was a real culture shock.

I had felt my mum's presence all the time there. Sounds a bit weird, but I think I just felt so sad and guilty that she wasn't alive to see me on a stage in the likes of Chichester, with actors of the calibre of Siân Phillips and Patricia Hodge (she would have been so chuffed). I felt her everywhere and couldn't explain it. My favourite designer label is Ghost and there was a Ghost shop in the town, which I cleared of merchandise on many occasions, especially during the sale. It wasn't until later that I realised that I'd picked Ghost perfume for my character to wear (I always have a different perfume for each of the shows I do). Generally, I have to say that I felt a bit haunted.

My mum's sister, Margaret, who had moved south all those years ago, actually came to see the show and I was so pleased, as it felt like a real connection to Stella. I decided to go back with her for a couple of days to where she lived in Brighton, and when I called her to make arrangements, I said that I felt strange, as if Stella was all around me, and I kept finding white feathers everywhere. Maybe I was just a bit bonkers. Aunt Margaret laughed and said, 'Well, Stella did adore Chichester.' I replied, 'But I never knew she'd been here!' Margaret went on to tell me that they had gone for a day trip to Chichester when Stella was down for a holiday in Brighton. They'd walked the city walls and gone into the theatre, but were too late for the matinee of the show, so had just had dinner in the Minerva restaurant instead. I was sitting in the Minerva restaurant at that very moment, having a coffee, and you could have knocked me down with a feather. I swear I could hear Stella's voice say, 'That's what I have been trying to tell you since you bloody arrived – I am here!' Cue spooky music again.

As we got nearer to opening night, we started previewing the show. The entire run was sold out there, so we at least knew we had an audience that were on our side, but that brings its own pressure and expectations. Bob came to the first preview and we were nervous as hell. He walked into my dressing room at the interval and said, 'Total hit, a total hit!' I looked aghast and said, 'Is it?', as by this time none of us had a clue what we were doing. He said that it was an absolute smash, but a lot of work still needed doing to it (not least the set, which was on hydraulics and was supposed to lift and move, but most of the time didn't; and the sound system was problematic, as we had no mikes and were screaming our heads off for most of the show). When I got onstage and heard the level that Lynda and Siân were at and that she was getting a great reaction, I realised that I had to raise my pitch, too. Even though it was completely exhausting, the reaction we received from the audience was terrific and more than made up for it. We were far from finished, though, and were given more rewrites and cuts almost every day as the writer and production team saw what worked and what didn't.

The best performance was actually the night that all the girls – the real Calendar Girls, Tricia, Angela, Ros, Chris, Beryl and the fantastic Lynda – came to view the show. At the end we got them to stand up and the audience gave them a standing ovation, and deservedly so, as out of their loss Leukaemia Research has gained over £2 million and still rising. It wasn't lost on me that some of that money would have gone into research that helped save my sister's life. We all met afterwards and they were, and are, the most fantastic set of women. The beautiful Lynda approached with her husband, Terry (who did all the original photos), and said to me in a broad Yorkshire accent, 'I'm Miss July and I like you, you're funny!' And we had a great laugh after that. So, we officially opened to apparently solid, indifferent reviews, but I never read any and instead trusted what I knew to be working. We left Chichester to the news that the entire tour was almost sold out. The phenomenon that was and is *Calendar Girls* had started.

The first stop on the tour was the Glasgow King's Theatre, my spiritual home! We had to play these big venues to bankroll the rest of the tour, as this was an expensive cast, in an expensive show, and the producers needed 'bums on seats' to make sure everyone was paid. It was sold out in Glasgow, and I mean sold out. All 1,750 seats for the entire week were gone. I had to put my family in a box with limited views, as there were simply no seats at all to be had. Most of the cast had played Glasgow in various touring shows but were a bit worried about what a Glasgow audience would make of this quite twee and very English story. Granted, I did always feel that in the first three scenes I was in *The Vicar of Dibley*. I actually had no doubt of the response, because the show had great heart, was based on a true story and had a cast of people that they liked. I wound them all up a bit with tales of Glasgow audiences and told them not to worry about the chatting during the show, or the clinking of glass and sounds like 'Ptshhshh', as that would just be the cans opening and the drink being passed along the row with whispers of, 'Naw, take it Betty, the drink's too dear in here!' There was also a strong possibility that they would try to get up and join in the strip scene, just to be part of the action. The ego of the Glasgow audience knows no bounds and sees no reason why there should be a barrier between the stage and the stalls – slightly different from that of Chichester, where they sat back and observed the show rather than got involved. I was also aware of a certain pressure on me from the audience, a sort of hometown thing, and knew that I had to hold steady and stay in character and within the play – no acknowledgement of the audience, even if they pulled me towards them. There is a sense of ownership between the Glasgow audience and me, as I am one of them, and they are therefore both proud and a bit over-familiar at times.

I was nervous, but very calm and in control, as I started singing the first bars of 'Jerusalem'. I had consoled myself with the fact that I wouldn't get lynched for singing the adopted song of English rugby fans in front of a Scottish audience by telling myself that it was a fantastic song and that the sentiment was about all people with a true socialist heart. I was right, because the response of the audience was great. I could hear, 'Oh, there she is!' and 'That's her!' and just kept going. It was amazing; they just adored Lynda, Gaynor and the show in general, and when we got to the 'strip for the calendar' scene I thought they were going to explode. That sense of ownership about me bubbled over when it was my turn and there were actual screams from the audience as I said, 'Well, if I'm going to get my kit off, I'd better warm this place up a bit!' They were hysterical. It was as if their auntie had just decided to strip off in the front room! As I sat there at the piano, with my back to the audience, I couldn't hear anything but hysterics and screams. I turned to Siân and Pat and said, 'Hold steady, girls, this might take a while,' which it did, but we got it done in the end and they adored it. I could feel a sense of pride in me, as if they were saying, 'See, I tellt you she was good . . . and there she is up there with all they big stars and she's no' making an arse of herself . . . she's holding her own!'

We didn't know what had hit us; the response was amazing and we felt as if the show had suddenly taken on a life of its own. Pat Hodge turned to me in the wings and said, 'How do you cope with that? That love and that pressure from the audience?'

'I just ignore it,' I said. 'If I started to believe that it was real, I would go mad. I just do my job and let them have a great time – but if they don't like what I am doing, they let me know just as quick. So I try to keep a distance and a balance within myself.'

There were tears from the audience at the end and I felt very emotional. I was really proud that my city and these people had opened their hearts to what these women from Yorkshire had done, and that's what they were responding to. Yes, they loved the laughs and the play, but it was the truth of it that got to them and I could feel it. And to tell you the truth, that response continued for the next 20 weeks of touring. From Edinburgh to Plymouth, from Cardiff to Manchester, the response was the same – people on their feet every night. It was amazing.

News reached us that we were indeed going into the West End in April 2009, but it meant a bit more touring beforehand, which wasn't as welcome. Although we all got on really well, we worked together so didn't want to spend all our free time together too. So, many an afternoon I spent pottering around another shopping mall or city centre, or going to the pictures if I could, or writing my column, or even this book, to keep me sane. All 'normal' life goes out of the window and it is a strange existence. Starbucks and Caffè Nero became like second homes!

It is quite a lonely life, too, and can take its toll on a marriage. Bob and I were so used to working with each other and being together that many stresses and strains started to show up, as I would arrive home knackered and unable to do anything while he got hacked off at having to hold everything together at home. He had all the responsibility and pressure of the children, while I had pressure of a different kind, and that put a lot of strain on us. I think he may have feared that I was going to go off and start a new life somewhere else and must have asked questions about where we were going. He always worried that my life with him and the girls had somehow held my career back and that I should have gone off to London as a younger actress, but I personally never felt that.

My being away also meant that our production company was pretty idle after some very busy years and he was having to put together my next show for Christmas without my even being there to discuss it, and when I was I just didn't have the energy.

I had committed many months before to do 12 nights' stand-up over Christmas at Òran Mór in Glasgow, so was busy writing that show (with Kate Donnelly by email in Glasgow, with some additional material from the very funny Bruce Morton) and would be spotted wandering around towns talking to myself, trying to remember my lines. I flew back from Plymouth with all my Christmas shopping at the end of the tour on 14 December, started rehearsals the next morning and opened two days later. God, I was knackered, but it was great to be back in Glasgow and home for Christmas. The show sold out and after a few days off I headed back to London for a new set of rehearsals and rewrites before *Calendar Girls* opened in Aberdeen.

There was still a lot of work to do on the show, as when you do any production the flaws within it slowly appear, and as an actor you notice these things and realise what needs correcting, and we were all keen to get the show perfect. Changes were made, my character's storyline became clearer and better, and we also managed to cut certain things, as we had during the tour when we realised that they didn't really work, and we had time to work and change them.

Aberdeen was again a wonderful welcome home for me. All the cast and crew said that they wanted to go back to tour in Scotland, as audiences were just so warm and welcoming – yes, even in Aberdeen.

His Majesty's Theatre is such a beautiful theatre and the response to the show there was just terrific. Again the whole tour was sold out, but we could all feel the tension build as we got closer to the West End run. From a producer's point of view, it is very tricky to bring a show into the West End because of the expense and risk involved. It is still the one place in the country where reviews can play a huge part in getting punters in because there is a lot of competition and seats are expensive. Audiences are famously fickle, and so difficult to gauge. Musicals, or plays in smaller venues with well-known stars in them, tend to sell brilliantly. Transfers from the RSC or the National tend to have a guaranteed audience, but a show like *Calendar Girls* carries a lot of risk and no one knew if it would work there. Many shows have been very successful out on the road only to die a death in the West End, and that was a worry and put pressure on everyone. The advance sales were good, but we were there for a sixteen-week run, which would be difficult to sell without five-star reviews. And that's where I started this tale – heading for the show's opening in the West End.

As I settled into my dressing room, I could feel the sense of excitement but also fear running through the entire building – this was not just another performance, this was something else. When I remarked to Siân about it, that I was amazed at all the panic suddenly from the producers and everyone else, she quietly said, 'Oh, it's always like this. The West End seems to induce a sort of panic in them all.' We had several previews before our gala night, so there was much work to do. It felt like all we had achieved thus far was being abandoned, which left us all feeling very unsettled, as we only had a few days to adjust. We, as a cast, had all been together for a long time and some stresses and strains in relationships were starting to show under the pressure and, though that would be found in any job, it was difficult to deal with at times. The egos, the fear, the desperation all seemed to surface in those first few days and I learned to stay as far back as I could from it, though I was burned and hurt a couple of times by some daft and insecure behaviour. But I had been here before and dealt with worse egos and fear in my career, so I tried to just get on and do my job.

I can honestly say that's what I preferred to do, as I had no agenda and I didn't care about getting future jobs out of it (or great reviews):

I simply wanted to do well, and the show to do well too. Yes, the West End is a massive shop window for actors and it's great to get noticed and approved of, but if that's what you are chasing then I feel you are heading for disappointment, and I wasn't prepared to put myself through that.

I had a headache throughout the first preview, which just got worse and worse, probably caused by the tension of it all. The audience were very 'soggy arsed' (i.e. they sat back and were very reserved), so we were at times going off to the sound of our own slippers. This was an audience that took itself very seriously and wasn't prepared to engage. But I always felt that the story and the heart of the play itself would win through – but not getting laughs or rounds of applause in the usual places is very hard to deal with. I stood backstage waiting to come on, holding Lynda's hands, saying, 'It's all right, hold steady, they will come with us,' and eventually they did. I felt so relieved to get it over with.

The gala night was really a wonderful, traditional showbiz London night, with more limos than you could throw a stick at and an audience packed with celebrities such as Cilla Black and Sir Cliff Richard, the *Loose Women* cast and other famous actors, writers, producers, agents and, of course, the Calendar Girls themselves. A 'business' audience can be very tricky too, and can be very hard to please, but they gave us a standing ovation at the end, which was a real surprise. The reviews were mixed, as ever, and I avoided reading them, though apparently one critic remarked that the show was actually 'critic proof' and would work and pack them in regardless of what they said. I think there was a lot of truth in that. The show did indeed pack them in and most times got the same response as it had on the road, with audiences going out feeling better than when they had come in, and that's what always matters to me – that people pay their hard-earned cash and get a good night out.

I had a wonderful, exciting time for four months in London. Going from *GMTV* to *This Morning* to *BBC Breakfast* to *The Wright Stuff* (one of my favourite shows) and *Loose Ends*. My favourite was Paul O'Grady, though, whom I just adore and who was just as warm, genuine and kind as I had always imagined. We'd met years before in Glasgow when he was doing *Annie*, and I took the kids to see him backstage at the Palladium when he was in *Chittty Chitty Bang Bang*, and he was always so funny and lovely. What you see is what you get – my kinda showbiz.

Gaynor and I had our flat in Bloomsbury and could walk to work every day. We weren't hitting Stringfellows every night (though we did walk past it), but we were living the London life. It was fantastic to have my sisters, friends and family down for breaks and to come to the show. It made me very emotional and sad to know that Stella would never see her daughter on the West End stage, but Louise told me that when she came to see it she had some of my mum's ashes in her locket around her neck, as she felt she had to make sure that Stella was present. In truth, I believe that she was always with me. In Nicaragua all those years ago, I attended a Mass where the dead were remembered and the congregation responded with '*presente*', meaning 'here with us'. Stella was, and always is, '*presente*'.

So, it's all over now and I am home. Well, actually, I am back in beautiful Cape Cod writing this and to try and make sense of what has happened to me in these last few years. Have I learned anything? Am I changed? Have I grown? Well, yes, I would say I have.

I have learned that many of the old clichés remain because they are, in fact, true. Life does pass too quickly and there is no way to control what happens to us. The random nature of life is what seems to terrify us all and makes us reach for religion, booze, drugs, you name it; all to make us feel better about the fact that we don't know what's around the bend! We all have to find a way to make sense of the world. I have no answers or pearls of wisdom to impart, but the lesson keeps coming back to me, 'seize the day' and in the end 'love is all that matters'. A week after I got back from London, we were again rocked by the sudden death of Allan, my sister's brother-in-law. A fit, healthy, handsome man with two kids and a lovely wife, tragically killed in a kite-surfing accident in a matter of seconds. There is no sense or logic in it, no rhyme or reason. It only reinforces the message to live our lives to the full, all the time. This ain't a rehearsal, folks!

As a performer, I have learned that I am actually good enough to do what I do – I am not better than others but am as good as anyone on a stage and I have nothing to apologise for. I have given myself a seal of approval and that's the one that really matters. When you put the price on your own head, then you have truly arrived – never let anyone else put it there and settle for it. Well, as long as it's not over-inflated. It makes a whole lot of difference to work and life when you respect yourself.

Where am I going? Who knows? But that's how the hell I ended up here at 51 in Scotland with those I love close by and doing a job that I love. I am, after all, my mother's daughter.

Thanks, Stella. This is for you.

ACKNOWLEDGEMENTS

I would like to say here and now that this is my version of my life story. There will be people who disagree with what I've said and my version of things, but I have done my best to be accurate and true to my version of the truth and I have tried not to speak for anyone else unless I have checked details with them. It goes without saying that I would not misrepresent anyone on purpose and wouldn't wish to hurt anyone – especially my family. If I have, then I am sorry, but it certainly wasn't my intention.

Thanks to the McGarrys and the Smiths. The Mortons for welcoming me into their family. Margaret and George McCulloch for helping to bring up my girls and for their kindness and generosity to us all. Claire Edwards for just being the best friend and cousin (no offence to other cousins!).

Andy Gray – 'nuff said! Thanks to my dear friend, dedicated adviser and manager Lynne Crossan, who has been an absolute star since she walked into my life 22 years ago. She and her assistant, Susan Gibson, are great friends and supporters, making sure I turn up at the right place, on the right day and hiding all the crazy letters sent to the *Sunday Mail*. My agent Sally Long-Innes, and Zoe, Lizzie and Oliver and all the team at Independent Talent Group in London. Allan Rennie, David Ross and the team at the *Sunday Mail*.

Vicki McKenna and Jenny Pearson for keeping me upright and semi-sane. Lisa, for all the massages and great gabs. To my dear friends Christine Dinwoodie, Kathleen Benham, Angela Connor, Babs Rafferty, Pauline Murphy, Joan Brear, Hilary Lyon, Ruth Wishart,

Dave Amos, Madeleine Hand, Christine and Cathie Lindsay for all their love and support, and all the tennis girls (Rhona, Maureen, Ina, Val and Lynda).

Kate Donnelly, for just being the best and wisest and most talented woman, whom I adore. Kennedy Aitchison and Irvin Duguid for being simply fabulous musical directors, and Gordon Wilson, the bestest drummer in the world, as well as all the fabby musos I have had the privilege to work with. A huge thanks, too, to all the crews in theatre and TV over many years who have worked so hard, for not much reward. To Seumas and all the team at Café Gandolfi in Glasgow for being my 'other office'. And gratitude and heartfelt thanks to all the actors and performers I have shared a stage with over the years. Many thanks also to the cast and crew of *Calendar Girls*, and Abby, Francis, Gary Lilburn, Amy (my dresser), Emily and all the other girls.

Thanks to all the charities I have been – and am presently – associated with, and to those workers who slog away fighting the good fight and making the world a bit better for those at the 'sharp end'.

And to Iain MacGregor, my editor, who has painstakingly gone through this tome with me, for his advice and for being tough too. Also to Bill Campbell and all the team at Mainstream and Random House for believing that I had a story worth telling.